The Decline of the Castle

M. W. Thompson

The Decline of the Castle

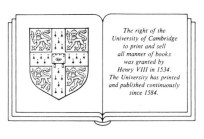

*The right of the
University of Cambridge
to print and sell
all manner of books
was granted by
Henry VIII in 1534.
The University has printed
and published continuously
since 1584.*

Cambridge University Press

Cambridge   New York   New Rochelle   Melbourne   Sydney

Published by the Press Syndicate of the University of Cambridge
The Pitt Building, Trumpington Street, Cambridge CB2 1RP
32 East 57th Street, New York, NY 10022, USA
10 Stamford Road, Oakleigh, Melbourne 3166, Australia

First published 1987

Printed in Great Britain by Scotprint Ltd., Musselburgh, Scotland

British Library cataloguing in publication data
Thompson, M. W. (Michael Welman)
The decline of the castle in England and Wales.
1. Castles – England – History
I. Title
942   DA660

Library of Congress cataloguing in publication data
Thompson, M. W. (Michael Welman)
The decline of the castle in England and Wales.
Bibliography.
Includes index.
1. Castles – England – History.
2. Castles – Wales – History.
3. Great Britain – Antiquities.
4. Great Britain – History, Military – Tudors, 1485–1603.
5. Great Britain – History, Military – Stuarts, 1603–1714.
I. Title.
DA660.T46 1987   942.05   86–32642

ISBN 0 521 32194 8

Frontispiece: the round keep and moat of the brick castle built by
Sir John Fastolf at Caister in Norfolk in the 1430s (RCHM).

WD

Contents

	List of abbreviations	vi
	Preface	vii
Chapter 1	Introduction	1
2	Fifteenth-century contrasts	17
3	Warfare in England and France	32
4	A rival – the courtyard house	43
5	A martial face	71
6	Accelerating decay	103
7	A continuing theme	117
8	Destruction	138
9	Nostalgia	158
Appendix 1	Derelict or abandoned castles in the fifteenth century	170
2	Condition of castles mentioned in Leland's *Itinerary*	171
3	Parliamentary demolition, proposed or executed, 1642–60	179
4	Demolition of Montgomery Castle, Powys, June to October 1649	186
	Notes	194
	Select bibliography	200
	List of illustrations	203
	Index	206

Abbreviations

AJ	Archaeological Journal
Ant J	Antiquaries' Journal
CA	D. J. King, *Castellarium Anglicanum*, 2 vols. (New York, 1983)
CCR	*Calendar of Charter Rolls* (HMSO)
CIM	*Calendar of Inquisitions Miscellaneous* (HMSO)
CIPM	*Calendar of Inquisitions Post Mortem* (HMSO)
CJ	Journals of the House of Commons
CP	G. E. C., *The Complete Peerage . . .* , 2nd edn, 13 vols. (London, 1910–59)
CPCC	*Calendar of the Proceedings of the Committee for Compounding Delinquents*
CPR	*Calendar of Patent Rolls* (HMSO)
CSPD	*Calendars of State Papers, Domestic* (HMSO)
DNB	*Dictionary of National Biography*, Compact edn (London, 1975)
EHR	*English Historical Review*
JBAA	*Journal of the British Archaeological Association*
KW	H. M. Colvin (ed.), *The History of the King's Works*, vols. ii–iv (HMSO, 1963–82)
Leland	L. Toulmin-Smith (ed.), *Leland's Itinerary*, 5 vols. (London, 1910)
LJ	*Journals of the House of Lords*
MA	*Medieval Archaeology*
RCAHM	*Royal Commission on the Ancient and Historical Monuments in Wales, Inventories* (HMSO)
RCHM	*Royal Commission on Historical Monuments in England, Inventories* (HMSO)
Rushworth	J. Rushworth (ed.), *Historical Collections, Abridged and Improved*, 6 vols. (London, 1703–8)
TAMS	*Transactions of the Ancient Monument Society*
TBG	*Transactions of the British and Gloucester Archaeological Society*
VCH	*Victoria County Histories*
WW	J. H. Harvey (ed.), *William Worcester, Itinerarii* (Oxford, 1969)

Preface

'I am king of the castle', building sand castles, castles in Spain, castles in the air, 'an Englishman's home is his castle' – the image is introduced from earliest infancy, and nursery books abound with pictures of castles. By the time he reaches adulthood the normal Englishman or European has the idea deeply embedded in his mind, although the image that exists there is often at variance with reality. The fierce controversies about the nature of the castle at the time of the Norman Conquest at the turn of this century were partly psychological: the average historian could not bring himself to believe that the earthworks belonging to the earth-and-timber structures described by Round or Mrs Armitage would really have to be substituted for the vision of 'cloud-capped towers' that he had imbibed from his early childhood. It offended common sense. The image he cherished derived from the final period of the castle's history when function played less and less part and display or even fantasy ever more part in the minds of the builders. Fantasy which outlived the real thing was given a new lease of life in the eighteenth and nineteenth centuries and, in the present century, by cinema and television.

This book attempts to relate the particular course of events in this country from when castles stopped being erected anew, through the period of decline in use but survival in fantasy, up to the final destruction in the Civil War. Events took a very different course on the Continent and in Scotland and Ireland, and by drawing attention to the contrasts the colours of the picture are sharpened and the development made more intelligible, no more so than by differing response to the new weapon, artillery, here as opposed to that on the Continent. Some attempt is also made to relate alterations in design to contemporary social changes, without, I hope, trying to climb too far up the greasy pole of socio-architectural history! Special attention has been paid to the systematic destruction of the Interregnum, far more extensive than is usually appreciated, while the concluding chapter briefly describes the extraordinarily enticing quality the image has continued to hold over the last 300 years.

My interest in this subject was first aroused when I was able to demonstrate that the great brick entry tower at Farnham Castle, Surrey, which so dominates the town, was not a Tudor addition but was erected in the fifteenth century, apparently as a direct imitation of the tower at Tattershall Castle, Lincolnshire. Later events brought me into a position of guide-writer to the latter and I also had considerable dealings with Lord Cromwell's manor at South Wingfield, Derbyshire. Over some years I had seen the demolished stump of Bolingbroke Castle emerge from the turf, and subsequently I had not a little to do with the great Jacobean and Carolean edifice at Bolsover, Derbyshire, and afterwards with the remarkable reconstruction of the Marquess of Bute at Castell Coch, Glamorgan. Peter Smith's map of tower-houses concentrated my thoughts, and a first essay in this field was a contribution on the abandonment of the castle in Wales and the Marches. The subject clearly needed further treatment.

The appendices that provide the material on which the book is in no small measure based will, it is hoped, have independent use for reference. As we are venturing into new ground the reader has to be supplied with the information that is not available in published sources. The illustrations have been chosen to further understanding of the text rather than purposefully to beautify it. There is always a temptation to do the latter; the library shelves groan under the weight of lavishly illustrated volumes that seek precisely to do that and not much else. If the fantasy element is to be discussed it is perhaps as well for the author not to be drawn himself too much into the fantasies!

Acknowledgement is made in the list of illustrations to those who have kindly allowed their use. However I must record my gratitude to those colleagues (alas, not all alive today), inspectors and architects, in the government service, from whom I have learnt so much. I am particularly beholden to my former colleague Mr J. K. Knight, for the material used in Appendix 4, to Dr D. F. Renn for drawing my attention to a number of useful articles, and to Mr A. Emery for advance loan of his article on South Wingfield. My wife has carried the burden of typing the text, and has taken most of the photographs.

M. W. Thompson

Cambridge, 1986

Introduction

The English traveller in France seeking the local castle and asking for the *château* may be surprised to find himself directed to an eighteenth- or nineteenth-century mansion, for he should have added the adjective *fort* or *féodal* in order to be understood. Although the English *castle* (old French *chastel*, from Latin *castellum*) is derived from French, and no doubt had exactly the same sense for French speakers on both sides of the Channel in the twelfth century, there has been a divergence since that time. In French the word denotes the status of the building and its owner, a seigneurial seat, which is close to the original meaning, while in English of today the word has an almost exclusively functional meaning, a residence with massive defences. There is perhaps an analogy with German where the word for medieval castle is *Burg*, although there is no English equivalent for the German *Schloss*, a post-Renaissance seigneurial seat. We shall have to return to the question of status implied in the castle, but first the English functional definition can be employed to eliminate what does not fall within the scope of this book.

A castle is a fortified residence in which the fortifications predominate over the domestic aspect of the structure, and the occupant normally owns or controls a large territory around it. This cuts out tribal hill-forts, Roman forts, Tudor and later coastal forts and so on. The very photogenic forts of Henry VIII are often called 'castles' (Wardour Castle, Deal Castle, St Mawes Castle . . . etc.), but were really defended batteries, i.e. forts with a master-gunner in charge. The distinction between a castle and other forms of residence can perhaps be best illustrated by the two Wingfields. Only the moat, gatehouse and parts of the curtain wall survive at the late fourteenth-century castle of Wingfield, Suffolk (fig. 1), but, in spite of the 'flushwork' ornament on the gatehouse towers, the portcullis groove, arrow slits, moat and most important the curtain wall with wall-walk and parapet, were not ornamental. South Wingfield, Derbyshire (fig. 44) has very properly been called a 'manor', since it was erected in the fifteenth century, for it has no moat, no portcullises, no arrow slits and, most important, no wall-walk and parapet. It is the existence of a massive wall encircling the site, thick enough for defenders to stand on its top behind the shelter of a parapet, that as rule of thumb is the distinguishing feature of a castle. The disposition and form of the residential buildings within the castle had to be adapted to fit within this wall to which they played second fiddle; the story in this book is very largely one of the house trying to escape from this crippling prison.

There remains one very important category of late medieval structure that has to be brought into the definition: the tower-houses of Scotland, Ireland and the Border areas erected between the fourteenth and seventeenth centuries and known as castles. They are most familiar to us from the first two volumes of the great work of MacGibbon and Ross. Where they occur on the Continent, in the Basque area of the Pyrenees for instance,[1] they fall below seigneurial status and so are not counted as castles by the French definition. However on the English functional definition, as permanently occupied residences whose form is entirely dominated by defence, they clearly must be classed as castles. They are perhaps best described as a different *species* within the same *genus*: *Castrum turris* as opposed to *Castrum castrum*.

John Leland writing in *c.* 1540 commented with some surprise that the manor house at South Wingfield far surpassed the castle at Sheffield. He was shocked at the presumption, the status of a castle being so much higher than a manor. Castles had their origin in a society where land was held by military service and a fortified residence was a privilege accorded to great landowners. Only a very restricted social level were entitled to construct them, and normally they served as the administrative centre for a large area. They might be the *caput* (head) of an honour, often associated with the earldom of a county. As the Middle Ages advanced, the social changes by which military tenure was replaced by a cash relationship between tenant and landlord undermined the position of the castle, to some extent depriving it of its social significance; its occupant became simply a great landlord. By the sixteenth century (particularly on newly-acquired monastic lands), it was possible for English noblemen to live in ordinary houses (Burghley, Longleat etc.) using them as their main seats, although it was difficult for Tudor antiquaries to adjust themselves to such changes; in the more rigid society of France the nobility overcame the problem by using the old name for a new type of structure. The status conferred on its owner by a castle not only prolonged the life of the real object but gave almost indefinite endurance to the forms associated with it, like towers and machicolations.

Enough has been said to show that the word 'castle' has had very different connotations in different countries at different times. In the period

1400–1660 with which we are concerned it will be increasingly apparent that its history took a very different course in this country from that of our near neighbours; our understanding will be much greater if an eye is kept on them to compare and contrast their experience with ours. Most of the generalisations that are made about the period will certainly need to be modified. For example, artillery was in very active use in France in sieges in the early fifteenth century but castles multiplied, not decreased, in numbers, while in England, where artillery was only slightly used in sieges until the Civil War, castles freely expired of their own accord in the fifteenth century. Comfort is said to have been the main motive for abandoning castles in this country but it can hardly have weighed heavily in the minds of the constructors of tower-houses in Scotland and Ireland in the fifteenth, sixteenth and seventeenth centuries. The insular position of England is said to have given it special advantages, but the insular position of Ireland only led to a tower-house culture analogous to that in Scotland. The French monarchy was hostile to castles and under Henry IV, or more especially under Richelieu, took active steps to demolish them, while the English Government (until the Interregnum) not

1 The gatehouse of fourteenth-century Wingfield Castle, Suffolk; although it has ornamental features like the flushwork and window tracery, the portcullis groove, arrow slits, moat and curtain wall on either side imply serious defence.

only took no action to restrict them but also seems to have deplored their accelerating decay. These apparent contradictions will only be understood if we go beyond the simple generalisations and try to reach the underlying factors.

The two main institutions that we associate with the Middle Ages, castles and monasteries, are so often thought of together (at least since the Romantic period) that the fundamental differences are forgotten. A monastery was founded on a piece of land given in perpetuity so that the religious, supported by their endowments, could celebrate the divine office there for evermore. It was permanent – perpetuity was its business. A castle, a fortified residence, had no such claims to permanence. The costs of its erection, the estate organisation that grew up about it or the village or town with which it was associated might make it difficult to abandon it and move elsewhere, but there was certainly no inherent reason why this should not be done. The history of the castle is indeed largely a history of abandonment, very frequently in its early history when it was usually constructed of perishable wood that required frequent renewal, less frequent when the walls were built of stone so that its capital value or costs of renewal on an alternative site were infinitely greater. It is not abandonment that is new, although this no doubt accelerated in the fifteenth century, but the virtual end of any kind of replacement of those structures that had become ruinous by new ones built on a new site, or even on the old site, that is distinctive of the period under review.

In the last few years the arithmetic of castles has become a little clearer; according to a recent list[2] there would have been about 1,700 examples in England and Wales, excluding some 270 tower-houses in the Border areas. Some 14,000 castles (5,500 earthwork remains) have been listed for the German-speaking areas of Europe,[3] although no doubt an underestimate. If one allows for France, the homeland of castles, Italy, Spain and so on, perhaps a reasonable guess for a total in western Europe (the Slavic *kremlin* of eastern Europe is not a castle but more akin to a Greek *acropolis*) could be 75,000 to 100,000. The total for England and Wales is then only a tiny portion, 2–3%, of the European total.

About 700 of the 1,700 castles in this country have visible masonry, although masonry may lie concealed beneath the turf in a good many cases in the remaining 1,000 earthworks. The vast majority of these castles have no written history of any kind; in 1959 an historian was able to tabulate only 327 castles recorded in the written sources of 1154–1216.[4] The earthworks are usually, not invariably, of the motte-and-bailey form, a conical mound with a flat top (the motte) and an attached embanked enclosure (the bailey). The timber defences that crowned them no longer survive but are vividly portrayed for us in the Bayeux tapestry. Figure 2 shows the distribution of mottes throughout the British Isles. Their great density on the Welsh border or in Dyfed no doubt reflects the prolonged struggle of their Norman builders with the native Welsh. Further west in Ireland they are common in the eastern part of the island but die out in the west; the Norman invasion began in 1169 so it is almost as if during the process of conquest the practice of erecting mottes died out.

The figures for the large annual expenditure on castle construction recorded by the sheriffs of each county in the Pipe Rolls, tabulated with

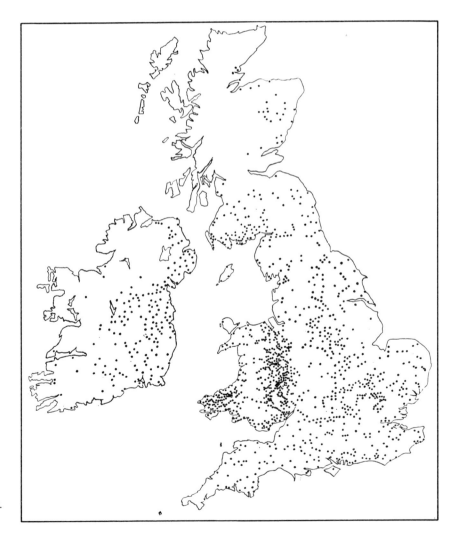

2 A map of Norman mottes in Great Britain and Ireland; note their thick distribution on the Welsh border and rarity in west Ireland, which was invaded from the east in the late twelfth century. (D. F. Renn)

painstaking care by modern historians, confirm the evidence of our own eyes that, in the second half of the twelfth century, Henry II went a long way towards transforming the nature of the castle in this country. By the end of the century the term could hardly be applied to a structure that was not stone. Cheap and hastily erected earth-and-timber fortifications were out, and expensive stone structures, only within the means of the rich, were in. Although not provable, it is reasonable to assume that the construction of mottes had ceased by *c.* 1200 and their use, unless fortified with stone, had virtually terminated by the end of the following century.

Most of the sites marked on the map therefore exist today as grass-grown mounds plotted by the Ordnance Surveyors on their sheets, but otherwise unknown to historians. The vast abandonment that led to this

3 Speed's map of Ely in 1611 showing in the foreground the long-since abandoned Norman motte with a windmill on top.

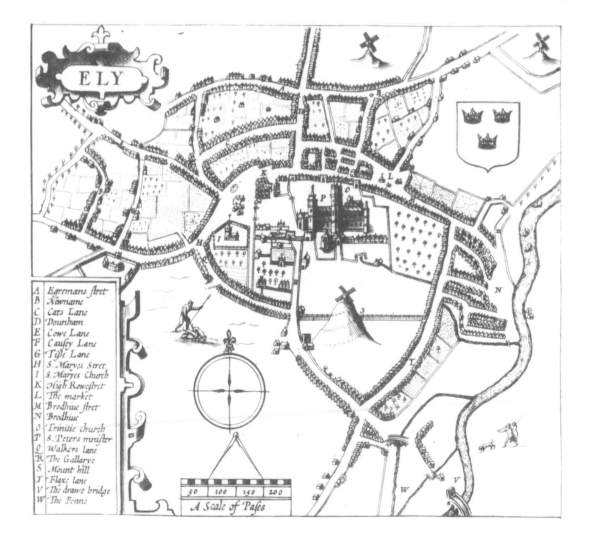

A	Egremans ſtret
B	Nowname
C	Cats Lane
D	Downham
E	Cowe Lane
F	Cauſey Lane
G	Tiſte Lane
H	S. Maryes Stret
I	S. Maryes Church
K	High Roweſtret
L	The market
M	Brodhiue ſtret
N	Brodhiue
O	Trinitie church
P	S. Peters mniſter
Q	Walkers lane
R	The Gallarye
S	Mount hill
T	Flaxe lane
V	The drawe bridge
W	The Fenne

50   100   150   200

A Scale of Paſes

must have taken place in the course of the twelfth and thirteenth centuries. Speed, in 1611, showed the motte at Ely with a windmill on top when the true nature of its origin had been forgotten (fig. 3). He showed other abandoned mottes at Bedford, Stamford and Worcester. His concern was of course with towns but the vast majority of the abandoned sites are in rural areas.

So, in the period after 1400 with which this book is concerned, the castles still in use were the survivors of a much larger number that had existed in the twelfth and thirteenth centuries. Abandonment was not a new thing but a continual process, a sword of Damocles, as it were, that had hung over most castles since their erection.

4 Speed's map of Worcester in 1611 showing the abandoned castle with a prison in its bailey (16, 17).

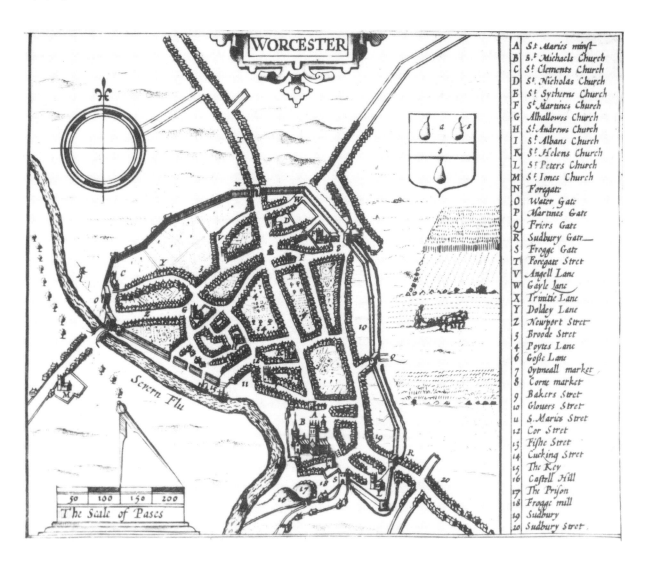

Monasteries associated with castles in the Middle Ages

Religious order	11th C.	12th C.	13th C.	14th C.	15th C.	16th C.
Benedictine	14	13	—	1	—	—
Cluniac	7	6	—	—	—	—
Alien (Benedictine)	15	7	—	—	—	—
Augustinian	2	27 (1 alien)	2	3	—	—
Premonstratensian	—	6	—	—	—	—
Cistercian	—	13	1	1	—	—
Others	1	2	3	2	3	1
Secular canons	6	6	3	16	8	2
Totals	45	80	9	23	11	3

A very interesting light is thrown on the general history of castles in the medieval period by looking at the monasteries associated with them.[5] Throughout the Middle Ages it was felt desirable for the owner of a castle to found a religious house nearby. This was often done at the time of the foundation of the castle, or sometimes by the founder's widow, or sometimes long afterwards. It was not obligatory and by no means all castles had them. The house by its prayers provided intercession for the souls of the founder and his successors, while it could furnish a burial place for the family, as well as providing other services. The table above sets out 170 cases where such a relationship between castle and religious foundation seems to have existed (it is almost certainly incomplete).

As might be expected the great period of foundation was during the eleventh and twelfth centuries, when the majority of parent (and other) castles were also founded. At that time a good many of the new houses (Cluniac and Alien) were dependencies of foreign monasteries which no doubt led to the introduction of many compatriot monks of the Norman castle-builders. A favoured method of foundation was indeed to give the parish church, or sometimes a piece of land, to a monastery at home or abroad and leave it to the house to set up and maintain a 'cell' of the mother house. In the twelfth century, foundations by the new orders, Augustinian, Cistercian and Premonstratensian, were the order of the day, the black canons (Augustinians), being ordained priests and so able to take services in the castle chapel, being particularly popular. From the point of view of the subject of this book, however, it is the striking changes that took place in the thirteenth to sixteenth centuries that deserve special attention.

The remarkable fall in the total number of foundations in the thirteenth century reflects in part a falling-off in monastic foundation as a whole, if we exclude friaries, the mendicants not being very suitable associates for a castle. Nevertheless, even without supporting figures, for the reasons given above, it may be suspected that there was a dramatic fall in castle foundations in the thirteenth century, although there must be caution in using the table to support this view since during this century, castle foundation without an accompanying monastery seems to have been more common. Wales offers the most impressive evidence of this; in the eleventh and twelfth century, castles (Chepstow, Monmouth, Carmarthen etc.) had associated monasteries, but the dozen or so castles founded or rebuilt by Edward I in the conquest did not.

The fourteenth century saw an increase in the number of monastic foundations, and, as we shall see, there may also have been an increase in the number of castle foundations (in England, not in Wales) at this time. The characteristic religious foundation of this period was the college of secular canons, very often attached to the parish church which was sometimes rebuilt at the same time. The canons were celibate priests living in a community but not by a regular rule like the 'regular' monks and canons. The constitution and the physical appearance of their buildings very much resembled that of a college at Oxford or Cambridge surviving from that period. There were a master and fellows, the latter living in cellular lodgings arranged around a court, a plan analogous to that of the large house of the period (as at Oxford or Cambridge) and not connected with the monastic plan. There was an educational aspect to their work (there were boy choristers) but prayers of intercession on behalf of the founder played an important part. The recital of benefactors on the Founder's Day at a Cambridge college most closely reproduces the atmosphere of such an institution. In the rivalry between castle and courtyard house that we shall be describing it is well to remember that in these religious foundations of the castle-builders the traditional medieval monastic plan had already been discarded.

There were Arthurian overtones in the chapel and associated college founded in Windsor Castle by Edward III, who created the new knightly Order of the Garter, and there may well have been an element of deliberate archaism in other foundations. It was a matter of status: the authentic castle required a religious house to accompany it. One feels this at Tattershall, Lincolnshire, although the actual creation of the college and reconstruction of the parish church were carried out by the castle-builder's executor. At Thornbury, Gloucestershire, a large college was planned just a few years before the Reformation, no doubt to confer suitable status on the splendid 'castle' (if we may use this term) then licensed and being built by the unfortunate Duke of Buckingham at the time of his execution in 1522.

To Tobias Hunt Esq.
This Prospect is humbly Inscribed by his Obedient Serv.
Sam. & Nath. Buck

THIS Castle appears to have been of considerable strength. It was first built by John de Norwich, who obtained a License from K. Edward III. to make a Castle of his House here. He left it to his Grandson, John, and he to his Cousin & next Heir Catherine de Brews, or Bruze; but, she taking on her the Habit of a Nun, soon after Robert de Ufford E. of Suffolk, & Son of Margaret de Norwich, entered it as next Heir. From the Uffords it came to the Wettenhams, who from hence took their Name. In this Castle was a College or Chantry, founded by S. John de Norwich, K. Vice Admiral of England, dedicated to God & y. Blessed Virgin. Annual Value 202. 7. 5. — Tis now the Property of Tobias Hunt Esq. 1 College.   Sam. & Nath. Buck del. et Sculp. Publish'd according to Act of Parliament Mar. 25. 1738.

Unhappily, very few of the buildings of such colleges survive, since, like the monasteries, they were formally dissolved by statute. The best example is at Windsor Castle with its great chapel and cellular lodgings built for the canons by Edward IV. At Mettingham in Suffolk the castle and college were founded by Sir John de Norwich in the middle of the fourteenth century, but subsequently the college was moved into the abandoned castle, an unusual turn of events. The gatehouse and few fragments that survive belong to the castle rather than the college (fig. 5).

The fortunes of a particular castle were of course bound up with the family history of its owners. No two were alike and even when we know the family tree this does not mean the castle experienced the same vicissitudes, particularly if it was held in plurality. The lack of male heirs with the division of the estate among daughters could (then as now) have serious consequences. Richard's Castle on the borders of Herefordshire and Shropshire traces its history back to the pre-Conquest period and its position on the Welsh border ensured it a lively history in the twelfth and thirteenth centuries.[6] In the fourteenth century it appears to have been in full vigour with some kind of attached borough, but the lack of male heirs caused division of the property among four daughters. What was a misfortune in the twelfth and thirteenth centuries could be a disaster in the contracting society of the later Middle Ages; by the time of

5 View in 1728 of ruins of Mettingham Castle, founded as a castle in the fourteenth century but later taken over by a college of secular canons.

Leland the ruined walls enclosed a timber-framed farmhouse. No doubt other factors played a part, such as its position on a hill away from the main road, but the absence of a resident lord, it may be suspected, was the main one. This fate, degradation from a seigneurial seat to a farmhouse, was undoubtedly the experience of a very large number of castles in the later Middle Ages and no doubt for not very dissimilar reasons.

In the eleventh and twelfth centuries it was probably not difficult to set oneself up in a motte and bailey on the Welsh border, but with changes in the later part of the twelfth century the maintenance of a castle became a much more costly and demanding business. Nevertheless, a castle that remained occupied by its owner rather than being absorbed into a large group of estates may in the long run have had more chance of survival; a building that is inhabited by its owner is much more likely to survive than one maintained by local officers. A striking case is Berkeley, Gloucestershire where the castle and its owners have shown the most astonishing ability to survive.

The major castles of the Middle Ages were not however held singly but in plurality, as is at once apparent from the 'Domesday Book'. At that time the same person might hold castles in different parts of England, as well as on the other side of the Channel. The Crown held the largest number, and for various reasons – forfeiture, the conquest of Wales, absorption of the Duchy of Lancaster etc. – this number increased progressively, possibly encouraged by deliberate policy. The sovereign could not possibly live in such a large number of castles or indeed visit them all; their maintenance was entirely in the hands of local officials and as their principal motive for erection, defence, diminished or vanished in the later Middle Ages so the drift towards dereliction and decay was almost irresistible. For most of the time the principal rooms of the castle were disused, and while an annual visit by the lord might keep staff up to the mark, infrequent or no visits at all were a recipe for neglect. Only those parts in active use for a prison or courthouse would have to be properly maintained. The inspections of the Duchy of Lancaster in the fifteenth century or the countless Tudor surveys of Crown castles well illustrate this. The greater number of Crown castles made them more vulnerable to neglect and its progress is better documented, but the same factors must of course have operated to some extent in all cases of plural ownership.

From a very early date castles served other purposes than that of just a residence for a lord; not only were they centres of administration for the extensive estates whose profits formed part of the lord's income at a time when land was the main source of wealth, but from very early times they also served as the seat of justice for the surrounding region. The hall provided ample accommodation for the court, as it still does at Oakham and Winchester, while the towers provided strong rooms to secure prisoners. Many castles served as prisons into modern times: Norwich, Lincoln, Lancaster, York, Flint, Carmarthen, Haverfordwest. These ancillary functions may have conduced to their survival, but in county towns increasing business of this kind must have made them unpleasant places to live in. The prime example of a castle where the resident lord was crowded out by its use as a prison and for numerous Governmental activities was the Tower of London. Built by William II as a royal residence, even in early times the proximity of the City must have made Westminster and Windsor more agreeable residences; by Tudor times the accumulation of activities within it led to its virtual abandonment as a royal residence except for special occasions such as the coronation procession.

6 The great mound at Thetford, the superstructure of which was destroyed by Henry II in 1173.

A factor leading to abrupt abandonment that we cannot ignore, although very difficult to quantify, is punitive demolition. Information about the construction of castles in Stephen's reign and their subsequent demolition by Henry II is given in fairly general terms by chroniclers. Wooden structures can be burnt fairly easily but also reconstructed without much difficulty. Probably a fair number of the dots on the distribution map (fig. 2) are sites of castles abandoned after demolition but it would be rash to guess at how many. We are on firmer ground at Huntingdon and Thetford where the Pipe Rolls (Sheriff's annual accounts) record costs of tearing down the timber structures[7] and the sites have apparently been desolate ever since (figs. 6, 7). The Pipe Roll for 1155 records purchases of picks for demolishing the Bishop of Winchester's castles, and at

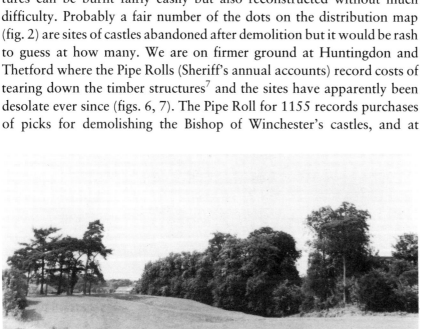

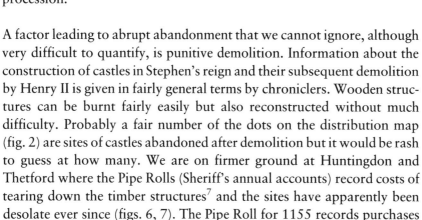

7 Earthworks of Huntingdon Castle, the superstructure of which was destroyed in 1174.

Farnham, Surrey, eloquent testimony to this has been found in his castle in the form of the stump of a great square stone tower on top of the motte.[8] In this case the castle itself was not abandoned; later in the century the motte was enclosed with a massive stone wall. In the list previously mentioned of 327 castles documented between 1154 and 1216 nearly 10% were recorded as having been demolished.[9]

In the twelfth century the castle was a resilient, robust institution that could recover from demolition by reconstruction as we have seen at Farnham. In the later Middle Ages this vitality had been lost and demolition terminated its life. A remarkable case is Bedford Castle deliberately dismantled following the hanging of the garrison after the successful siege in 1224,[10] and although Bedford was an important town its castle was never reconstructed; Speed shows the motte and a low ruinous wall in 1611 (fig. 8). The important castle at Malton, Yorkshire, had been

8 Speed's map of Bedford in 1611 showing the ruins of the castle (S, 9) demolished by Henry III in 1224.

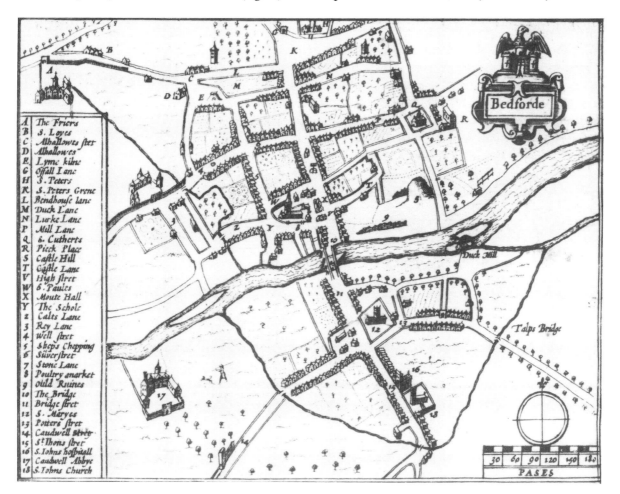

seized by the Scots in 1322 and after demolition seems simply to have become pasture by the fifteenth century.[11] Carreg Cennen Castle in Dyfed was partially demolished in 1462 and never recovered.[12]

Punitive demolition (as opposed to robbing stone from already ruinous structures) certainly played a part, prior to 1642, in the abandonment of castles, but I doubt whether it should be rated as more than a significant contributory factor.

Anyone concerned with large buildings will know that they do not survive simply of their own accord; in order to function properly they require minor maintenance almost continuously and major operations at longer intervals. Gutters become blocked, drains overflow, woodwork rots, thatch, tiles and lead have finite lives, walls crack, tilt or move because of subsidence, and so on. There are unpredictable vagaries of weather to contend with: storms and wind; medieval accounts make frequent mention of havoc created *a magno vento*. Medieval buildings were at much greater risk than modern ones: erected often with inadequate (or even no) foundations, set near the edge of a large ditch or moat, sometimes built on made-up ground, relying completely on lime mortar (no concrete), built often of easily weathering stone, lacking a damp course, vulnerable from many open fires, not to mention braziers for casting lead on roofs . . . the recital need not be prolonged. There was no possibility of recouping loss by insurance in the event of an accident; the cost of repairs had to be met from income. A moment's reflection on the problems and costs of operating the intricate waterworks (without flooding during a storm), not to mention maintaining the multitude of buildings, at Kenilworth Castle, Warwickshire, is sufficient to kindle our sympathy for those who had to do it.[13]

The exuberant construction work of the earlier Middle Ages had left a wealth of buildings to the later Middle Ages, so it is not surprising that with their reduced resources and somewhat different requirements a large part of the load was shed.

A castle normally stood at the centre of an estate the function of which was to make money, not to spend it. The revenue came from direct farming, rents, various feudal dues and so on. An account was drawn up each year at the castle by the reeve or bailiff or other responsible officer. Many hundreds or rather thousands of such accounts survive, known as Ministers' accounts. The charges for the maintenance of the castle are usually recorded and of course deducted from the revenue. There was then a constant annual reminder of the burden that the maintenance of its buildings represented. This was not so serious a matter when the castle was in active use. For example at Pickering Castle, Yorkshire[14] Thomas, Earl of Lancaster, ordered the construction of a new hall in 1314 and in the summer of 1323, just after the Scottish invasion, Edward II spent three weeks at the castle when he ordered the construction of new fortifications. Special money had to be made available of course for such large works. In the fifteenth century it was a very different story: there was no sign of the lord (it was Duchy of Lancaster property) for decades on end and although minor works are recorded in great detail one must suspect that this was something of a cover-up for widespread neglect and deterioration. It is reasonable to assume this from Leland's description of its decayed state in *c.* 1540.

A castle yielded no revenue in itself except for a pittance for leasing the *herbage* or pasture in the ditches. In frequent inquisitions or surveys of the later Middle Ages there is often written against it *valet nihil* (it is worth nothing). Antiquaries often erroneously interpret this as meaning its capital value was nothing and therefore that it was ruinous; it merely means that it yielded no revenue. It is nevertheless indicative of an unfriendly state of mind that the services it allegedly provided (accommodation and protection) were overlooked and attention was drawn to the fact that it produced no revenue. The phrase has an ominous ring to it!

A concrete example may help to illustrate the point. The great castle at Devizes, Wiltshire, had been founded by Bishop Roger of Salisbury early in the twelfth century. An Inquisition of 27 January 1405 found of the castle 'which is no net yearly value because it needs much repair from year to year'.[15] This must have been followed by accelerated abandonment since by the time of Leland's visit in *c.* 1540 it was a total ruin.

Bishop Roger of Salisbury, who also built castles at Old Sarum (abandoned by the fourteenth century), Sherborne in Dorset and Kidwelly in Dyfed evidently set an example to his colleagues in the sees of Lincoln and Winchester. According to the chronicler, that great twelfth-century Bishop of Winchester, also abbot of Glastonbury, Henry of Blois, erected six castles in 1138 at Farnham, Winchester (Wolvesey), Merdon and Bishop's Waltham (Hampshire), Downton (Wiltshire) and Taunton (Somerset).[16] The annual accounts of the forty or fifty manors of the bishopric, the so-called Winchester Pipe Rolls, have survived with intermittent gaps, not alas from the time of Bishop Henry but from the reign of King John to Tudor times. Bishops' estates enjoyed a high degree of continuity of ownership with intervals only after the death of a bishop and before the appointment of his successor when the king enjoyed the revenues. Since they were not subject to the varied fortunes of private estates the accounts should provide an unrivalled insight into the history of the castles over that period of 300 years, although unfortunately they have never been studied with that object in view.

We have seen that Henry II demolished the castles of Bishop Henry of Blois; they seem all to have been rebuilt except Downton which disappeared from sight before the thirteenth century.[17] Merdon was the next casualty, disappearing in the fourteenth century. Farnham and Wolvesey were in most active use and fared best, for Bishop's Waltham (a palace rather than a castle) and Taunton it was perhaps more of a struggle. The *Custus domorum*, costs of the houses, that occurs year after year in each manor impresses on one's mind what an unrelenting task the upkeep of such buildings represented for their owners. The size of the entries is no clue as to the scale of the work carried out – almost the opposite is the case, the thirteenth-century entries being laconic and the fifteenth-century verbose! There were however major works of great interest in the fifteenth century like the construction of the large brick entry tower at Farnham Castle which did so much to alter both the accommodation and appearance of the castle.[18]

In this introduction an attempt has been made to give the background arithmetic of abandonment and the mechanics – one might almost say natural processes – by which it took place. The limited but not insignificant part played by punitive demolition has been discussed. The really central subjects were touched on in the opening section when trying to disentangle the three constituent elements; fortification, residence and status, which part company as the castle draws to its end as a fully functional structure. The necessity for fortification will be the starting point, for it is from this that the rest flows; this must be the first concern and the other subjects will follow in the later chapters. Did fortification cease because it was no longer necessary or because a new weapon of such power had been introduced that it was no longer practicable? In the next two chapters it will be argued that the evidence points towards the first reason in this country although perhaps the second on the Continent, but in neither case is there a straight and simple answer to the question.

Chapter 2

Fifteenth-century contrasts

The twentieth century has offered some dramatic examples of building types that have suddenly ceased to be erected: flamboyant cinemas were constructed in every town in the 1920s and 1930s but their construction stopped in 1939; more significantly the great country house (the French château), for centuries the dominant feature of the English rural scene, ceased to be constructed after 1914. The changes were not the direct result of the wars (the Second World War indeed promoted the cinema), but were due to alteration in the form of entertainment sought after in the first case and profound social and economic changes in the latter. In both cases the existing buildings have continued in use in dwindling numbers since there are no replacements for losses. There is a striking analogy between these events and the experience of the castle in this country in the early fifteenth century, made the more interesting in that the country house is the direct heir and successor to the medieval castle.

The change could hardly have been foreseen in the fourteenth century when a great deal of castle construction took place. Although it is not easy to quantify there may indeed have been an increase over the previous century (in England, not in Wales). There were of course the massive reconstruction works at Windsor, Warwick and Kenilworth, although these were perhaps not so much new works as expressions of dissatisfaction with old ones. There were however many new foundations.[1] Some were for a specific purpose: on the south coast, after the French raids, at Bodiam, Sussex, and Cooling, Kent, and Queenborough built by the Crown in Sheppey. The latter, of rather idiosyncratic circular shape, recalls the later artillery forts of Henry VIII, but its real affinities are with the petal-like plans of Old Wardour, Wiltshire and Nunney, Somerset. Compact tower-like plans were now favoured although courtyard plans were still popular. There are other examples in the south like Wingfield, Suffolk or Hemyock, Devon, but it is the prodigious amount of castle-building in the northern counties during the last decades of the century that attracts notice: Sherriff Hutton, Bolton, Cawood, Harewood, Wressell (Humberside) in Yorkshire, Raby and Lumley in County

Durham, Doddington and Macclesfield in Cheshire, Penrith in Cumberland. This still excludes tower-houses which start at this time and continue to the seventeenth century.

The abruptness of the cessation of castle-building is that much more impressive in the North because of its intensity in the decades immediately preceding 1400. An historian who has examined the records of the Percy family from the fifteenth century has told us: '... Of large-scale expenditure on building the surviving accounts make no mention. The castles of Alnwick and Warkworth belong to the fourteenth century ...'[2]

During the eleventh, twelfth and thirteenth centuries the leading founder of castles had been the Crown: castle construction had often been associated with the execution of royal policy both in England and Wales. In the fourteenth century this was not so: although major works were carried out on royal castles, new foundations were largely a matter for the nobility. This was in marked contrast to the French monarchy. Between the construction of Queenborough in the 1360s and the great series of new coastal forts erected by Henry VIII, no major fortification on a new site was undertaken by the Crown. Alterations and additions to existing structures were made, sometimes substantial, but the principal architectural works that come to mind associated with royalty in this period are not military: Sheen or Richmond Palace, King's College Chapel, St George's Chapel, Eltham Palace ...

The demolition of castles by Henry II has been mentioned (p. 12); the right to fortify was a privilege granted by royal licence, the wording of the licence being copied on to the back of the Patent Roll. These licences by Letters Patent should therefore provide a clue to the amount of fortification carried out in the fourteenth as opposed to the fifteenth century.[3] In some sense they do but unfortunately many works appear to have been unlicensed (or recorded elsewhere, in some cases on the Charter Rolls) and in any case the licence was not like modern planning permission. They seem to have been sought after as conferring a certain prestige, like a modern 'listing'. Many were for fairly minor alterations, rather than new foundations. Until recently the figures available were 305 licences for the fourteenth century and 15 for the fifteenth, but by extending the search beyond the Patent Rolls the current figures are 380 for the former and 80 for the latter. However we may judge 'licences to crenellate' these figures are fairly suggestive.

In chapter 5 new foundations will be discussed to which I have given the generic name of 'show castles', since their object was evidently mainly to impress by a martial face rather than act as a serious fortification; the contrast with the formidable defences of the structures just described from the previous century is evident.

Turning from new castles to old ones, any assessment of the condition of already-existing ones is fraught with difficulty. Decay or disuse, dereliction, ruin do not attract the attention in the way that new construction does, by the physical upheavals for digging ditches, bringing in materials, the arrival of craftsmen and labourers, quite apart from the administrative aspect of costs etc. The silent advance of decay passes unchronicled and escapes the attention of the auditor, which is indeed what the local officers in charge of maintenance may particularly wish! Prolix descriptions of minor repairs are often a way of concealing major deterioration.

The most revealing information comes from observers from outside who saw the matter with a fresh eye so to speak, that is surveyors and travelling topographers. Detailed surveys abound from Tudor times but are less common in the fifteenth century. The large body of evidence from early Tudor times, either in surveys or mentions by Leland, show castles in a condition that can only have been reached by a long period of neglect extending over much of the previous century. Fuller reference will be made to this in chapter 6.

The only topographer of the fifteenth century to help us, William Worcester, a native of Bristol and later secretary to Sir John Fastolf, who therefore had experience in the south of England, has left us an account of his journeys in 1479–80.[4] One might be pardoned for thinking that in Cornwall castles were normally ruined and in Wiltshire often so. He was liable to confuse prehistoric hill-forts with castles, but nevertheless the fact that he felt so strongly about the matter is in itself suggestive of the contemporary state of affairs. His description which is detailed (he was a man who paced out the measurements) of the castle in his native town of Bristol with its hall in total ruin can leave no doubt that it had not seen proper residential occupation for a very long period of time.

In Appendix 1 (see p. 170), forty castles are listed which were reported to be derelict or ruinous in the fifteenth century by Worcester himself, or where I have come across original evidence or have relied on the authors of the *History of the King's Works*. It should be regarded as a sample and in no sense exhaustive. The list includes castles at major towns like Norwich, York, Bristol, Cambridge etc. Some castles had passed out of use long before, like Bedford or Malton, but the mere fact that they had not been reconstructed is suggestive. At Worcester the castle probably went out of use in the thirteenth century but in the fifteenth century its materials were being used to repair the town walls, perhaps an indication of the relative importance of the two types of fortification at this period.

There can be no doubt that neglect, decay and ruin were very widespread, which must imply disuse. By the very nature of their discontinuous use, castles could suffer long periods of neglect and even fall into decay, but ruin has to go a long way before a structure is entirely beyond rehabilitation. Leland was told that Castle Hedingham (included in the list) had been brought back into use in early Tudor times when its domestic buildings were reconstructed in brick. Long periods of neglect can be the first stage of permanent disuse. It is to this matter that we must now turn.

At the time of Owain Glyndŵr's rebellion, which soon affected the whole of Wales, the Government placed reliance upon the occupants of castles in southern Wales to defend themselves. In September 1403, the king, Henry IV, then at Worcester, ordered the owners of 22 castles in South Wales from Manorbier in the west (Llawhaden, Llandovery, Laugharne, Crickhowell, Tretower etc.) to Gwent and the English borders in the east (Abergavenny, Usk, Caerphilly, Caerleon, Stapleton, Snodhill etc.) to fortify and supply their castles.[5] It was evidently considered that the buildings were sufficiently well-maintained for them to be used in this way during the emergency. Seventy years later Parliament petitioned the king 'to consider the intolerable extortions, oppressions and wrongs' suffered by his subjects in this area due to 'the outrageous demeaning of Welshmen, favoured under such persons as have the keeping of castles and other places of strength . . . '[6] Some of the castles of 1403 (Clyro, Caerphilly, Snodhill, Caerleon) were found by Leland to be ruinous sixty years later; we may suspect indeed that it was not so much the 'favour' of their keepers that was the problem as that the condition of their fabric rendered them unfit to exert such control. As a result of the petition the elder son of Edward IV was created Prince of Wales and in due course an organisation arose at Ludlow that became the Council of the Marches in Wales, effectively transferring authority from the largely defunct marcher castles to the Yorkist and royal seat whose life was prolonged for two hundred years.

Information of this kind has to be acquired indirectly, as in this case, but particularly illuminating are the remarks of foreign observers who were usually surprised by the situation in this country compared with that in their own. Thus a Milanese envoy writing in 1497 said of Henry VII: 'He garrisons two or three fortresses contrary to the custom of his predecessors who garrisoned no place. He has neither ordnance nor munitions of war, and his bodyguard is supposed not to amount to one hundred men, although he is now living in a forest district that is unfortified.'[7] No doubt this is a little (but probably not much) exaggerated; there were garrisons at Calais, on the Scottish border and in Wales. The contrast with Renaissance Italy must however have been impressive extending to the nobility who according to Polydore Vergil in England built no castles nor repaired old ones.

Another Italian writing at about the same time has often been quoted (my italics): 'In former times the titled nobility, though, as I said before, they possessed *no fortresses* [*fortezze*], nor judiciary powers, were extremely profuse in their expenditure, and kept a very great retinue in their houses (which is a thing the English delight in beyond measure), and in this manner they made themselves a multitude of retainers and followers with whom they afterwards molested the Court . . . '.[8]

Here it is not the king but the nobility that is referred to; fortresses played no part in their lives we are told. Something will be said about the large retinues that the nobility liked to keep in their houses when discussing the courtyard house, but the important point here is that it was the large bodies of retainers that 'molested the Court'. There had been Government legislation between the time of Edward I and Edward IV seeking to restrict 'livery and maintenance', the misuse of large bodies of retainers wearing the lord's livery. This was reckoned to be the cause of much civil disorder and abuse of the courts, but there was no legislation against castles, nor indeed any suggestion that they were the cause of disorders. The misdeeds of the 'overmighty subject', a phrase coined by Sir John Fortescue in the fifteenth century, were never attributed to misuse of his castles. In view of the blame that was heaped on castles in the reign of Stephen or in the Civil War (contrast the attitude of the French monarchy in the sixteenth and seventeenth centuries) it is most unlikely that they would not have been made the scapegoat for the troubles if there was any likelihood of making the charge stick. Had they been in very active use we would have expected them to have been citadels of unrest.

The remarkable fact that now requires attention is the divergence that took place in the development of the castle in the later Middle Ages in most of this country as opposed to that in Scotland and the Border area together with Ireland on the one hand, and to that on the far side of the Channel in France on the other. The rest of this chapter will concentrate on this subject starting with the former region.

Travellers in the Border area, Scotland or Ireland will be familiar with the tall square stone towers that form such a prominent feature in the landscape of those regions. The English visitor at first tends to think that they are twelfth-century Norman keeps of the type with which he is familiar. This is not the case; they are towers for living in, tower-houses, erected between the fourteenth and seventeenth centuries. Although there are considerable variations between and within the different areas, the towers are normally twenty to sixty feet square and two to five storeys high. There is usually a stone vault over the ground floor room and sometimes over other floors. The principal living room with fireplace, for they were permanent homes not places of temporary refuge, was above the vault. Sometimes they had a stone roof. They can be rectangular and much larger, while the Scottish ones developed annexes giving an L- or Z-shaped ground plan. Later Scottish ones have the most elaborate corbelled projections bearing turrets (*bartisans*) or flues. They could have the entry at first floor level reached by external steps, or were entered at ground floor level through a door closed by a grill (a *yett*). The ground floor room sometimes had a separate entry and was evidently used for animals. The top of the tower was crenellated and there is no doubt they were designed to be defended against at least a raid. In the regions where they were in use they superseded more orthodox enclosure castles, and were the homes of a wider social range than the latter, from the top down to quite modest landowners. They have a date range corresponding to courtyard houses and halls with cross wings in England.

The accompanying map (fig. 10) prepared by Mr P. Smith, Secretary of the Royal Commission on Ancient and Historical Monuments in Wales, shows the distribution of tower-houses throughout the British Isles, the size of the black circle corresponding to the number of examples in each county. It will be seen that they are virtually absent from England except the Border counties, common in Scotland south of the Great Glen, common in Ireland occurring in great profusion in Munster. An example drawn by Speed at Enniskillen is illustrated (fig. 9). The three different areas will be briefly discussed.

The Elizabethan antiquary, William Camden, who had no doubt about the military origin of the towers, remarked speaking of Northumberland:

> The country itself is mostly rough and barren and seems to have hardened the very carcasses of its inhabitants: whom the neighbouring Scots have rendered yet more hardy, sometimes inuring them to war, and sometimes amicably communicating their customs and ways of living; whence they are become a most warlike people and excellent horsemen. And whereas they have generally devoted themselves to war, there is not a man of fashion

9 Speed's view in 1611 of the Irish tower-house at Enniskillen on Lough Earne.

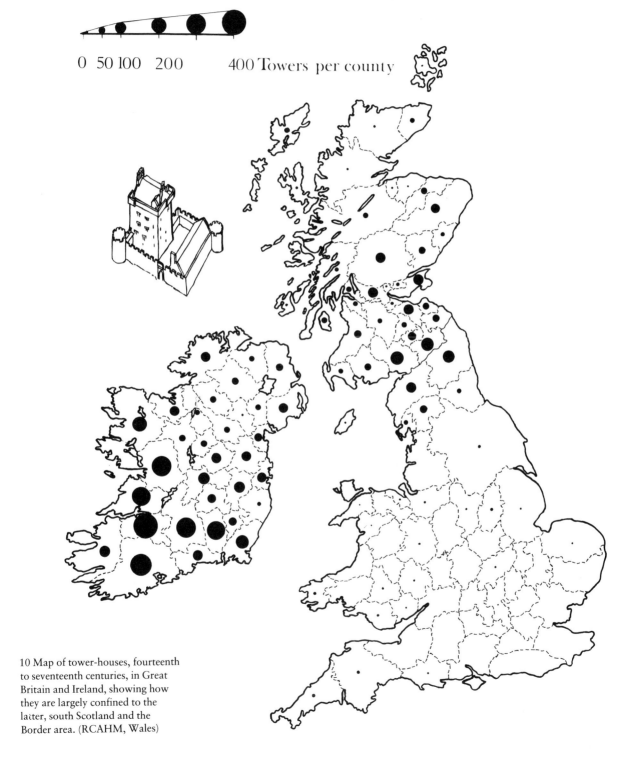

0 50 100 200 400 Towers per county

10 Map of tower-houses, fourteenth to seventeenth centuries, in Great Britain and Ireland, showing how they are largely confined to the latter, south Scotland and the Border area. (RCAHM, Wales)

among them but has his little castle and fort; and so the country came to be divided into a great many baronies . . .[9]

We are very well-informed from surveys made of the area in 1415 (seventy-eight towers) and 1541 (much decay but towers still being constructed) which allows us to amplify Camden's observations.[10] The tower at Dacre, Cumberland, is a good early example of three storeys vaulted over two rooms at basement level with principal living room on the first floor (figs. 11, 12).

Drawings of numerous Scottish towers were made by MacGibbon and Ross in the last century;[11] a fine fifteenth-century example at Comlongon, Dumfriesshire is illustrated (figs. 13, 14). The vaulted basement, the great fireplace in the living room or hall above, the two floors above, the stone roofs and machicolated parapet should be noted. It is a massive structure with walls twelve foot thick at the base.

Of castles in Ireland Camden commented:

. . . and some other castles of less note which like those in other parts of Ireland are no more than towers, with narrow loop-holes rather than windows; to which adjoins a hall made of turf, and roofed over with thatch, and a large yard fenced quite round with a ditch and hedge to defend their cattle from thieves . . .[12]

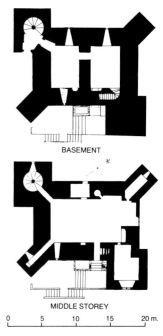

BASEMENT

MIDDLE STOREY

0   5   10   15   20 m.

11 Dacre Castle, Cumberland, an early (fourteenth-century) tower-house, plan at both floors, the lower being vaulted.

13 Comlongon Castle, Dumfriesshire, a fifteenth-century tower; note its massive nature and elaborate machicolations and corner turrets.

14 Comlongon Castle, Dumfriesshire; plan and section show it has three storeys over a vaulted basement, and stone-roofed galleries at roof level.

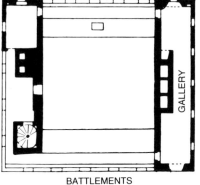

BATTLEMENTS

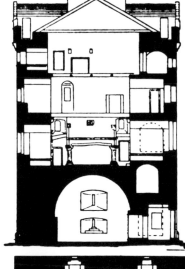

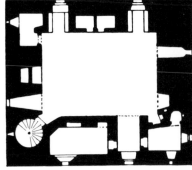

SECOND FLOOR

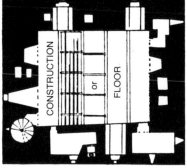

CONSTRUCTION   or   FLOOR

THIRD FLOOR

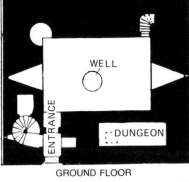

WELL

ENTRANCE

DUNGEON

GROUND FLOOR

0   5   10   15   20 m.

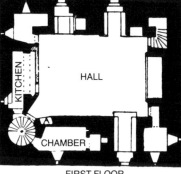

KITCHEN   HALL

CHAMBER

FIRST FLOOR

◀ 12 (left) Dacre Castle, Cumberland, a nineteenth-century view of the fourteenth-century tower, its windows being seventeenth-century insertions.

Some of these are known as '£10 castles' from the bounty of £10 that the Government offered to people to build castles in those areas which it could not control, a fairly explicit admission of the conditions prevailing that required such defences. The Irish towers are less robust and far less ornamented than the Scottish ones although being narrower look taller, but perhaps represent a common Gaelic response to a background of clan disorders.

The example illustrated (figs. 15, 16) at Clara, County Kilkenny, had five storeys and an attic. The ground floor is not vaulted, the only vault being at third-floor level. To judge by the fireplaces there was a principal living room at fourth floor level over the vault, with further living accommodation on the second floor. Note the square-headed windows and the characteristic Irish battlements with stepped merlons.

15 Clara Castle, Kilkenny; a view of the five-storeyed tower. Note the stepped 'Irish' merlons.

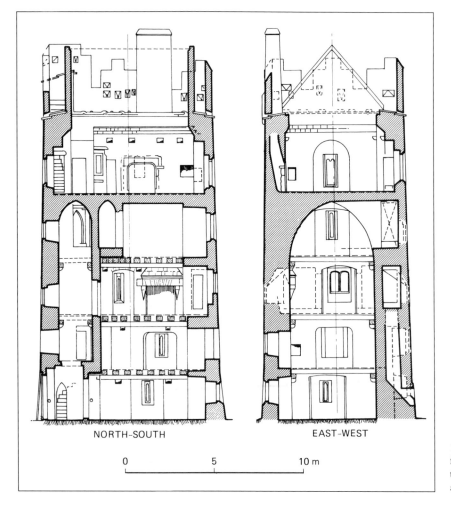

NORTH–SOUTH

EAST–WEST

0   5   10 m

16 Clara Castle, Kilkenny; a five-storeyed tower vaulted at third-storey level. Note fireplaces at second and fourth storey.

At first sight the contrast between France and Scotland and Ireland could hardly be greater, but there was one very important feature in common: the dwellings of the nobility required defence to a much later date than in England, into the sixteenth or seventeenth centuries. England was indeed in a happy position by being largely able to dispense with such defences in the fifteenth century and entirely in the sixteenth.

In the fourteenth century there is some resemblance between England and France in that there was an outburst of castle-building in its last decades, although in the latter case on a far grander scale than in this country. One thinks of Vincennes, or the great Pierrefonds (Oise) or Le Ferté-Milon (Aisne), the unfinished masterpiece by the same builder, Louis d'Orléans. The luxurious castles of this period have been compared to the famous châteaux of the Loire of the Renaissance era, and indeed the period has been spoken of as the preface to the Renaissance. To some extent the buildings are recaptured for us in their pristine glory in the Calendar of the *Très riches heures* of the Duke of Berry with its exquisite illuminations by the Limbourg brothers: Vincennes, the Louvre, Clain, Saumur, Etampes, Mehun-sur-Yevres.[13] Most of these had been rebuilt recently and in the illuminations are of quite breath-taking beauty. The Berry Herald (Gilles de Bouvier) described the provinces of France in almost exultant terms, one of the chief criteria being the strength and beauty of their castles.[14] It is the high point of the castle in European history. Unhappily England he says had few walled towns and few castles in spite of being thickly populated! The contempt in which the French held the English in this respect was voiced by the French herald speaking to his English colleague: 'But in England you have only simple manor houses, or if you have any castles for every one that you have we have fifty.' This was written in *c.* 1450 and if the author was Charles of Orléans he certainly knew both countries well.

The almost passionate feeling aroused by a fine castle in France is expressed in this verse from *The Castell of Labour* published in Franch in 1501 and translated into English in 1506.[15] In the morality story a man assailed by evil sees the Castle of Labour as his true objective:

> Then saw I this castle fair and pleasant
> Most rich, strong and sumptuous
> When I it saw so resplendent
> Soothly of heart I was full joyous

An important point to remember is that there were a large number of Englishmen in France in the early years of the fifteenth century during the period of the heady French 'Renaissance'. The English monarch claimed to be king of France, the child Henry VI actually being crowned in Paris. After Agincourt, Charles d'Orléans was brought back a prisoner to England where he remained for twenty years, and there were other prisoners of this kind. The English armies were raised by indenture between a lord and the king, the object of the campaign not being to protect territory so much as to acquire booty from ransoms, taxes, impositions etc. mulcted from the unfortunate natives. The indenture indeed specified that a fraction (a third) of the profits would go to the Crown.[16] Many young Englishmen returned therefore from France with their heads full of the dazzle of French castles and their purses full of gold. Among the 'castle' builders the names of Fastolf, Cromwell and Boteler come to mind. The French experience gave an impulse to the attraction and glamour of castle symbols that lasted until Tudor times, if not later.

The contrast between the countries is no less, indeed more, marked in the fifteenth century. Looking through the lists in Enlart's *Manuel* one might be pardoned for thinking that the major period of castle-building in France fell in the fifteenth century, not only reconstructions but new foundations.[17] There were considerable regional variations: the greatest volume of construction was in the south west (Anjou, Poitou, Berry, Orléanais, Angoumois, Limousin), the Ile de France and the north (Flandres, Artois); the east of France was less affected. According to one authority, in the areas freed from English occupation 'hundreds upon hundreds' of castles and town walls were erected or reconstructed.[18] This is hardly an exaggeration; in Enlart's list I counted nearly 500 new foundations or reconstructions in eleven departments in the south-west. The social status of some of these is no doubt not much more than a manor house in this country, since, except in certain areas, the equivalent of English manor house was not common in medieval France.

Fortified castles continued to be constructed into the early years of the sixteenth century so that the well-known adage at the time of the French Wars of Religion (Huguenots versus Catholics) in the latter part of the century is readily understandable: *Trop de châteaux et par là trop de pauvres* (Too many castles and so too many poor). The complete contrast with the situation in England hardly needs emphasis.

The style of castle varied, certainly not on the grand scale of the previous century, block or courtyard in plan, always moated with drawbridge and portcullis at entry, round towers with very tall conical roofs (a French speciality) and machicolations, their walls with large windows (introduced in the fourteenth century). They can be very handsome buildings which become increasingly less war-like in the latter part of the fifteenth century. Few are closely dated but the still-inhabited example

17 Rambures Castle, Somme; a general view of this north French early fifteenth-century castle; note the *chemin de ronde* and tall conical roofs, especially French features.

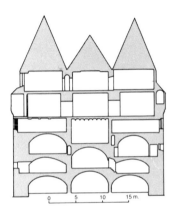

18 Rambures Castle; the section shows vaults at two or three levels which, together with the round shapes of the towers, were perhaps intended to resist artillery impact.

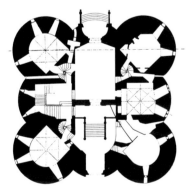

19 Rambures Castle; the ground plan looks like six towers pressed together.

illustrated, at Rambures (Somme) in northern France, which is built of brick, probably belongs to an early part of the century.[20] It is a tower-like structure with circular corner towers united by chords (recalling Nunney, Somerset). It has a broad deep moat and the three lower floor levels are vaulted (figs. 17–19). The towers have conical roofs set in wall-walks rising above the *chemin de rond*, a covered passage running round the tower below the summit corbelled out giving an additional fighting plat-form at a lower level, but also a highly ornamental feature giving the tower a sort of crown, a Gallic speciality. The two lower floors are below the level of the ditch but at second floor level there are windows with gunports below facing the outer lip of the ditch. The walls are nine feet thick, so it is a formidable structure, incapable no doubt of resisting a siege train but not easily taken by a mob or troops without artillery.

The fifteenth-century château was not quite the same thing as it had been in earlier centuries, except in one area where something like the thirteenth-century castle persisted.[21] Socially and culturally Brittany was distinct from France (only united to it politically at the end of the century) expressed in the harsh granite walls of its castles with their old-fashioned ground plans. Hunaudaye Castle (Côtes du Nord) in the plan (fig. 20) shows the smaller dark-shaded towers of the thirteenth century with the later obliquely-hatched towers of the fifteenth century.[22] The decidedly thicker walls of the latter were probably designed to counter the impact of shot from artillery.

However, that Brittany was not so isolated is shown by the well-known highly decorated lodgings at Josselin (Morbihan) (figs. 21, 22) in the courtyard of the castle contrasted with its grim exterior walls enclosing them. It is as if the ornament was trying to break out from the constraint imposed upon it, as indeed it would do in the following century.

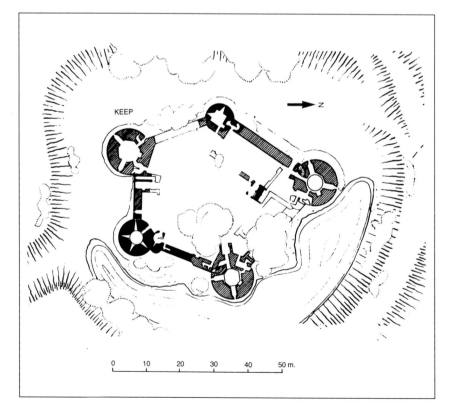

20 Hunaudaye Castle in Brittany; the plan shows two small thirteenth-century towers and three large fifteenth-century towers, the thickened masonry probably intended to withstand artillery shot.

21 Josselin Castle in Brittany, highly ornate lodgings of *c.* 1500.

22 Josselin Castle in Brittany, the exterior view of the lodgings shown in fig. 21 to point the contrast. Note also the conical roofs on the towers.

Chapter 3

Warfare in England and France

'... for he hath no defence of his own except his castles and fortresses.'[1]
Sir John Fortescue (*c*. 1400–76) in contrasting the English and French
monarchs said of the latter that he had to rely on his mercenaries (a little
unfairly perhaps in view of Joan of Arc) and castles, while the former had
extraordinary expenses to 'make new buildings, when he will, for his
pleasure and magnificence'.[2] The English monarch apparently had no
need of garrisons and castles, although he might need to raise an army to
resist invasion. Warfare in the first half of the fifteenth century illustrates
the observations of Sir John.

The battle of Agincourt (*Azincourt*) is so deeply impressed on our
minds, as much by the event itself as by Shakespeare's play, that it has
coloured our view of the nature of the fighting in France at that time. In
fact, the circumstances that led to the battle were peculiar: the French
tried to intercept the English army on its way to Calais, relying on
superiority of numbers to give them victory. In the event, contest in the
open field had a considerable advantage for the English because it allowed
them to use massed discharges of arrows from their longbows, the English
armies of the time being composed predominantly of archers. This kind of
open-field fighting gave full play to the preferred weapon and when
English fought English later in the century both sides preferred it almost
to the exclusion of siege warfare. The French on the other hand did not
employ archers in this way, preferring to counter with fortifications from
which they had rashly emerged on this occasion.

The voluminous material collected by Jehan de Waurin (from Artois)[3]
deals with the English armies throughout the period right up to 1471, and
so includes the earlier part of the Wars of the Roses. There is no need to
describe the tedious series of sieges that constituted the fighting in France,
nor the dramatic change to field fighting that took place when the scene
shifted to England. John or Jehan had fought on the French side at
Agincourt when his father and brother had been killed and later on the
Burgundian side, so he worked from first-hand knowledge of events in
France, and he had been in England. The English were quite skilled in

siege warfare up until the siege of Orléans, the turning point of the war, after which they were outclassed by the French, mainly apparently because of the quantity and quality of French artillery and the skill of their gunners. A mixture of bombards and the old *trebuchets* (slings) and *mangonels* (catapults) seems to have been used in the English assault on Harfleur with good effect.[4] At Orléans twelve years later, when the French were again the defenders, levelling the suburbs to improve the field of fire and constructing earthworks for cannon have a decidedly modern sound.[5] However the English became increasingly sceptical about the value of laying sieges, perhaps because of their lack of success; Fastolf in his report on the management of the war thought further effort should not be wasted on this.[6] The French advance continued relentlessly, culminating in the re-conquest of Normandy in a year and six days after a series of most rapid assaults with artillery on the chief strongpoints. The success of French arms has been attributed, no doubt rightly, to the discipline of the troops and the excellent provision of artillery, it being reported that the French king had so many guns and of such a variety that no one had seen the like.[7]

Sieges had been regarded as a normal part of the fighting in the early fifteenth century: '. . . no archer or any of the common soldiers make assault to any castle or fortress without the presence and will of some captain . . .' the statutes of Henry V had laid down.[8] That had been in the period of advance; in the period of retreat the English showed themselves to be increasingly incapable of withstanding sieges mounted by French forces, it is true, that were better equipped and more strongly motivated. It is time to turn back to England to see how warfare was conducted here in the second half of the century.

That the form of fighting was different in England from that on the Continent the well-known passage from Philippe de Commynes referring to the Wars of the Roses makes clear: '. . . the realm of England enjoys one favour above all other realms that neither the countryside nor the people are destroyed, nor are buildings burnt or demolished. Misfortune falls on soldiers and on nobles in particular . . .'.[9] What is meant is that the fighting was largely confined to battles in the field outside towns and that the buildings and people who were not contestants went largely unmolested. No doubt there must be some qualifications – St Albans, Stamford or other places can hardly have escaped damage – but the studies by historians, and there have been several in recent years,[10] go a long way to support this.

Just as Shakespeare's *Henry V* may have misdirected our attention on the nature of the wars in France, so the description of the famous siege of Caister Castle, Norfolk, in the Paston Letters[11] may have blurred our vision of the real nature of the fighting in the Wars of the Roses. The siege had nothing to do with the dynastic wars then in progress, except that perhaps in the late summer of 1469 Edward IV was hardly in a position to support Paston. The manor of Caister with its castle which had been bequeathed by Sir John Fastolf to Sir John Paston was claimed by the Duke of Norfolk as his property, and so determining to establish his claim by force he sent a small army to besiege the castle. Both sides used firearms in the ensuing siege, in which there were some fatalities, but John Paston the Younger who was defending the castle was obliged to surrender it to the Duke in September 1469 due to 'lack of victual, gunpowder, men's hearts, lack of surety of rescue' (Letter 732). The chance survival of the account in the letters should not mislead us into thinking that an event that was quite unusual in two respects, a siege, and moreover a siege of a recently constructed castle, was by any means typical of the fighting of the period.

Sieges occurred in the peripheral areas during the Wars of the Roses: St Michael's Mount, Harlech and Bamburgh to name the principal ones. Indeed there was something like siege warfare in 1464 in Northumberland, Bamburgh being taken by bombardment and assault.[12] The Border area was culturally closer to Scotland and can hardly be taken as typical. The considered view of the latest historian of the Wars of the Roses is: 'The Wars of the Roses have the appearance of wars of movement in which most commanders sought a speedy decision, if necessary by risking all in battle, rather than attempting to maintain a static defence in fixed fortifications'.[13] In the last resort, particularly where a town was involved, as with the Bastard of Fauconberg and London, there was not much choice, but there are several examples of sieges being deliberately avoided, as for example when Warwick and the Lancastrians took refuge in Coventry pursued by Edward IV. The castle at Northampton played no part in the battles. The most interesting case undoubtedly was at Ludford Bridge in 1459.[14]

The Yorkist centre, the seat of the Duke of York, was Ludlow, where there were a splendid castle and a walled town, but instead of fortifying themselves within the town and castle the Yorkists crossed the river Teme and erected an earthwork base, a sort of artillery laager on the other side. The object clearly was to provoke a field battle with the Lancastrians, which in the event never took place. Few episodes illustrate more clearly the shortcomings of a castle in fifteenth-century warfare: no doubt its vulnerability was a consideration, although much less than an open laager, but the constraint it imposed upon the defender to use his own artillery was the chief disadvantage. You could not hit back at the enemy.

Contemporary accounts reveal how unsuited the favoured form of fighting was to castle warfare: at Barnet ' . . . did blow up trumpets, and set upon them, first with shot, and then and soon, they joined . . . '; at Tewkesbury 'the king's ordnance was so conveniently laid afore them, and his vanguard so sore oppressed them with shot of arrows, that they gave them a right-a-sharp shower . . . '.[15] It was a very aggressive style of fighting in which preliminary discharges of artillery and arrows were followed by hand-to-hand fighting on foot, a conclusive result being reached within a few hours.

It can be argued that the issues in dispute in England were dynastic, who was to occupy the throne, and as the two sides did not differ in religion, language and race there was a real risk of people changing sides unless the matter was settled quickly. As there was no question of ransoms (distinguished prisoners were executed) or levying money from the population (as in France) there was no point in prolonging the struggle. The circumstances of the wars in the two countries in the first and second half of the century were very different, having more or less contradictory consequences for the castle. In France, defence of the homeland seemed to give it a new and vigorous life, particularly in those areas where there had been English occupation, while in England the civil wars, if they did not actually demonstrate its superfluity, did nothing to arrest its accelerating decline.

There is a major contrast between the two countries in the architectural reaction to artillery. In England there was no significant response to the new arm; it is difficult to point to any major adaptations made to older structures to allow them to withstand or deflect the impact of shot, while the gunports of the period do not mark any significant advance on those of the previous century. Indeed, one of the most cogent arguments for believing that artillery played a very small part in the abandonment of the castle in this country is the almost total absence of any serious effort to combat it. How different to France where the new weapon was accepted with enthusiasm both for attack and in devising methods to resist its effects. The accounts of the recapture of Normandy are full of descriptions of breaches blown in the English walls or adding bulwarks (French *boulvarts, boulevardes*) to existing structures. Bulwarks were simply earthwork or masonry additions on the outer face of an earlier wall designed for the mounting of guns. Indeed it is worth remarking that where the English were confronted with a permanent French adversary at Calais, adaptation of the defences to counter artillery had to be made.[16]

The differences between France and England in their response to artillery, conspicuous in the fifteenth century, became even more marked in the following one; it is to this subject that attention must now be turned.

Although gunpowder had been known to Roger Bacon in the thirteenth century, the first recorded use of its explosive force as a propellant for a weapon is from a manuscript illumination of 1326 which shows a large arrow in a vase-shaped 'gun'. Records of its use in warfare begin soon afterwards and multiply over the next 100 years.[17] There seems little doubt that guns were used by the English at the battle of Crécy in 1346. Such bulky and cumbersome weapons were more easily employed in static warfare at a siege where they could serve the valuable purpose of battering the walls. Bombards, mortar-like guns, that threw a very large shot were much favoured in the late fourteenth and early fifteenth centuries. The older machines for projecting missiles, *trebuchets* (slings) and *mangonels* (catapults), which were still in use, could hurl missiles of much the same size as those from the firearms, so that there was no need yet for the military architects to change their designs. However, firearms of smaller calibre had considerable advantages as anti-personnel weapons, so that the first evidence of an architectural response to firearms is the provision of gunports in buildings which were being newly erected. English examples of this are of particular interest.[18]

23 Cooling Castle, Kent; note the late fourteenth-century gunports (like inverted keyholes) on both the corner tower and gatehouse beyond.

During Richard II's reign (1377–99) there were not only French raids but, according to Froissart, proposals for invasion.[19] The castle built on the Isle of Sheppey at Queenborough by Edward III has unfortunately vanished, but it possibly had provision for the use of firearms. Pre-1400 gunports are found almost exclusively in structures of the south coastal region (the Cow tower, built of brick for the defence of Norwich right at the end of the century is an exception). The new castles at Bodiam, east Sussex, Cooling, Kent, on the lower Thames estuary and the town gates at Canterbury (figs. 23–25), Winchester and Southampton are noteworthy examples. Shapes vary, but usually a round hole, 20–30 cm in diameter, with a slit above was the basic design, the hole being for the discharge of the weapon and the slit for sighting. The openings could be at several levels, as in the West Gate at Canterbury, but it was soon found that raking (horizontal) fire at the height of a man above ground level had more chance of hitting, if not the target, then an adjoining one (in a body of men), than plunging fire which if it missed would simply go into the ground. Although usually forming a feature of new defences they could also be added to older ones: Corfe Castle, Dorset, Porchester Castle and Southampton town wall are examples.

24 Bodiam Castle, Sussex; note gunports in the gatehouse of the 1390s now set just above ground level to give raking (horizontal) fire.

25 Close-up view of gunport of late fourteenth century in West Gate, Canterbury.

Two significant points emerge from the occurrence of these gunports of the last years of the fourteenth century. They are almost exclusively confined to the south coast and are not known in the great castles then being constructed in the north of England. It was clearly assumed that the French raiders would be using firearms and suggests that firearms were still hardly used in the north. The second point is that, with the possible exception of Queenborough, the design of the new buildings was traditional: there is no indication that it was felt necessary to modify the shape or form of the structure to counter the impact of shot. This was also the case in France but in the fifteenth century there was a clear divergence between the two countries: in England until the time of Henry VIII gunports on traditional buildings were the continuing but feeble response to ever-improving artillery; in France an attempt was made to grapple with the problem of altering the building to cope with the new weapon.

That there were improvements in the performance of artillery during the fifteenth century there can be little doubt, although the evidence is elusive and has led to some disagreement among the experts. The earliest cannon barrels made of iron rods hooped with metal bands were replaced by cast iron guns, or those made of cuprum or latten, that is bell-metal, or brass. Ammunition continued into the early fifteenth century to consist of dressed round stone balls, as frequent references in the records testify (just as it had been with the torsion and gravity weapons). The critical change was from stone to cast-iron shot, which could be more accurately calibrated, but, the fundamental point, had a density 2.9 times higher than stone. The density of lead is slightly higher but it is softer, not so serious against human bodies which it could easily penetrate, but liable to flatten on impact against sound masonry.[20] Cast-iron was almost as dense as lead, much harder and unlike stone not liable to shatter on impact, although much more expensive. Its extra density required a heavier charge to propel it and during the century the increased size of charge required improvements in the barrel to withstand the heavier explosion. The quality of the gunpowder was also greatly improved by experience so that the proportions of saltpetre, sulphur and charcoal in it were nicely adjusted to give the greatest force to the shot.

There seems to be general agreement on the Continent that by the second quarter of the fifteenth century these improvements had so enhanced the penetrative power of artillery that it had become a serious menace to the masonry of the time. The natural reaction was to thicken the stonework and as we have seen this is the probable explanation for the great thickness of the walls in the fifteenth-century reconstruction at Hunaudaye (p. 30), and may indeed have also played a part in the choice of shape at Rambures, the curved surfaces being more likely to deflect shot. These were new structures but what could be done with old ones to render them better able to resist artillery?

Soil piled up in a bank behind the wall, rampiring as it is called, not only deadened the shock of impact but if raised high enough would allow the defender to use his own artillery. The impotence of the defender to use his own cannon was perhaps the main disadvantage of using a medieval castle. The wall-walks were far too narrow for guns while the roofs on the towers were not capable of being used as gun platforms even if the masonry had been capable of standing up to vibration from the detonations. The simple solution was to pull down the upper part of the tower and fill up the lower part with its debris to form a platform for the guns. One of the most vivid examples of this to be seen today is at the great French castle of Angers, although there it was apparently done by order of Henry III in the late sixteenth century. The snag about lowering the height of the defences was that it made them very much easier for the enemy to scale. The other solution was that already mentioned of leaving the masonry as it was but constructing *boulevardes* or bulwarks outside to serve as gun platforms. The chroniclers leave us in no doubt that this was the method normally adopted. The outer lip of the ditch could also be raised to create a *fausse braye* to protect the lower part of the wall. Another device, said to be especially used by the English and which may have had some influence on some fifteenth-century work in England was the *bastille*, a round island a little way out from the wall surmounted with guns enfilading the walls and particularly the entries to the castle.

Only a few castles constructed in France in the fifteenth century with adaptations for artillery have survived into modern times, of which two will be mentioned here. Viollet-le-Duc's reconstruction drawing of the castle at Bonaguil (Lot-et-Garonne) erected by Charles VII (1422–61) at first sight seems to be a concentric castle with a decidedly eccentric keep dividing it into two wards, but with towers with *chemin de ronde* and so on (fig. 26). In fact closer inspection shows that there is a complicated

26 In Viollet-le-Duc's reconstruction drawing of the fifteenth-century castle at Bonaguil (southwest France) the traditional plan has been modified to allow the defenders to sweep the approaches to the castle with their guns, but elevations are unaltered.

arrangement of horizontal gunports (splayed on the outside) covering an intricate access route with barbican. It is an attempt to meet the problem of maximising the defender's retaliatory fire against an enemy who could concentrate his wherever he wished, but without discarding the essential medieval form of the buildings.

The next example from Northern France, Ham (Somme), shows a later and far more sophisticated adaptation (figs. 27–29). It had been a thirteenth-century castle largely rebuilt in the fifteenth century, shown here in plan and prospect with a section through the keep.[22] Masonry of the thirteenth century is black on the plan, while the towers on the west front and the keep on the north-east are fifteenth-century, first and second half respectively. Unfortunately this noble monument was demolished by the Germans in 1917 but plans had been made before the war.

27 Ham Castle, Somme; in the reconstructed view it can be seen that the tall towers and roofs have been swept away to be replaced by squat forms in the fifteenth-century determination to cope with artillery.

The first feature that strikes one about the prospect is its frightening bleakness: all the frills of Bonaguil such as machicolations, tall towers, conical roofs, have gone. Even the crenellations have vanished because the flat roofs of the towers are platforms designed to carry guns resting on vaults below. The windows are tiny. All the projections or openings that were vulnerable to gunfire have been removed. The section of the keep illustrates a dramatic change in construction; its walls are thirty-five feet thick, every floor and passage vaulted to resist impact and sustain vibration. Apart from the guns on the roof there were casemates (chambers) for guns in the thickness of the wall at lower levels. It causes no surprise to find that although built as a private château (not like one of Henry VIII's batteries) it became a barracks as the later buildings in the view show.

Since Viollet-le-Duc, Ham has been regarded as the starting point for artillery fortification in Europe. At this stage, round shapes were believed to be the best because of their powers of deflection; the real solution proved to be the angled bastion discovered soon after 1500 in Italy. The

28 Ham Castle, Somme; this section of the circular keep shows it vaulted at all levels with a wall thickness of some thirty-five feet and casemates for guns.

29 Ham Castle, Somme; the plan shows the castle in a river bend has undergone massive reconstruction in the fifteenth century from the original thirteenth-century structure.

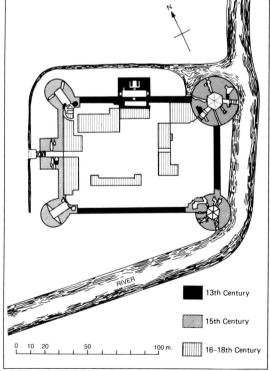

13th Century

15th Century

16–18th Century

0 10 20   50   100 m.

angled bastion allowed the defender to hit back and made protection against artillery a feasible proposition for the next 300 years, until advances in the weapon rendered even that solution untenable. However the dilemma before the owner of a castle or anyone who proposed to build one was acute: did he want a massive structure that could resist the new weapon but was ugly and almost uninhabitable, or did he prefer to keep all the beautiful frills – tall towers, conical roofs, machicolations, *chemins de ronde*, window tracery etc. – that had made the castle so magnificent a sight since the fourteenth century? It is not surprising that he normally opted for the latter, leaving his castle vulnerable to artillery. It was of course only one step from this to decide that there was no point in keeping up the pretence of defence which could be left either to towns with greater resources and whose citizens did not have to live among the bastions, or of course to the state whose centralised monarchies now disposed of ample resources and men for such undertakings. There was far more resistance to such abnegation in France than in England, partly no doubt because the need for protection persisted in France to a much later date, and partly because of the far greater weight attached to the castle as a status symbol in France.

Chapter 4

A rival – the courtyard house

There is perhaps an analogy between the creation of the courtyard house in the fourteenth century and the formation of the monastic cloister 500 years before in Carolingian times. The latter was no doubt more deliberately designed, while the former had the appearance of having arisen accidentally, although even here there may be more deliberate design than at first meets the eye. In both cases buildings that had hitherto been dispersed were pulled together to form a coherent whole, the monastic church being the axial base in the one case, and the traditional hall with appurtenances in the other. The plan of the monastery of St Gall which is the only clue as to where the conventual cloister was born was soon adopted for its particular purpose all over Europe. The secular courtyard plan which so far as we can tell is a local development in this country, far from being restricted to the house, was adopted by hospitals, inns, colleges and was indeed employed universally on houses and institutions alike.

The Saxon hall is known to us dimly from references in *Beowulf* and Bede or perhaps more concretely from the excavations at Yeavering in Northumberland or Cheddar in Somerset. It was evidently constructed of wood and one-storeyed. This place of gathering, of the whole household and guests, for eating once or twice a day (which could no doubt serve other functions at other times as a courthouse or even a dormitory) was a basic feature of medieval life, and up to Tudor times other buildings were regarded as derivative and subordinate to it. At South Wingfield, Derbyshire, in the fifteenth century it was the hall that was built first, all other ranges of the two courtyards following later.[1]

Halls erected after the Norman conquest were sometimes of stone and so could survive up to the present day: there were two varieties, those on the first floor above a basement that was usually vaulted, and those at ground level, often aisled like a church to provide a wider roof span.[2] The first-floor halls were usually divided at both levels into two rooms, the ground floor or semi-basement perhaps being a kind of servants' hall. The ground-floor variety normally had a two-storey block built at right-angles to it at one end, at first without direct access from the hall, although it was usually situated at the end near the hall doorway or rather the two opposed doorways at one end of the hall that gave a passage through (the later screens passage). In due course a doorway was opened in the gable end of the hall and a way made through on the ground floor out to the kitchen beyond, while the rooms created by this on either side became the time-honoured pantry (literally bread room) and buttery (bottle room) each with its own door from the hall. Hence the three-door arrangement at the lower end of all halls in the later Middle Ages. The first-floor room of the transverse block was the lord's private room; historically in origin – and often in the later Middle Ages also – the lord's private rooms were at the lower, not the upper, that is at the kitchen end of the hall. A beautiful example of this survives in the west hall of the Bishop's Palace at Lincoln. In due course cross-wings developed at either end, while at the upper there was a raised dais for the high table and a projecting oriel window.

At a lower social level than that of the castle, the familiar late medieval hall-house, widespread in much of England and Wales, with separate cross-wings, or under one roof with hipped gables in the case of the 'Wealden house', has left abundant survivals. It is at this time (if not before), in the fourteenth century, that the Border, Scotland and Ireland with their tower-houses parted company with England and Wales where the blank areas on the map show that hall-houses either with cross-wings, or at the highest social level with attached courtyard, held sway (see fig. 9).

In the eleventh to thirteenth centuries there was no problem about accommodating the house in the castle bailey. A point facing south could be chosen on the curtain where the hall, the starting point for any domestic arrangement, would be erected, and then from this there could be expansion outwards from either end as the required ancillary buildings multiplied. By the late twelfth century the extensions had reached a point where the two could meet at the keep or gatehouse. Indeed this kind of development imposed a sort of discipline that was absent from the jumble of buildings in undefended houses or palaces like Clarendon or Westminster. We are not of course dealing with continuous ranges but disconnected buildings set against, probably as lean-to's, the same continuous massive curtain or defensive wall. At the lower end of the hall there might be pantry, buttery, scullery terminating in a quite elaborate kitchen with huge fireplaces, at the other end a chamber block and other buildings ending in a chapel at the gatehouse. These were the sort of arrangements at Conisborough or Kenilworth Castles.

There was a high degree of flexibility and the resulting chain of buildings would bend to take whatever shape the bailey of the castle required. An irregular courtyard was thus formed, but when from the late thirteenth century it became usual to give the castle itself a square or rectangular form, so this courtyard took perforce the same shape. This is well illustrated at Harlech Castle in west Wales, erected in 1283–9 following the conquest of Gwynedd by Edward I (fig. 30). The hall and kitchen are on the west side (both now ruinous) and there were other buildings on the north and south linking up with the immense gatehouse on the east side. A glance at the plan shows how the shape of the castle determined the disposition of the buildings, not vice versa: they have no independent existence. It has been suggested that the square castle forced the buildings into a square shape, thus when they were erected independently it could be the genesis of the courtyard house of the same shape. The matter cannot be ignored but I doubt whether it is sufficient explanation of itself.

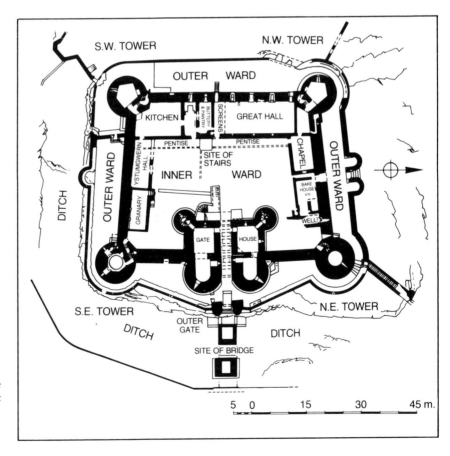

30 Harlech Castle, Gwynedd, erected in 1283–9 by Edward I; the internal buildings, hall etc. against the curtain wall have taken the shape of the geometrically regular castle, not vice versa.

The point can be illustrated by comparison of the plan of Stokesay Castle (fig. 31), more of a manor house than a castle, roughly square within a deep ditch but with hall and towers erected in most irregular manner, with Treago Castle (fig. 32) in the adjoining county of Herefordshire. The latter, which is of fifteenth-century date with later reconstruction of the internal buildings, is almost exactly square, illustrating very well the craving for this kind of symmetry in the later Middle Ages, even in a modest building like that at Treago.

However there are chronological difficulties in accepting the square castle as the father of the courtyard house. During the fourteenth century the plan of the castle was in something of a state of flux: in the Border areas and Scotland the tower-house was born, and in England there was a decidedly vertical element in many castles such as Nunney and Bolton. It was almost as if there was uncertainty as to which way to go. The fundamental feature in the courtyard plan was the long lodging ranges with parallel walls, which were perhaps used first in institutional buildings rather than private houses. A person who played a formative role in the matter was William of Wykeham, Bishop of Winchester whose work at Windsor Castle, New College, Oxford and Winchester College all contained such lodging ranges.[3]

The ordinary late medieval manor house did not need to adopt a courtyard shape since the hall did not have enough ancillary buildings to create four ranges. The need for a four-sided plan arose when there was a demand for ranges of cellular lodgings (bed-sitting rooms or small suites) to house a substantial body of household officers, retainers, or members of an institution who by their rank or importance required separate accommodation. A late medieval college where the ownership was vested in a group of fellows (*socii*) of more or less equal status with a master who was *primus inter pares* is the sort of model that inevitably comes to mind. The time-honoured and rigid arrangements of a hall and chamber did not allow the insertion of extra floors so the straightforward and simple solution of adding flanking wings on either side to provide such accommodation was adopted. If the fourth side was closed by another range with a gatehouse then the courtyard was complete. It was a very flexible and simple design, which merely by adding three new ranges on any of the four sides allowed expansion in any direction, no doubt the main reason for its retention in the Oxford and Cambridge colleges.

150–200 years after its creation, Andrew Boorde (born 1490) described the courtyard house in his *Dietary of Health* (*c.* 1542) in terms that could apply to it throughout its history:

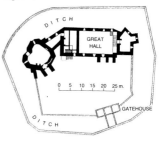

31 Sketch plan of Stokesay Castle, Shropshire, a thirteenth-century fortified manor house; note its complete irregularity and lack of long straight ranges (contrast fig. 35).

32 Treago Castle, Herefordshire, a strictly square fifteenth-century plan with one corner tower larger than the others.

Make the hall under such a fashion that the parlour be annexed
to the head of the hall. And the buttery and pantry be at the lower
end of the hall, the cellar under the pantry, set somewhat lower:
the kitchen set somewhat lower from the buttery and pantry,
coming with an entry by the wall of the buttery, the pastry house
and the larder house annexed to the kitchen. Then divide the
lodgings by the circuit of the quadrangle and let the gatehouse be
opposite or against the hall door (not directly) but the hall door
standing lower down and the gatehouse in the middle of the front
entering into the place.[4]

Some details can be discussed later but the general lay-out can be seen at
Pembroke College, in the view by Loggan (fig. 33): gate on to the street,
doorway on the far side of the court leading to screens passage with hall
on the right and buttery and pantry on the left. The college had two
parallel courts but by the time of this view the one on the right had been
pulled down for the construction of the new chapel. The college was
founded in 1347 and except for the upper storeys lit by dormer windows
was probably in this state by the end of the fourteenth century.[5] The rows
of chimneys in the side ranges served the numerous fireplaces in the
cellular lodgings below. Ranges of lodgings of this type deserve special
attention.

The earliest rows of cellular lodgings erected in a castle belong to the
mid-fourteenth century, forming part of the work of Wykeham for
Edward III[6] in the upper ward of Windsor Castle (fig. 34). Along the
eastern and southern curtain walls are two-storeyed rows of cellular
lodgings within the space formed by the erection of a wall about twenty
feet out from the main (and much older) defensive wall. The staircases are
internal. They are not free-standing ranges, the essential characteristic of
the courtyard house, for they take advantage of the fact that the south curtain wall happened to be straight and there was only a slight bend on the
eastern wall. Account had to be taken of the existing divisions created by
towers on the wall. At New College, Oxford, his own foundation,
Wykeham took the next step by not setting the north range against the
adjoining city wall but building it as a separate range.[7]

By the end of the fourteenth century the design was mature: two
parallel walls, say 2–3 feet thick, set 15–25 feet apart and running for 50
to 300 feet. The intervening space was subdivided horizontally all along
its length into two, or occasionally three, floors, and vertically by
partitions into numerous compartments. Omission of the latter divisions
on the first floor could create a Tudor long gallery, as at Haddon Hall,

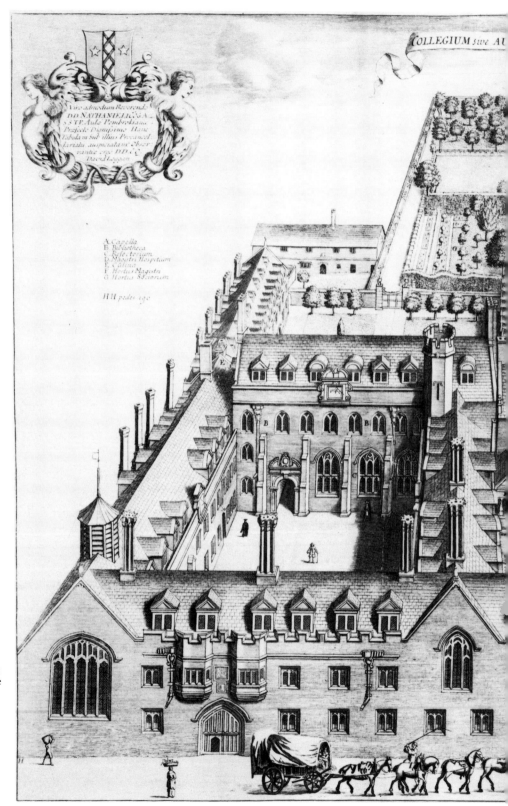

33 Pembroke
College, Cambridge;
founded in 1347, the
left hand court in
this view of *c.* 1690
shows an early
courtyard plan with
entry opposite the
hall and the cellular
lodgings served by a
multitude of
chimneys.

BROCHIANA apud Cant.

David Loggan delin. & Sculp. Cum Privil. S.R.M.

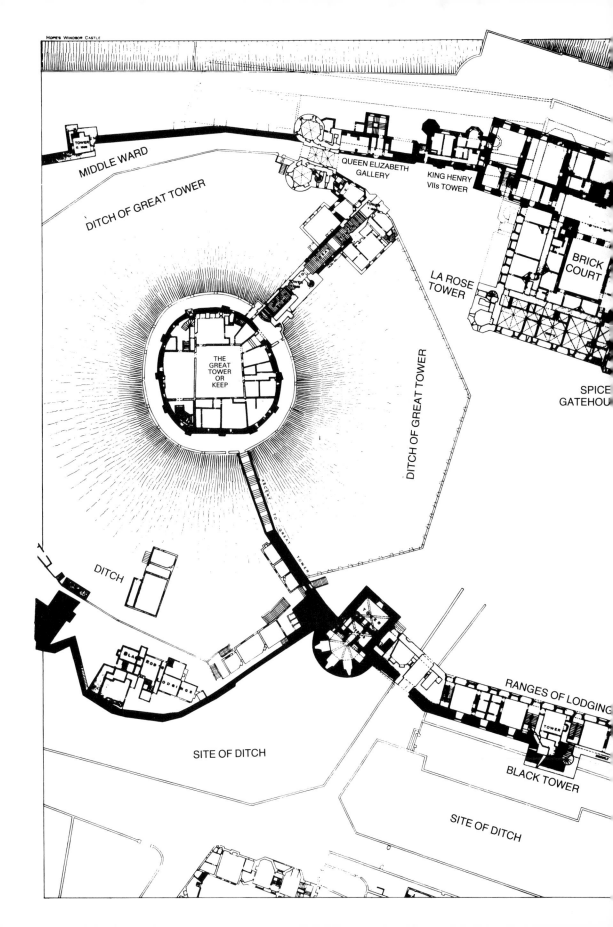

HOPE'S WINDSOR CASTLE

MIDDLE WARD

DITCH OF GREAT TOWER

TOWER

QUEEN ELIZABETH
GALLERY

KING HENRY
VIIs TOWER

LA ROSE
TOWER

BRICK
COURT

SPICE
GATEHOU

DITCH OF GREAT TOWER

THE
GREAT
TOWER
OR
KEEP

ASCENT TO GREAT TOWER

DITCH

BLACK
ROB
LODGE

RANGES OF LODGING

TOWER

SITE OF DITCH

BLACK TOWER

SITE OF DITCH

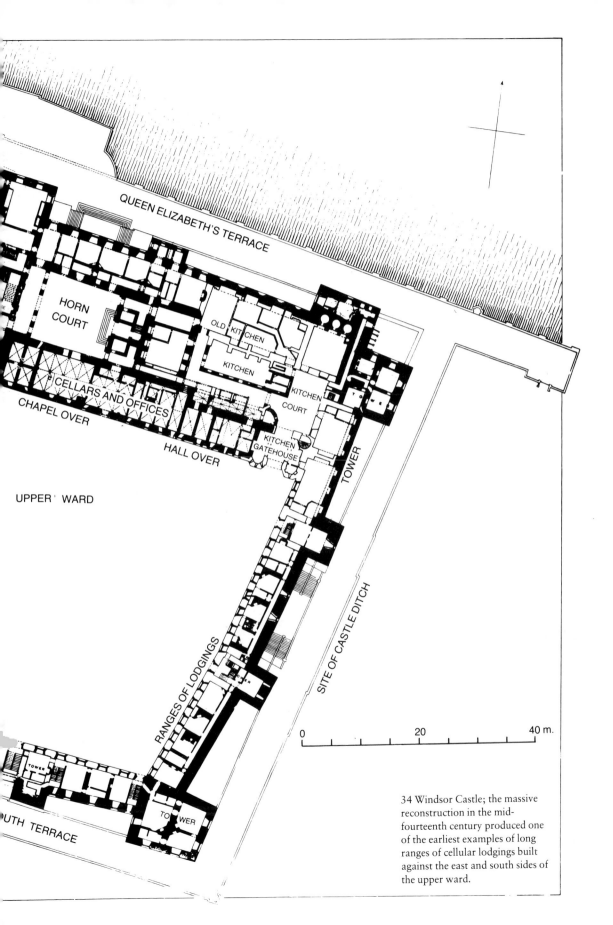

QUEEN ELIZABETH'S TERRACE

HORN COURT

OLD KITCHEN

KITCHEN

KITCHEN

KITCHEN COURT

CELLARS AND OFFICES

CHAPEL OVER

HALL OVER

KITCHEN GATEHOUSE

UPPER WARD

TOWER

TOWER

SITE OF CASTLE DITCH

RANGES OF LODGINGS

0　　　　　　20　　　　　　40 m.

TOWER

TOWER

SOUTH TERRACE

34 Windsor Castle; the massive reconstruction in the mid-fourteenth century produced one of the earliest examples of long ranges of cellular lodgings built against the east and south sides of the upper ward.

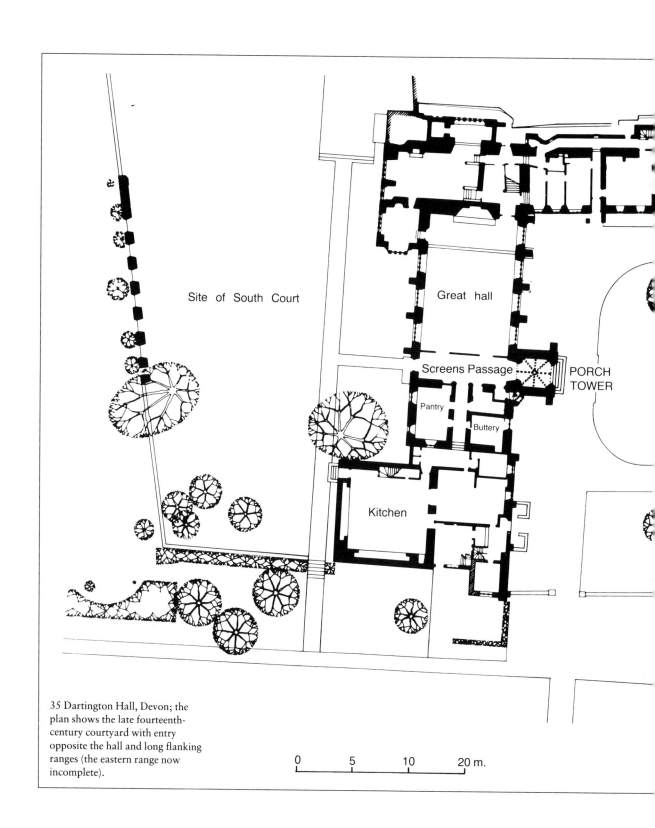

Site of South Court

Great hall

Screens Passage

PORCH TOWER

Pantry

Buttery

Kitchen

35 Dartington Hall, Devon; the
plan shows the late fourteenth-
century courtyard with entry
opposite the hall and long flanking
ranges (the eastern range now
incomplete).

0   5   10   20 m.

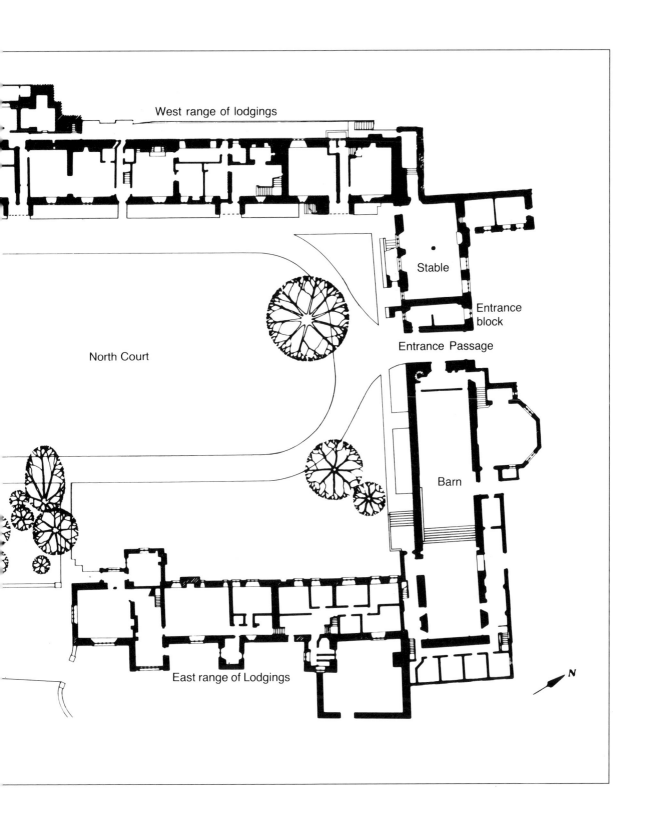

West range of lodgings

North Court

Stable

Entrance block

Entrance Passage

Barn

East range of Lodgings

N

Derbyshire or Kirby Hall, Northamptonshire. The compartments were the cellular lodgings normally arranged in pairs sharing one external door or with paired doorways, those on the first floor being reached by either an external staircase or steps or sometimes an internal one. Each cell had its own fireplace (hence the forest of chimneys on such ranges) and sometimes its own latrine discharging outside the building (particularly where there was a moat or ditch).

There are odd survivals of fourteenth-century lodgings in the older universities, as in Corpus Christi at Cambridge, but the only domestic example from before 1400 that has come down to us is at Dartington Hall, Devon.[8] It possibly had two courts from the beginning. The main court is designed exactly as Boorde recommended, long flanking ranges of lodgings with the gateway opposite the hall door (figs. 35, 36). The lodgings are paired with external steps to reach the first floor, recalling access to some first-floor halls. The lodging ranges were slightly askew from the hall block or rather one of its flanking wings, suggesting they are a slightly later addition. However there seems no reason to doubt but that the entire work is a complete design of the last decade of the fourteenth century. There is a surprising maturity about the whole structure as if it had been at the end of a long period of development. However, it may have been directly inspired by new constructional work in the institutional field such as New College, Oxford. The builder in this case, John

36 Dartington Hall in an eighteenth-century view looking across the courtyard, hall on the left and entry on the right, towards the lodging range with paired rooms and external stairs to upper sets.

Holand, later Duke of Exeter, came from the highest social level, who certainly owned castles but preferred to erect and live in a type of structure that evidently better satisfied the domestic requirements of the time.

The surviving west range is over 200 feet long, the outer wall being a little thicker than the inner, probably to accommodate the flues, since there are no projecting stacks. A glance at the plan shows how these immensely long pairs of parallel walls that formed the lodging ranges lay at the basis of the courtyard house – it was not a miscellaneous grouping of buildings round a courtyard. The monastic plan had of course contained very long ranges formed by pairs of parallel walls on both the east and west side of the cloister, particularly the former. In Cistercian houses the need for accommodation of lay-brothers could give rise to immensely long west ranges – one thinks of Fountains. Perhaps the ultimate ancestry of our ranges is monastic: the old common dormitories were indeed being split up into cubicles at this time, but the separate entries – as in modern flats – constitutes a fundamental difference between the monastic and secular ranges.

The second point about these ranges, a central one to our subject, is their incompatibility with castles. It was not just a question of geometry: all castles built before 1250 (the overwhelming majority) were irregular in shape and, unlike Windsor, limited in space, which was already filled with buildings. Problems of conversion were formidable and very costly (as at Windsor), but there were also problems of design in a new structure: the services for the individual lodgings (flues, latrines, windows) interfered with the defensive wall (the windows in the curtain wall of the late fourteenth-century castle at Wingfield, Suffolk, illustrate this) and equally defensive features on the wall, like towers, interfered with the lodgings. One solution was to put the bed-sitting rooms in the towers: Bodiam, a small castle, has eight towers with up to three levels of cellular lodgings in each (cf. also Warwick).

Unfortunately the palace at Sheen where Henry V carried out so much work does not survive so that our only information about royal palace plans comes from Eltham, Kent where the Elizabethan architect, John Thorpe, made a plan (upon which fig. 37 is based). The hall built by Edward IV and the bridge are all that survive today. The palace was in active use by sovereigns from the fourteenth century until early Tudor times so that it underwent changes, the cellular lodgings being of the fifteenth century. The Lord Chancellor's lodgings rebuilt in Henry VIII's time as a hall-house suggest an interesting development: the replacement of a group of cellular lodgings that were permanently assigned to the Lord Chancellor *ex officio* by a real house. The inference would seem to be that in other courtyard houses certain lodgings belonged *ex officio* to certain household officers, which is indeed what we should expect.

Bishops had from early times lived in open palaces as well as castles; there is evidence from this period for courtyard palaces of the new style at Southwell, Nottinghamshire, Croydon, Surrey, Sherburn in Elmet, Yorkshire, and Knole in Kent.[9] In the latter case the two courts built by Archbishop Bourchier in *c.* 1450 still survive; they are the two courts in the back of the bird's-eye views by Kip in the early eighteenth century

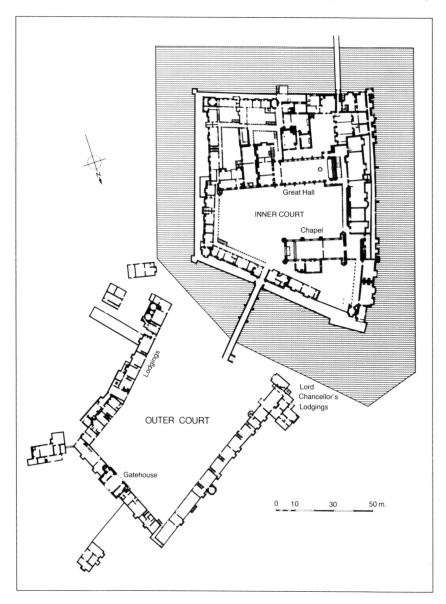

37 Eltham Palace, Kent; note the extensive ranges of cellular lodgings in the late medieval royal palace with projections for flues and the conversion of the Lord Chancellor's lodgings into a house in Tudor times.

(fig. 38). The large court in the front is sixteenth-century, an interesting example of how easy it was to extend a building by adding a new court in the Oxford or Cambridge fashion. By the time of Kip there were immense gardens adjoining the house; as gardens became more important in early Tudor times there was a tendency for the external face of the range to be treated more lavishly, as at Thornbury where the external façade was clearly more important than the internal face in the courtyard.

Among secular examples that survive substantially three may be mentioned: Gainsborough Old Hall, Lincolnshire (fig. 39), South Wingfield Manor, Derbyshire (fig. 43) and Haddon Hall, also Derbyshire (fig. 40). Only three sides survive of the first; its lodging ranges have an internal corridor, recalling the galleries of contemporary inns, and occurring elsewhere. The missing range no doubt contained the gatehouse and the building has a fine brick tower in one corner. South Wingfield will be discussed below. Haddon Hall is still inhabited, now by a duke but in the fifteenth century by a modest family, the Vernons, who evidently intended to raise the status of their home. A new court which was added to include the parish church, the Lower Court, allowed the provision of cellular lodgings of the new style on its north and west sides. The changes recall another splendid fourteenth-century hall with cross wings built by a merchant at Penshurst, Kent, transformed into the cross range of a great courtyard house by its aristocratic owners in the next century, although the plan is now scarcely recognisable.

There was a tendency for the courtyard house to be adopted at a lower social level, where there was no need for lodging ranges. An early Tudor example is the attractive manor house of Compton Wynyates, Warwickshire, which reproduces the standard plan with internal corridor on the north side but has limited lodging accommodation. It was constructed about 1520: twenty years later Boorde knew only one type of house, with one or two courts and optional moat. He distinguished between *mansion* and *house* built on the same plan, varying no doubt in scale but also for Boorde marked by certain seigneurial additions: a park, a dovecote, in particular a bowling green. Manor house and castle had merged into one, but it is suggested here that it was not a case of the former replacing the latter, so much as the large aristocratic courtyard house of the fifteenth century replacing the castle and at the same time forming a new model for the manor house. That this was the case has been lent support by the recent excavations at the More, near Rickmansworth, where three phases of irregularly designed manor houses were overlain and replaced by a courtyard house following a licence to crenellate in 1426.[10] Such an abrupt change has also been inferred elsewhere.

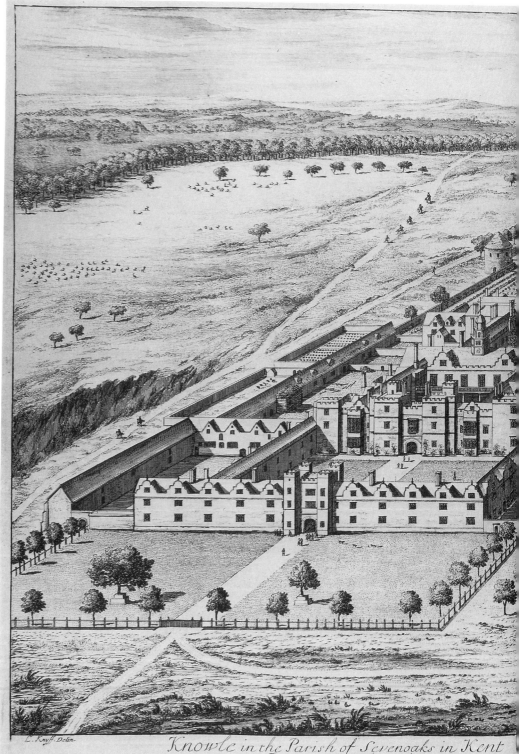

L. Knyff Delin.

Knowle in the Parish of Sevenoaks in Kent
Viscount Cranfeild Earle of Dorsett & Middlx. &c. Knight of the Garter, & one

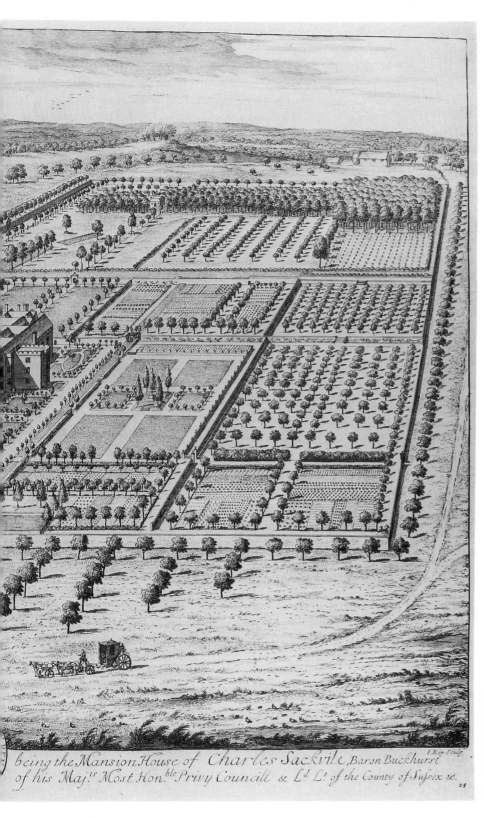

being the Mansion House of *Charles Sackvile*, *Baron Buckhurst*
of his *Maj:ts* Most Hon.ble *Privy Councill* & L.d L.t of the County of *Sussex* &c.

I. Kip Sculp.

38 Knole, Kent; the two back courtyards are fifteenth-century, the front one a Tudor addition with great gateway. Note also huge formal gardens in this early eighteenth-century view.

The merging of house and castle is perhaps best illustrated by
Thornbury Castle, Gloucestershire. It was described by Leland and bears
an inscription, apart from two sixteenth-century surveys, so it is exceptionally well dated.[11] The Duke of Buckingham started to construct it in
1511 and work stopped upon his execution in 1522, although an
Elizabethan survey indicates that further work was carried out. The
partially-built remains which still survive are occupied. A very telling
point is that the surveyor who made the survey immediately after the
Duke's execution was actually uncertain whether to call it a manor or a
castle and gives it the alternative titles in the survey. The fact that the
owner had a licence to crenellate and a licence to found a college of canons
to accompany it can leave no doubt that the builder assumed that it would
be of castle status. It was to consist of an outer court of two and a half
acres enclosed by ranges of servants' lodgings, not completed, and an
inner court of half an acre. At the Duke's death an earlier hall range on the
east side, on which the whole plan was laid out, still existed. A new south
range to contain a new hall had been built in magnificent style with
splendid external façade facing a garden. There were to be octagonal

39 In Gainsborough Old Hall,
Lincolnshire, several stages of
fifteenth-century work produced
this plan (one range missing):
lodgings with external corridor
and projecting kitchen and brick
tower. Cf. corridors in galleries
of contemporary inns.

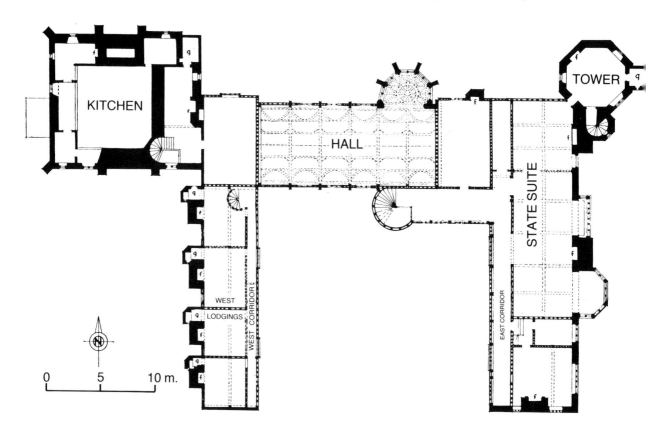

40 At Haddon Hall, Derbyshire, the hall and upper court are fourteenth-century, the lower court with its cellular lodgings a fifteenth-century extension.

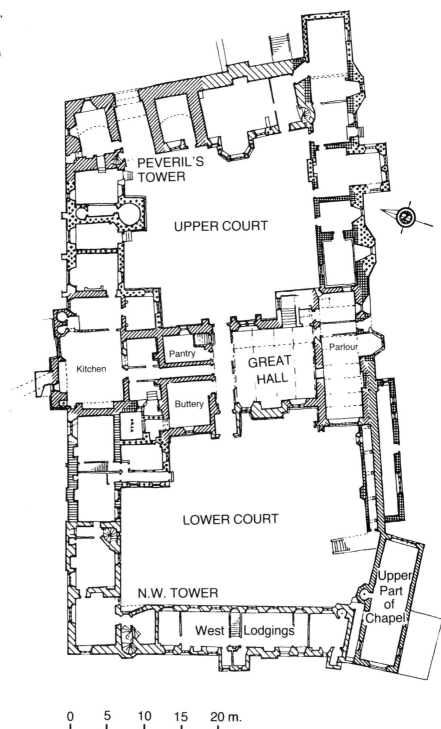

PEVERIL'S TOWER

UPPER COURT

Kitchen

Pantry

Buttery

GREAT HALL

Parlour

LOWER COURT

N.W. TOWER

West Lodgings

Upper Part of Chapel

KEY:

- ■ 12th Century
- ▥ 13th Century
- ▨ 14th Century
- ▧ 15th Century
- ◨ Late 15th
- ▤ 16th Century
- ▦ Later 16th
- ▧ 17th Century

0   5   10   15   20 m.

towers at the corners and an imposing gatehouse. The stonework was exceptionally fine in quality while the roof line was enlivened with decorated brick chimneys. The cellular lodgings were to be in the outer court (a significant Renaissance change) after the French fashion. The incomplete buildings imply a sequence of building which recalls that at South Wingfield. At the latter there had been a small triangular garden adjoining the hall but at Thornbury there were to be two gardens, an ornamental orchard, a new park four miles in circuit containing 700 deer,

41 The completed south range at Thornbury Castle, Gloucestershire, indicates the very fine building that it was proposed to build here in c. 1515.

THIS cannot be so properly call'd y Remains of a Castle as the Remains of a very Magnificent unfinish'd one design'd by Edward Stafford Duke of Buckingham Lord Constable &c. He began it An. 1511. 2. Hen. VIII. as appears by an Inscription over y Gate but he liv'd not long enough to compleat it being beheaded An. 1521.

42 An eighteenth-century view of Thornbury showing south front of inner court and unfinished outer court.

another three miles about and a rabbit warren. Although incapable of serious defence (in spite of gunports) we are certainly dealing with a château, even if a manor in English, although in fact in this case 'castle' has been kept in the title.

The need for cellular accommodation in an inn or a college is self-evident but what purpose did it serve in a domestic context? Why was it primarily required in aristocratic households, that is of those who owned castles? Most important, why did this cellular accommodation become a requirement in the fourteenth century that was no longer needed in the late sixteenth or seventeenth century? It was the changes in the household, induced no doubt by social changes outside, that should provide answers to the questions.

Cellular lodgings clearly met a permanent, not a temporary need, and equally they were not for mere servants but for people of a higher social level. It is probably safe to assume that they were principally for senior members or officers of the household. We have seen that at Eltham some cellular lodgings had probably been thrown together and converted into a house for the Lord Chancellor, a royal officer frequently in attendance on the king. No doubt also some of the lodgings were in use for guests, as this instruction from a fifteenth-century courtesy book describing the duties of the marshall and usher makes plain: he 'shall assign all other men their lodgings, as well as strangers as men of the household; and he shall assign them bread, ale, wine, wax, tallow and fuel to their lodging after the season of the year and their degrees, and reckon for it daily and weekly as the lord's books be made'.[12] The quotation is very interesting because it shows how self-sufficient both officers and guests were expected to be, with their own fire, lights and food and drink. It was essentially a bed-sitting room life punctuated by communal gathering in hall for the two main meals of the day, resembling that of the student in one of the Oxford or Cambridge colleges, except of course that the officer had daily duties to perform. No doubt the question of status ('degrees' in the courtesy book) was very important.

The great ruin at South Wingfield, Derbyshire, one of the most remarkable of the fifteenth-century courtyard houses of which large parts survive, was erected in 1439–50 by Ralph Lord Cromwell, Lord Treasurer and one of the dominating political figures in the middle of the century.[13] It was set on a spur, the ground sloping away on three sides, and consisted of two courtyards, the outer or southern containing the entrance and the inner at the point with a triangular garden at the apex adjoining the hall. The outer court consisting mainly of service buildings was separated by a cross-range containing a gateway and a high tower at its west end, from the smaller inner court which contained the hall with vaulted undercroft, a great audience chamber and Lord's apartments at the lower or west end. The east range is missing but the surviving account indicates the parlour adjoined the hall at the upper end, as at Gainsborough Old Hall or Haddon (probably a messroom for senior members of household like senior 'parlours' at Oxford or Cambridge), and an eastward projection on the range suggests the chapel adjoined the parlour to the south like Compton Wynyates or indeed Haddon. On the west side was a range of cellular lodgings, three-storeyed, with projecting octagonal staircases on the inside (only surviving as a foundation) and latrine chutes and chimneys projecting on the outside.

A fundamental interest is given the remains at South Wingfield by the single building account that survives for the period 1 November 1442 to Christmas 1443, since construction work which had been going on for some four years now allowed Lord Cromwell to come into residence. The account makes clear that only the hall range and the west range of cellular lodgings had been constructed, which gives an indication of their importance; not only the lord's accommodation but that for his chief members of household had to be ready before the building could come into use. No doubt there was a good deal of *amour propre* involved! It is very revealing. At Thornbury, Gloucestershire, the cellular lodgings were in the

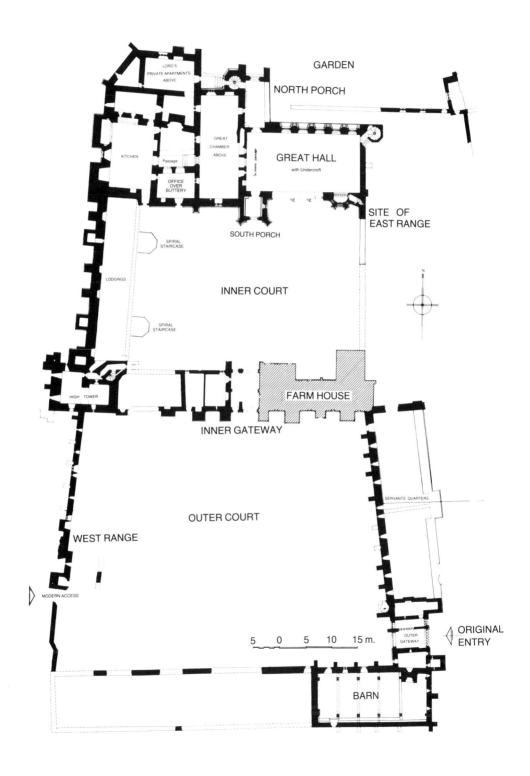

GARDEN

NORTH PORCH

LORD'S
PRIVATE APARTMENTS
ABOVE

GREAT
CHAMBER
ABOVE

KITCHEN

Passage

Screens passage

GREAT HALL
with Undercroft

OFFICE
OVER
BUTTERY

SITE OF
EAST RANGE

SPIRAL
STAIRCASE

SOUTH PORCH

LODGINGS

INNER COURT

SPIRAL
STAIRCASE

N

HIGH TOWER

FARM HOUSE

INNER GATEWAY

SERVANTS' QUARTERS

OUTER COURT

WEST RANGE

MODERN ACCESS

5   0   5   10   15 m.

OUTER
GATEWAY

ORIGINAL
ENTRY

BARN

outer court and had not been completed when work stopped; in a Renaissance household no doubt a different relationship between lord and officers obtained. One range in the outer court of Wingfield survives, a long one of two storeys without cellular accommodation possibly serving as a dormitory for servants. Reading backwards so to speak from the later adaptation of some monastic lay-outs after the Dissolution (Leez Priory, Essex or Jesus College, Cambridge) when the cloister became the inner court of the courtyard house and the great court of the monastery its outer court it may be that the origin of two courts, an inner domestic and a large outer one for offices, drew its inspiration from the monastic lay-out.

Direct information about households is provided by their accounts of which a number of those that survive have been published. In 1465, Sir John Howard had 158 persons in the household, men and women,

44 South porch of the hall of South Wingfield Manor, with the adjoining window of the great chamber.

ranging from ploughmen and maids to quite senior men who bore the title 'sir'.[14] Of these about half were to be provided with two or three yards of black material to be made up into mourning garments for the funeral ceremonies of Lady Catherine Howard. There was evidently a crucial social division between the two groups, those who took part in the mourning ceremonies and those who did not. There are many other references to providing gowns or red cloth for making up clothes for certain individuals. The provision of gowns or material introduced subtle divisions of rank. Even if not wearing livery, that is the badge of their lord, it must have been apparent to whose household they belonged.

A great deal is known about the royal household at the time of Henry VI and Edward IV from the Ordinance of 1445, the Black Book and the Ordinance of 1478.[15] Presumably the practices in the royal household, albeit on a grander scale, were similar to those of a noble household. Much of the detail is concerned with the entitlements of people at court, whether household or visitors, from dukes and archbishops downwards: how many servants and how many liveried retainers they were entitled to, how much food and drink was to be allocated to them and so on. It is abundantly clear that above a fairly modest social level everyone was expected to have his own rooms, and although he took one or two main meals in hall each person was issued with 'night commons' to feed himself not only at night but probably at breakfast; evidently he occupied a sort of bed-sitting room perhaps with two or three retainers or servants. Not only the architecture but also the way of life has persisted at the colleges of Oxford and Cambridge. It held together in a domestic unit a substantial but varying number of people while allowing them quite independent lives.

The rhythm of late medieval life is nowhere better displayed than in precious kitchen accounts, a few of which have survived, because they record the number of people served in hall at the three main meals of the day. Attendance in hall was a declaration of membership of, and loyalty to, the household, when the whole body assembled to express their unity as they enjoyed their food and drink; it survives in an attenuated form in colleges, the Inns of Court and the City Livery companies. What strikes one indeed is the constant variation by numbers present between the three meals each day during the year: a handful at breakfast (except at harvest time), twice or three times as many at dinner (our lunch-time) and slightly less at supper (our high tea).[16] Clearly people came in from the outside for the main meals of the day, but the most reasonable explanation for the discrepancy is that a number of guests or household officers took their breakfasts in their rooms. It is very difficult to envisage this happening unless they were accommodated with bed-sitting rooms such as the cellular accommodation just described could provide.

The first question may have been answered and it is time to turn attention to the second and third: the aristocratic level at which the cellular lodgings were required and the time span during which they were in use. On the face of it aristocratic households were likely to have required more accommodation but why in this form? A digression is necessary here.

During the earlier Middle Ages, land had been held by military tenure, so much land being worth so many knight's fees and so on. Gradually, as money became the nexus of such relationships, other ways of establishing a mutually intelligible bond between lord and liegeman arose, at first by crude cash payment but later replaced by 'good lordship' in return for services.[17] A formal document, an indenture, would be drawn up and both sides entered into a binding agreement for life; in return for 'good lordship' the other party solemnly bound himself in peace and war for the rest of his life. The arrangements are best known from the considerable number of surviving indentures written in English entered into by Lord Hastings, 1461–83. The practice had started in the previous century and continued well into the next. Agreement by indenture, a formal document in two copies divided between two parties was a favourite way of arranging new building, going to war or other activities in late medieval times. It was essentially a form of contract. In this particular form it is often referred to as 'bastard feudalism', although a kinder, more accurate term to apply to it might be 'contract feudalism'.

In some respects it was like a throwback to the early days of feudalism with analogies to 'commendation' or the bond between a Saxon thegn and his followers. The government looked askance at the practice because it clearly encouraged retaining displayed by wearing 'livery' and leading to 'maintenance' which promoted intimidation and interference with justice or worse crimes, challenging the authority of the government itself. Consequently, between 1305 and 1468 legislation was introduced aiming to discourage livery and maintenance. An act of 1390 restricted those who might enter into such agreements to the peerage (dukes, earls, barons and bannerets) who could only retain knights or esquires for life. This particular form of contractual relationship was thus restricted to closely defined social levels, the top and the next one down. There was some latitude in practice for the indentured retainers of Lord Hastings consisted of twenty gentlemen, fifty-nine esquires, nine knights and two peers. An act of 1468 was much more stringent and seemed to imply that retainers had to be resident in the household (they were called servants in the indentures). In fact most indentured retainers did not live permanently in the household, although presumably this was necessary from time to time, while the 1468 act made occasional residence a sensible precaution to keep within the law.

While not provable there must be a strong suspicion that there was a close relationship between courtyard houses with cellular accommodation and contract feudalism of this kind. Chronologically the two coincide closely. Both continued into Elizabethan times. The peers who built the houses were the only people allowed to have indentured retainers, while equally the retainers themselves were of a social level that expected certain minimum standards of accommodation and the sort of quasi-independent status that cellular accommodation presupposes.

45 At Tretower, Gwent, the juxta-position of the twelfth-century castle (containing farmyard) and the fifteenth-century 'Court' dramatically contrasts the different styles of living accommodation in early and late medieval times.

It may be felt that the castle has been rather left behind in the discussion, but the courtyard house is central to the subject of its decline. The fact that a large structure like South Wingfield Manor could be raised in the middle of the fifteenth century says a great deal about the confidence of the builders in the security of the countryside around it, since it was virtually undefended. There had of course been undefended palaces or simply 'houses' (*domi*) in earlier centuries but that was a general term for a group of buildings subservient to a hall. The courtyard house offered an articulated unit designed for the social needs of the time, and not surprisingly its charms beckoned many to leave the crude quarters inserted into fortifications that were no longer needed. At Tretower, Gwent (Monmouthshire) the twelfth- and thirteenth-century castle lies only three or four hundred yards from the fifteenth-century courtyard house, a modest one with wooden galleries more like an inn, that we may assume superseded it in the later Middle Ages (fig. 45). No one who examines the two buildings will have any doubts about the motives for such a migration.

Chapter 5

A martial face

The chapter title refers to a group of fifteenth-century buildings in which certain features characteristic of castles were displayed in an exaggerated form, or sometimes introduced into an essentially domestic setting where they were out of place. These non-functional, theatrical elements occurring in the buildings which I have dubbed 'show-castles' have parallels in other aspects of the life of the period, notably costume and heraldry but also in the tournaments and ceremonies known from the written records of the time. They were general but took a particularly exaggerated form in the Burgundian court. This hot-house, almost caricature, 'chivalry' was described by the Dutch historian Huizinga in his famous book *The Waning of the Middle Ages*, which has so moulded our views of the period. Recently Professor Colin Platt has coined the expression 'castles of chivalry' to describe buildings exhibiting these features.[1] The subject is of such interest that it deserves some discussion before turning to the buildings themselves.

The outlook, the code of conduct, the morals, one might say, of west European aristocracy between the twelfth and sixteenth century was governed by a set of beliefs that can be given the general title of chivalry.[2] It found its most overt expression in tourneys and jousts, but the mythology or series of legends associated with it are perhaps equally important. What is suggested by the term 'castles of chivalry' is that an element of make-belief was introduced into the construction of the castle, so that it served as a theatrical backdrop for the fantasies, particularly the legends, associated with chivalry.

Edward I after his conquest of Wales held an elaborate tournament at Nefyn in the Llyn peninsula.[3] The three great castles that he began to build at Caernarfon, Conwy and Harlech in 1283 have a well-documented construction.[4] Caernarfon with its banded masonry and octagonal towers was singled out for special treatment, not only as the intended capital of the new province but evidently having some regard to Welsh legend about its imperial past. No doubt the king would have built a castle in any case in the town, like Harlech or Conwy, so it was only the form that was varied. To that extent it may be accounted a 'castle of chivalry'. Edward I's grandson was influenced by Arthurian legend in the great works carried out at Windsor in the middle of the next century; the knightly Order of the Garter is chivalry in its most explicit form.[5]

There is no documentary evidence to associate chivalry with the buildings to be described, although there must be a strong suspicion that it was in the minds of some of the builders. The work of Ralph Lord Cromwell is a case in point. His manor constructed at South Wingfield has already been discussed (p. 64), but his work at Tattershall, Lincolnshire, his main seat, is also well documented.[6] In the latter case he apparently demolished a thirteenth-century castle, the stumps of the towers of which survive, and erected an enormous brick tower to replace it, evidently as a residence for himself. It is very difficult not to believe that the self-dramatisation that this implies did not owe something to chivalric fantasy, especially in view of the profuse heraldic blazons in the overmantels of the fireplaces throughout the tower.

The contrast with France is illuminating. A French castle with round towers and conical roofs, moat and drawbridge, gunports and machicolations was an imposing object, its purpose quite unmistakable; the English courtyard house was a shambling, rambling group of buildings of decidedly unimpressive appearance. An Oxford or Cambridge college makes a very poor showing against the castles in the *Très riches heures* of the Duc de Berry. It was not just a question of appearance but of status. Leland was shocked by the manor at South Wingfield overshadowing the castle of Sheffield, and most Tudor topographers (Lambarde for instance) showed a special reverence for castles. The more the real castle disappeared the stronger the craving of the nobleman to give his house extra dignity and status by the addition of towers, gatehouse or keep or even to dress it up to look like a castle. There were therefore strong motives for emphasising or exaggerating the castle aspects of an aristocratic dwelling in this period. Caution must be exercised in attributing all sham features to chivalry, while functional features that were capable of military use should of course be treated as serious unless there are good reasons for not doing so.

I have employed the term show-castle in preference to 'castle of chivalry', which seems to recall a phrase from one of Horace Walpole's letters! Nor am I certain that chivalry was always, or was at any time, an overriding consideration, in the minds of the builders of the structures to be discussed in this chapter. Nevertheless it is certainly essential to bear in mind the peculiarly florid and exhibitionist forms in which chivalry expressed itself during the period when they were erected.

Before considering individual buildings a few general points deserve to be made.

First, as regards the builders themselves we are not normally dealing with royalty or indeed the highest nobility, but lesser noblemen who had made good and were determined to give material expression to this success; the brashness of the results may owe something to this. A number of the builders of the middle years of the century – Fastolf, Boteler, Cromwell – had had youthful military careers in France where their appetite for castle forms had no doubt been whetted, and from where – if we are to believe Leland – the money for construction had sometimes derived.

Most of the buildings discussed were not raised on virgin ground but as additions to existing structures or over their foundations after demolition, so that there is no great originality of ground plan. It is the external elevations that are of chief interest, which is no doubt what the original builders wished, together with the internal lay-outs and materials used for construction. Although there is ample evidence for the use of firearms in the form of gunports there is no evidence for structural modification of the buildings to withstand the impact of shot such as thickening the walls, lowering the towers and so on.

The seigneurial emphasis in the buildings, and this is the main interest, was provided by a great tower or an imposing gatehouse, the two being usually mutually exclusive. Thus the imposing gatehouse at Herstmonceux, Sussex or Kirby Muxloe, Leicestershire, made a great tower unnecessary, but at Ashby de la Zouch, Leicestershire, Faulkbourne Hall, Essex, Tattershall Castle, Lincolnshire, Caister Castle, Norfolk or Buckden, Cambridgeshire, the towers are the centre of interest. It is not a hard and fast rule so that Raglan, for instance, has both. The gatehouse continues as the centre of interest through most of Tudor times, when keep-like towers more or less disappear (Compton Wynyates, Warwickshire, which lacks a gatehouse is an exception). The exclusiveness of the two was perhaps most clearly demonstrated by William Lord Hastings at Ashby de la Zouch and Kirby Muxloe; in the former case he constructed an enormous tower to give dignity to what was otherwise a rather pedestrian manor house, while in the latter case the incomplete remains show that the gatehouse primarily and the four corner towers secondarily were to provide the desired seigneurial emphasis.

Military gatehouses have of course a long history going back to the end of the twelfth century at about the time when the keep was falling out of favour. Imposing gatehouses with octagonal turrets were very popular in the later Middle Ages with monasteries and other institutions, but they usually had vehicular and pedestrian gates, the entry not being as narrow or so obviously flanked by the two projecting towers as in a military gatehouse.

The Scottish and Irish tower-houses differed from the great tower with which we are mainly concerned in that they were the principal, if not the only, residence on the site and designed to be occupied by the whole household. The English towers may have furnished a separate residence for the lord but they were essentially an additional feature to the standard medieval accommodation of hall and ancillaries. They could contain a vertical arrangement of grand rooms (Raglan, Ashby, Tattershall) or cellular lodgings of the familiar kind (Caister); it was the outward resemblance that was the crucial point, the internal function being to some extent optional. They were neither Celtic towers nor Norman keeps, but symbols of dignity and authority which they derived from their resemblance to the latter.

A very important change in building material was the employment of brick. Re-used Roman brick had been employed in the eleventh and twelfth centuries at for example St Albans Abbey or St Botolph's Priory at Colchester but went out of use in the thirteenth century (with certain exceptions like Little Wenham Hall, Essex) but came into favour again in the late fourteenth century (in Humberside at Holy Trinity Church, Hull, and Thornton Abbey gatehouse or in Norfolk at the Cow Tower at Norwich). During the fifteenth century it was widely used from Humberside southwards into the east Midlands, East Anglia, the Home Counties down to the south coast. In the mid-fifteenth century the dressings and mouldings, that is vault ribs, window and door surrounds, tracery, strings, quoins and corbels were usually in stone; the ancient tradition of stone carving died hard. Brick which cannot be easily dressed can be moulded before firing to the required shape; by the third quarter of the century buildings were being erected that had all their detail in moulded brick. The records show craftsmen from the Low Countries at work on the building sites and they no doubt passed on their skills.

In traditional building, kilns had to be constructed on the spot for making quicklime for the mortar so the construction of brick kilns was perhaps not quite so innovatory as might at first sight be supposed. The bricks were usually fired a short distance away from the building site and then carted to it. The cost of transport as compared with that of stone, particularly in stoneless areas, must have been greatly reduced, but probably the savings in costs were only a contributory factor to the use of brick; the bright red colour given to the building entirely fitted in with the craving for brightness and gaudiness that was the delight of this age. Instead of grey, brown or yellow walls they were bright red which could be enhanced by using haematite to redden the mortar and rouge the surface of the building. When freshly built such a building must have looked as though it had stepped out of a contemporary manuscript illumination. Further decoration could be applied by the use of vitrified bricks the blue ends of which could be arranged in the coursing to create patterns: simple diapers, mitres, initials and so on.

In the areas where flint occurred it could also be used to make 'flush-work' patterns, chequers or lilies or initials, by putting knapped flint and stone side by side. Though common on ecclesiastical buildings, it is rare in castles but not unknown, as on the gatehouse of Wingfield Castle, Suffolk (fig. 1), for instance.

46 The late fourteenth-century Guy's Tower at Warwick Castle.

Before turning to the fifteenth century there is work at Warwick Castle carried out in the previous half-century by Thomas Beauchamp and his son, also Thomas, both Earls of Warwick, that compels attention. The two great towers that the visitor sees as he approaches Warwick from the east were constructed between 1360 and 1390, the more southerly by the river, Caesar's Tower, being the earlier, and the more northerly, Guy's Tower, the later.[7] The very elaborate gatehouse with bridges spanning the corner turrets and barbican in front is of the same period. The whole structure has a verve and flamboyancy not encountered elsewhere in Britain, and there can be little doubt that it is an offspring of the French 'Renaissance' of the same period where spectacular towers of this kind are not uncommon. At Warwick one feels indeed that exuberance has taken the work well beyond the functional requirements of defence.

In some ways Caesar's Tower by the river is more imposing, being externally trilobate in plan and having the French *chemin de ronde*, a corbelled-out gangway or passage with crenellations below the top of the tower which rises to a wall-walk above it (fig. 47). It produces the effect of a 'crown'; it is also known from the very French castle of Nunney in Somerset and we shall meet it again in the mid-fifteenth century at Herst-monceux. Like Caesar's Tower, Guy's Tower was vaulted at each level, each floor having a large central and two side chambers. There were separate spiral staircases to serve the rooms and independently to reach the wall-walk on the summit. The tower is twelve-sided and was clearly intended to be a keep replacing the earlier keep on the eleventh-century motte on the opposite side of the castle. It has been suggested that the enormously thick vault over the top floor was designed to allow the use of cannon, but this must be regarded as doubtful. The term 'show-castle'

47 Caesar's Tower at Warwick Castle has the fourteenth-century French style of *chemin de ronde*, rarely found in England.

48 View of the late fourteenth-century gatehouse, Warwick Castle.

George Duke of Clarence was made Governour of this Castle, at whose death it being Seized into the Kings hand, continued in the Crown till the 17 of Hen. VII when Edn.d Belknap, Esq.r of the Body to the King, was made Constable. In the first of Edw.d VI. John Dudley was advanced to be Earl of Warwick; but upon his attainder in the 1 of 2. Mary, this Castle escheated to the Crown; yet through y.e especial favour of 2.Eliz. Ambrose his Son was made Earl & Governour thereof, he dying without Issue, it came again to the Crown, and so continued till the 2.d Year of K. James I. in which time it became very ruinous; but the K. bestow'd it in fee upon S.r Fhulk Grevill K.t who expended upwards of 20000 L. in repairs, which besides it's pleasant situation on the Bank of the River Aven, commanding a delightfull Prospect on every side, was accounted y.e most princely seat in that part of the Kingdom. This Castle belongs to y.e L.d Brook.

S.N & N. Buck delin.t & sculp.t 1729

49 An early eighteenth-century view of Warwick Castle shows (from the left) Caesar's Tower, the gatehouse, Guy's Tower and in the foreground Richard III's unfinished tower with circular openings for artillery.

can certainly be applied to both the towers and the gatehouse; they must have made a great impression on contemporaries.

Although vaulted at each level (most unusual in this country) the rooms in the tower were provided with fireplaces and their own separate access so that they are really cellular lodgings of the familiar kind rather more luxuriously appointed than those at Dartington Hall but essentially the same thing, arranged vertically instead of horizontally. The constrained access must have been a source of some inconvenience compared to that in a courtyard house but if you wished to live the chivalric life that was a penalty that you had to pay!

There is much else that deserves attention at Warwick, but mention must be limited to a construction on the north side of the castle erected a century later. The castle was in Crown hands from 1478–1547; Leland tells us that Richard III 'began and half finished a mighty tower, or strengthe, for to shoot out guns'.[8] It was a rectangular fort or tower, like other fifteenth-century towers with octagonal turrets at the corners, only two of which, the external ones, called the Bear and Clarence Towers, were completed, the rest of the building only reaching foundation stage. An eighteenth-century view by the Brothers Buck shows the circular apertures for cannon (fig. 49). The significant point is that the building was of traditional form in which no serious attempt was made to counteract the impact of shot against the fabric, so hardly suggesting any serious experience or knowledge of what was required when involved in an artillery exchange.

The fifteenth-century buildings now to be described divide broadly speaking into two periods, those from the second quarter and those from the second half of the century. Although we have fairly good dating evidence for most of them, licences to crenellate or building accounts, they cannot be taken in strict chronological order although this will be roughly followed. As might be expected there is more evidence of fortification among the earlier examples.

Raglan Castle, Gwent (Monmouthshire) is a natural starting point since it is perhaps the most ambitious work of this kind in the period, although unfortunately its date is controversial.[9] It has not been laid out on a rectangular plan as might be expected and the general resemblance of shape to a motte and bailey suggests that the builders were constrained by the ditches and earthworks of the earlier castle of which there is record. In other words it was a massive reconstruction on an earlier site, not piecemeal but conceived as a unity. Unfortunately there is no licence to crenellate, nor any building accounts, so that the date of construction has been a matter of dispute. There are three candidates: Sir William ap Thomas who had been in the French wars and after successful marriages became steward of the lordship of Usk and Caerleon under the Duke of York, or his son, William Herbert, and grandson (1469–79) who both became Earls of Pembroke. Family tradition, the recent experience of the Glyndŵr rebellion (a traumatic experience in Wales) and his experience in France favour the first, but the scale of work seems to fit better with William Herbert as does also the rather exotic style of the architecture. There is not sufficient evidence for a decision.

This is not the place for a full architectural description but a few salient points deserve mention. First the plan of the domestic buildings is entirely that of a fifteenth-century courtyard house divided into two by the central hall range with inner domestic (Fountain) court and outer court with offices. Tudor alterations may mislead as to original use of the buildings, particularly on the absence of cellular lodgings. The hexagonal shape of the keep, unusual in itself, was adopted for the impressive gatehouse and flanking towers or projections, and it may be that it was felt that it had special deflective powers against enemy shot for the profusion of gunports can leave no doubt that it was an attack with firearms that the occupants were expecting (figs. 50, 52). In the main castle the gunports are below the windows in the French style but in the keep they were at the bottom of a cross loop (fig. 50). The gatehouse shows robust machico-

50 A gunport on the keep of Raglan Castle with cruciform loop above, but the separation must have made sighting the gun difficult.

51 The hexagonal keep at Raglan Castle, a very finely built fifteenth-century tower, was 'slighted' by Parliament in 1646 by bringing down one side. It stands free of the rest of the 'castle'.

52 The hexagonal towers of the gatehouse of Raglan Castle, Gwent, with fine machicolations recalls fifteenth-century Continental work. Note two tiers of gunports below the windows.

lation, the corbels of which survive, and the keep also must have been a most imposing structure before the Parliamentary slighting (fig. 52).

It is still a very impressive sight. It is quite unlike the other great towers that we shall be examining in that it is not only strongly defended against an outside attacker but also against the rest of the castle. At first it could only be reached by a drawbridge across its own moat, and it has gunports facing that direction. The gunports are at ground level to give raking fire and face in all directions (the later construction of a causeway has rendered them useless). Inside it had four floors, perhaps to be interpreted as servants' hall on ground floor, hall above, audience chamber and then bedroom at the top. The upper part of the tower was removed at the time of the Parliamentary demolition.

One can only guess at the reasons for erecting such a strongly fortified tower at Raglan. The Glyndŵr rebellion may have caused extra apprehension about treachery among Welsh retainers. However its position so placed in front of the castle that its guns could rake any approach to the entries must raise the question as to whether there was not a functional explanation: it was perhaps intended to act as a permanent *bastille*, a sort of island fort set outside the main structure to prevent any direct assault on what was after all more of a house than a castle. The English were said to be proficient in the construction of such bastilles in France, although they were normally temporary works constructed of earth (fig. 53). Such an explanation might go some way to explain the rather puzzling plan of

53 Viollet-le-Duc's reconstruction of *bastilles* at Lübeck; perhaps the keep at Raglan and the exterior southeast tower at Caister had an analogous function.

the castle. The thickness of the walls, eleven feet, suggests that there was serious concern about impact. There is a distinctly continental feel (almost of the Italian Renaissance) about some features of Raglan, so it is most unfortunate that we do not know the circumstances of the building's construction nor the name of the master mason in charge of the work.

The date is known of the construction of the castle at Caister, near Great Yarmouth, since although there is again no licence to crenellate, some accounts of building expenditure have survived.[10] Work started in 1432 and continued for ten or fifteen years. The builder, Sir John Fastolf (Shakespeare's Falstaff although adopting his name did not bear the remotest resemblance to the real person), had a long career in the French wars from before Agincourt to the turn of the tide in the 1430s. A great deal is known about him from his records, from his secretary, William Worcester, and from the Paston letters, since John Paston was a close friend and the chief beneficiary in his will. It was the dispute over title that led to the famous siege in August 1469, when John the younger held the castle against an armed force of some 3,000 men of the Duke of Norfolk and eventually had to surrender (Paston letters 722–32). Permanent damage may have been inflicted on the fabric by bombardment at that time.

The castle which seems to have been laid out on a virgin site consisted of three elements (figs. 54, 55): a moated rectangular enclosure 160 by 140 feet defended by a brick wall with small square projections at three corners and a tall round tower at the north-west corner, a rectangular enclosure, formerly separated by a moat, roughly 200 by 100 feet on the north side with its own corner towers, and finally to the south a squat round tower adjoining the 'barge ditch' (really a canal). The remains of the castle are fragmentary but brick with stone dressings was used throughout. The bricks, fired locally, were brought by water transport to the castle, as well as stone and plaster of Paris from France. An eighteenth-century plan shows buildings lining the sides of the enclosures, and gate-houses on north and south, the former joined by a bridge to the outer enclosure. The tall slender keep and the plan caused Douglas Simpson to compare them with Schloss Kempen in the lower Rhineland and to suggest that the castle was a *Wasserburg* of the same type.[11] It is a plausible theory but as Fastolf's connections were entirely with France, over many years, and the master mason, Gravour, did not have a German name, caution must be exercised on this.

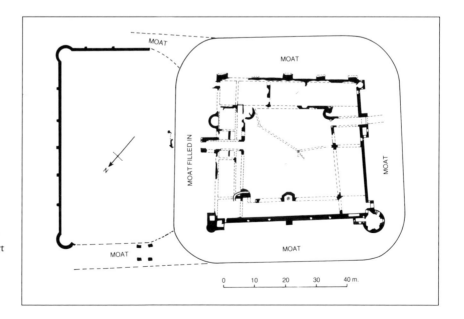

54 Plan of the castle at Caister by Yarmouth showing the inner court with round keep at southwest corner and the outer court on north; the exterior south-east barge-ditch tower is off the plan.

Several points deserve attention. The squat isolated tower to the south has a flat top as if to bear cannon, and although it had an important function to protect the canal head it was so placed that it commanded the whole of the south and east sides of the castle, including the entry, so it may have been intended to act as a protective *bastille* in the same way as has been suggested at Raglan. The northern enclosure was presumably intended to be the outer court of a normal domestic lay-out and the eighteenth-century plan shows an entry there. There are gunports in the surviving brickwork and we know that firearms were used in the 1469 siege. The gatehouse is not a dominant feature, the seigneurial emphasis being placed on the keep, which is ninety feet high, but only twenty-three feet in diameter (frontispiece). A hexagonal stair turret rises another eight feet above the tower. It is very thin-walled (four feet), about a third of that at Raglan, so its resistance to shot would be slight. It has brick machico-

55 Aerial view of Caister Castle, showing moat and round keep on the left and 'Barge Tower' – perhaps originally a bastille protecting the castle – on the right.

lations at its summit which are also carried by the surviving curtain. It has two rectangular projections on either side from one of which the stair turret rises. The tower contained five storeys of hexagonal rooms with their own fireplaces and rectangular windows, evidently cellular lodgings or bed-sitting rooms of the type to which we are now accustomed. In the building adjoining the tower there was a fairly grand room on the first floor, but the eighteenth-century plan leaves much obscure about the original layout, possibly having been already altered by that time.

Herstmonceux Castle, Sussex, now the Royal Observatory, lies near the south coast, an area vulnerable to foreign incursions throughout English history. In 1441 Sir Roger Fiennes received licence to 'enclose, crenellate, and furnish with towers and battlements his manor at Herstmonceux',[12] as recorded in the Charter (not Patent) Rolls. There was no such licence for our previous three castles, a fair indication of how fortuitous such a grant was. What was erected has some claim to be among the prettiest compositions that the late Middle Ages has to offer; the sun shining on the red brick of the south front reflected in the moat produces a sight that has been photographed many times!

Roger Fiennes, the eldest son of Sir William Fiennes of Herstmonceux, was somewhat outshone by his younger brother James Fiennes, created Lord Saye and Sele, who served long years in France and was Sheriff of Kent, Surrey, and Sussex, Warden of the Cinque Ports, Constable of Dover Castle and so on. Roger, although less distinguished, probably served in France like his brother, was knighted in 1422, was Treasurer of the Household 1439–46 (when the licence was issued), dying in 1450.[13]

The ground plan of the castle is extremely regular: within a broad moat a rectangle of 208 by 214 feet was enclosed by a brick wall with octagonal turrets projecting diagonally at the corners, and with three semi-octagonal turrets spaced along three sides, but on the fourth the central one was replaced by the gateway flanked by two octagonal turrets with a vaulted passage between (figs. 56, 57). There were two entrances, a postern with drawbridge in the middle of the north side, and the main southern gatehouse with its deep slots into which the beams of the draw-bridge fitted when it was in a raised position. The two octagonal towers have cross slits at three levels with circular gunports below the lowest tier at ground level. There are two-light windows above the gate arch at first and second storeys. The most striking feature of the whole structure is the battlemented *chemin de ronde* on both towers on a stage itself corbelled out, the crenellations carried over the gate passage, while the two towers rise one stage higher terminating in crenellated parapets. The archway is

56 Herstmonceux Castle, Sussex. Like Caister Castle it was built of brick in *c.* 1440.

four-centred and another tall arch encloses the beam slots and first-floor window. This very striking composition with an heraldic device at second-floor level provides the seigneurial emphasis for there is no keep. The wall towers are corbelled at the top and slope backwards lower down giving a distinct batter. There is a steep battered base sloping up from the moat all the way round. One-light (occasionally two-light) windows divided by a transom, taller on the first floor, punctuate the wall all the way round. Brick is used throughout except for the dressings which are of stone.

The interior of the castle was gutted in the eighteenth century but from a plan that was made before this happened it is known there were ranges all the way round with the hall in a cross-range about two-thirds of the way back, the hall itself on the east side with chapel just in front, the central wall tower containing its east end. The screens passage was almost opposite the main entry but to reach it you had to pass round a 'cloister' that occupied the south-eastern part of the interior.

What are we to make of this remarkable building? It is quite clear that the symmetry of the exterior was an overriding consideration: the internal buildings if a little cramped seem to have been more or less like an ordinary courtyard house. It cannot be said that the shape of the castle determined the disposition of the domestic buildings, as at Harlech (p. 45), but equally the latter did not determine the geometric shape of the castle,

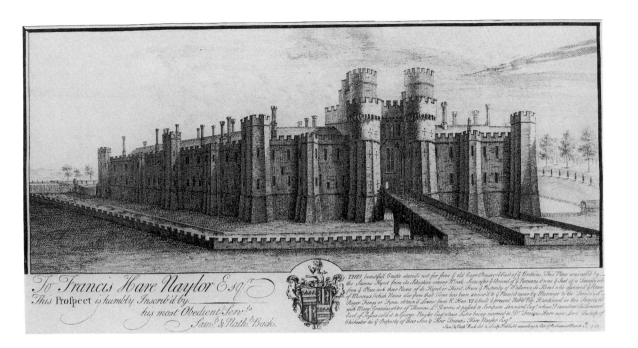

57 An eighteenth-century view of Herstmonceux Castle showing its symmetry with repetition of octagonal towers, as also the wealth of chimneys from the internal lodgings.

which suggests rather a handsome jacket for a courtyard house. It is situated in a vulnerable position on the coast, so it is probably a mistake to write off the defence capability. The lowest windows are well above the moat water level, the expanse of masonry being no small obstacle, and while there are no gunports, except in the gatehouse, one suspects that the lower tier of one-light windows could have been readily adapted for this purpose. The *Leitmotiv* was to leave the outside onlooker with an impression of a dreamlike ethereal castle – certainly a suitable back-drop for jousting and tournaments!

Two other buildings which have some resemblance to Herstmonceux should be mentioned here. Ampthill Castle, Bedfordshire has vanished, but a plan survives which shows that the inner courtyard was 220 feet square containing one large and two small courtyards, as at Herstmonceux, and that it had octagonal towers. It must have closely resembled Herstmonceux.[14] There was an outer ward according to Leland who also says that Lord Fanhope (Sir Richard Cornwall) built it 'of such spoils as it is said he won in France'.[15] He had a distinguished career both in France and the tournament field, married the sister of Henry IV and died in 1443.

The second example is at Bronsill, Herefordshire, which survives as a ruin.[16] There was a licence to crenellate issued to Richard Beauchamp in September 1460, so it is later than Ampthill or Herstmonceux. The enclosure is smaller, 120 feet square with an internal courtyard of 60–70 feet. It had octagonal wall towers.

The preference for polygonal shapes that we have seen in all cases except Caister may have arisen from the belief that inclined faces would cause the enemy shot to ricochet off.

Ralph Boteler, Lord Sudeley, who was born at the end of the fourteenth century, had business in France over several decades as a soldier and diplomat.[17] According to Leland he built Sudeley Castle, Gloucestershire, from 'spoils got in France', and, as he was pardoned in 1458 for not having obtained a licence to crenellate, there is independent confirmation of this.

The castle was largely demolished in the Commonwealth period while modern rebuilding in the outer court has even further confused our understanding of this impressive ruin. There were two courts, the outer slightly askew, and so perhaps built a little later (fig. 58). The inner courtyard, the earlier, which measures internally about 160 by 130 feet, originally had towers at each corner and keep (the Dungeon Tower) in the south-west corner (there does not seem to have been a prominent gatehouse). The magnificent ruined hall range on the east side was probably erected by Richard, Duke of Gloucester who had acquired the property when Boteler had to forfeit his estates to the Crown. The original hall was on the north or possibly the south side of the inner court. The east and west ranges of the outer court are Tudor and later in their present form. The

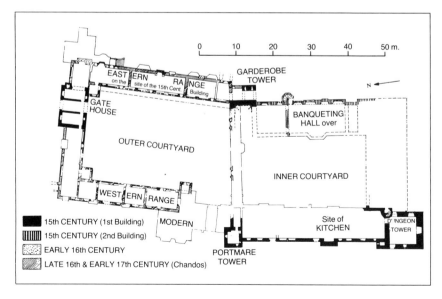

58 The irregular junction of the two courtyards at Sudeley Castle, Gloucestershire indicates that the outer one is a later addition.

gaunt ruins of today give a very poor picture of the palatial buildings as they must have been before the Civil War.

Another fortified site with licence of 1443 to crenellate, to impark and fortify the manor, was Rye House, Hertfordshire, where only the gatehouse and moats survive.[18] The early date makes it convenient to refer to it here. The licensees were Andrew Ogard, John Clifton, and William Oldehall, and as the manor is referred to as in the Isle of Rye, water and marsh were presumably the main defence. Brick was the building material and the plan was evidently a rectangle with octagonal turrets at the corners. The gatehouse, probably an inner one, has a three-bay vaulted passage, two first-floor oriel windows, and looped merlons with central oillet and splayed base (fig. 59). There are decorative diaper patterns on the brickwork, and the false decorative machicolation, window surrounds and dripstones are all in moulded brick. If the date of 1443 is reliable it is one of the earliest instances of moulded brick. The rather feeble gatehouse suggests that it was compensated for by a large tower somewhere on the site.

Ralph Lord Cromwell is already familiar from these pages as the builder of the great courtyard house at South Wingfield, Derbyshire (p. 64). Although the remains are much more fragmentary at Tattershall, Lincolnshire, the survival of the large brick tower which dominates the site, and the dramatic events that led to its acquisition by Lord Curzon together with the works of restoration, of re-flooring and re-roofing in this century have given this place much wider notice. One of the most remarkable discoveries of the restoration work was that the early thirteenth-century castle (licence to crenellate, 1231), no doubt an irregular polygon with round towers at the angles (like the recently exposed structure at Bolingbroke Castle of almost identical date only a few miles away), had been demolished by Lord Cromwell in the 1430s to begin the construction of his great tower. Some surviving building accounts, albeit rather laconic in character, were published by the late Dr Simpson in 1960.[19]

Lord Cromwell, who took his name from the village in Nottinghamshire, the third holder of the title, had served as a young man in France and achieved a position of great importance as Lord Treasurer in 1433.[20] The earlier castle with its stone towers was perhaps in decay, so that Tattershall as his main seat was judged to require something more imposing and flamboyant in red brick. The overall plan of the castle is by no means clear from the early eighteenth-century view of the brothers Buck (figs. 60–62). It is apparent that certain domestic buildings of the earlier structure had been retained, notably the hall, and the tower was laid out in relation to that. There are several long sections of brick foundations visible on the site from ranges of the courtyard house type but there does not seem to be a coherent plan. To an earlier enclosure measuring 250 by 200 feet a large moated L-shaped enclosure itself divided in the middle has been added. The engraving shows what looks like an inner, outer and possibly uttermost gatehouse. The inner one had octagonal corner turrets and portcullis, while within stood a building with large two-light windows (? chapel) and a three-bay hall with oriel and cross-wing immediately in front of the great tower which at this time still

59 The highly ornamented brick gatehouse with bay windows is all that survives of a large mid-fifteenth-century moated seat at Rye House, Hertfordshire.

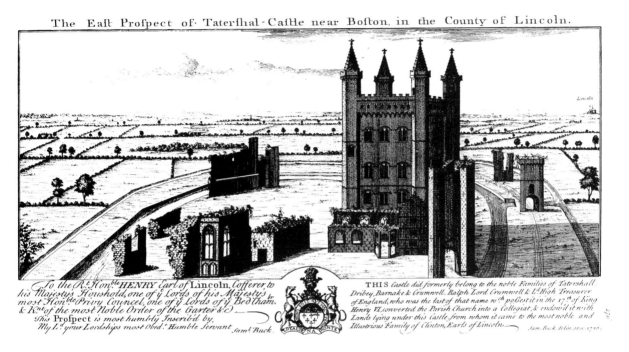

The East Prospect of Tatershal-Castle near Boston, in the County of Lincoln.

To the Rt Honble HENRY Earl of Lincoln, Cofferer to his Majestys Houshold, one of ye Lords of his Majesty's most Honble Privy Councel, one of ye Lords of ye Bedtham & Knt of the most Noble Order of the Garter &c — This Prospect is most humbly Inscrib'd by, My Ld your Lordships most Obedt Humble Servant Saml Buck.

THIS Castle did formerly belong to the noble Families of Tatershall Dribey, Barnake & Crumvell. Ralph Lord Crumvell & Ld High Treasurer of England, who was the last of that name wch possest it in the 17th of King Henry VI. converted the Parish Church into a Collegiat, & endow'd it with Lands lying under this Castle, from whom it came to the most noble and Illustrious Family of Clinton, Earls of Lincoln — Sam. Buck delin. et sc. 1726.

60 The ruins of the reconstruction in brick in *c.* 1430–50 by Ralph Lord Cromwell of Tattershall Castle, Lincolnshire, as seen in the eighteenth century. Note the conical caps on the turrets of great tower, the fragmentary gatehouses, and most important the earlier hall with oriel in front of the great tower which was built to serve it.

retained the conical roofs of its turrets. The hall which appears to be of stone, possibly decorated with flushwork, is evidently older than the tower behind. Presumably there was some kind of courtyard in front of the hall but its details are obscure.

The juxtaposition of the hall to the great tower is the key to understanding the latter. It was not designed as a defensible citadel as is the case at Raglan, nor as an independent domestic block as at Ashby de la Zouch, but as an ancillary building to the hall. There are three ground-floor doorways, that on the right, approached from the upper end of the hall, leading to the ground-floor room. By analogy with South Wingfield this room with a fine fireplace would have been the parlour or mess-room for senior members of household. The middle doorway leads down to a dark vaulted basement, probably a servants' hall, heated by braziers and lit by torches, analogous to the undercroft at South Wingfield. The left hand door opened directly on to a spiral staircase serving the three grand rooms on first, second and third floors, all furnished with splendid fireplaces with heraldic decoration on the overmantels. The rooms are probably best interpreted as private hall, audience chamber and bedroom for Lord Cromwell himself. The suite was approached from the lower end of hall, as at South Wingfield, Farnham, and probably fairly generally. At Ashby de la Zouch the underground passage from the keep came out at the lower end of the hall, probably so that the lord could enter the hall to process

along it majestically to the high table. The building accounts surprisingly do not refer to the *donjon*, evidently this tower, until 1445 and it may be that it was not so called until it reached a certain height, it being referred to as the parlour while work was still at that level. The rooms above the basement are well lit by large two-light windows, and the access from the staircase to the main upper rooms was evidently deliberately restricted with a long passage in the thickness of the wall to be traversed at 'audience-chamber' level. The octagonal corner turrets furnished three small supplementary rooms at each level.

However it is clear that the outside of the tower was meant to impress as much or even more than the inside. It is of brick with strings, windows, doorways, and machicolations in stone. The machicolations between the turrets carry a battlemented parapet on a platform above, giving a double-tiered defensive work. The tops of the turrets have a decorative brick corbel table and their conical roofs survived until the nineteenth century. There are no gunports and with three ground-floor doors and

61 Outer face of the brick tower at Tattershall. The large traceried windows, particularly at ground level, indicate that it was built not for defence but for show.

62 Inner face of great brick tower at Tattershall Castle, Lincolnshire; note machicolations supporting gallery below wall-walk and three doors leading (from right) to parlour on ground floor, vaulted basement (servants' hall?), and spiral staircase serving three great rooms on upper floors.

large ground-floor windows on three sides it can hardly have been intended as defensible.

As explained above (p. 72) it is difficult to put forward any reasonable motive for building the tower that does not include a large element of fantasy and self-dramatisation, a view that receives reinforcement from the heraldic displays on the over-mantels of the fireplaces. 'Castle of chivalry' would hardly be an inappropriate name for this most telling of fifteenth-century monuments.

In order to provide yourself with a dwelling of more martial appearance, either the earlier structure could be demolished and replaced, as at Kirby Muxloe and perhaps Raglan, or alternatively imposing additions could be made to the existing fabric or part retained after demolition of the rest, as at Tattershall, Buckden, Ashby de la Zouch, Farnham and Faulkbourne Hall, Essex. At Faulkbourne, Sir John Montgomery received a licence to crenellate in 1439.[21] The hall comprises buildings of two periods in the fifteenth century: a T-shaped group of timber-framed rooms, which the Royal Commission regarded as belonging to 1439 and the magnificent brick range of the north front which comprises a four-storeyed tower at the north-east, a vaulted oriel window in the middle and a semi-octagonal tower at the north-west (figs. 63, 64). All the detail is in brick: decorative corbelling, windows, diagonal buttresses on the tower with projecting turrets above, panelling and so on. The thorough-going use of moulded brick certainly lends weight to the Commission's view that the north front was not erected before the second half of the fifteenth century. There was a moat but no courtyard with imposing gatehouse; presumably the north-east tower supplied the missing seigneurial element.

If Ralph Lord Cromwell was the dominant figure in secular building in the second quarter of the fifteenth century, then the dominant figure in the second half was William Lord Hastings. Born in about 1430 he was more than a generation younger than Cromwell, without the exhilarating experience of Agincourt and the French wars of that period, although he had been in France and perhaps more significantly in Scotland. His indentured retainers have been discussed already (p. 68) and through his close friendship with Edward IV he was rewarded with a formidable list of appointments in England and Wales.[22] The dramatic circumstances of his death, when he was hustled away to execution on the orders of Richard III, have left a permanent monument in the unfinished remains at Kirby Muxloe, Leicestershire.

Like Cromwell, Hastings' main interests were in the Midlands; in April

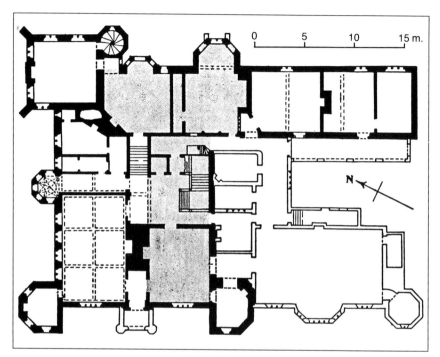

63 At Faulkbourne Hall, Essex, the south side (tinted) is timber-framed and probably earlier, while the north front is in brick and later. There is no gatehouse but an imposing tower.

64 The north front of Faulkbourne Hall; note the highly decorative, moulded brick, bay windows and bartisans on great tower.

65 The great stone tower built by William Lord Hastings at Ashby de la Zouch, Leicestershire; the portcullis groove at the door and the bartisans recall a Scottish tower of the period. Only the north side survives.

66 The south face of the great tower at Ashby de la Zouch; the whole side has been removed by Parliamentary 'slighting', and left exposed the four main floors in the tower and the doorways and windows of a vertical arrangement of cellular lodgings in its annex on the right.

1474 he received licence to fortify four houses in Leicestershire: Ashby de la Zouch, Bagworth, Kirby Muxloe and Thornton.[23] He had received the manor at Ashby a few years before and had probably started alterations before the licence was granted. There was already a hall with cross-wings and kitchen on the side. Hastings made a circuit on the east side of the chapel and a small set of cellular lodgings linked by a curtain wall to the great tower on the south side. This immense structure was split asunder by orders of Parliament after the Civil War so only its northern half survives, but enough still exists to merit special attention (figs. 65, 66).

It is about forty-five feet square with a rectangular projection on its eastern side. Of all the towers with which we are concerned it is the one that most recalls a Scottish tower-house; not just because it is in stone (rather than brick) but on account of the projection on the side, the portcullis at the entry (recalling the Scottish *yett*), the vaults over the two lowest floors and the corbelled-out turrets or bartisans at the corners. The four floors are probably best interpreted as unlit servants' hall, private hall, audience chamber and bedroom. The latter has a display of heraldry on the overmantel which recalls on a modest scale that at Tattershall. The parlour is missing in the vertical sequence here, no doubt because there was already a large room at the upper end of the main hall on the other side of the courtyard that could serve the purpose of mess-room for senior staff in the normal position of the parlour. The eastward projection was a sort of annexe with six floors of small rooms with their own separate entrances. Unfortunately, the destruction of the whole of the southern side of the tower has destroyed the evidence for fire-places with a common flue that we might expect, since these chambers are evidently the familiar cellular lodgings in a vertical arrangement. An underground passage leading from the ground floor comes out in a cellar near the kitchen on the other side of the courtyard, presumably to allow food to be brought direct to the tower but probably also to allow the lord to make an imposing entry at the lower end of the hall and process to high table. The top of the tower is machicolated and the projecting turrets bear panelled decoration. The portcullis at the entry may have been a serious defence because the rest of the 'castle' (really a house) was crudely defended, or for appearances.

Although Hastings had received the licence to crenellate for Kirby Muxloe in 1474, work did not begin until October 1480. From then until December 1484, £1,088/17/7 had been spent, although work was reduced to almost zero after his execution in 1483.[24] The earlier hall, the stone foundations of which survive in the courtyard, was retained initially but demolished later so as to use the stone in the foundations of the new buildings. A much more dramatic treatment was possible than had been the case at Ashby: a seventy-foot-wide moat enclosed a rectangular area about 180 by 120 feet which had square towers at the corners and rectangular projections in the middle of three sides with the gatehouse in the middle of the fourth (north) side (figs. 67, 68). The new material, brick, was used throughout except for the stone dressings. Most of the foundations had been laid, the gatehouse largely and the north-west tower wholly built when work was brought to an abrupt halt. The symmetry of the design is broken on the south side where the central projection is off-centre, evidently to accommodate the end of the screens passage opposite the gateway.

The gatehouse is more in the nature of a rectangular tower with octagonal corner turrets, those externally being larger, the overall shape recalling the structure erected immediately after this by Richard III at Warwick Castle (p. 77). The resemblance is made greater in that its outer face is amply provided with gunports (fig. 67). The two back turrets contain spiral staircases apparently to give access to cellular lodgings in pairs on the first and second floor (the latter not built), since there are fireplaces and latrines at each end. A drawbridge and portcullis guarded the central vaulted passage which was flanked by vaulted chambers and could be closed at either end by gates. The front of the gatehouse bears the initials W. H. (William Hastings) with his badge, a 'maunch sable' or black sleeve on the right hand turret, both picked out in vitrified brick headers; the seigneurial emphasis was on the gatehouse for there was no great tower.

The completed west tower had three storeys: gunports in the ground floor, but two floors above the rooms had their own latrines and fireplaces (fig. 68). The constrained space within the castle meant that full use of the towers and gatehouse had to be made for bed-sitting rooms. It is interesting that they were some of the first parts to be built; it has been suggested that at South Wingfield the provision of lodgings for senior members of staff had a high priority (p. 64). The gunports are so placed that they both enfilade along the moat and face outwards. They consist of a circular aperture in stone about eight inches in diameter for discharging the weapon through, and a sighting slit above (fig. 69). In order to give raking fire they had to be set to fire at a man's height, just above the outer lip of the ditch. In the gatehouse, the first gunports were set too low and another tier had to be put in above, presumably because of a change of mind about the depth of water required in the moat. The thinness of the walls, four feet, hardly suggests that serious artillery bombardment was expected.

The gunports at Kirby may make this a convenient point to mention three buildings of the period where there may have been a serious

67 The gatehouse of Kirby Muxloe Castle, Leicestershire, left unfinished by Lord Hastings at his execution in 1483; note gunports at ground level and decorative vitrified brick.

68 The only tower erected at Kirby Muxloe; note the gunports.

defensive intention. Lathom House, Lancashire, was destroyed in the Civil War but is said to have been built by Thomas Stanley, first Earl of Derby, in the second half of the century,[25] and to have had eleven towers, two courts, a keep and provision for artillery. Greenhalgh Castle in the same county was also destroyed at the time of the Civil War, although one small corner tower survives. The same Thomas Stanley had licence to 'build, crenellate and embattle' at the site in 1490.[26] Berry Pomeroy Castle in Devonshire has a gatehouse with pointed, semi-hexagonal towers linked by a rampired wall with apron to a U-shaped corner tower all protecting a large Tudor house.[27] The gatehouse recalls that at Raglan but the date is quite uncertain: provision for artillery to such a degree suggests a late fifteenth- or even early sixteenth-century date.

The Crown, although not involved in new castle foundation, continued to make additions and alterations to existing structures – Richard III's work at Warwick has been mentioned, but one thinks of the great gatehouse at Lancaster or that reconstructed at Carmarthen after Glyndŵr's rebellion. No doubt there was ostentatious work at Sheen or Richmond (engravings of the latter exist) which does not survive, but the brick gatehouse added to Hertford Castle[28] in 1461–5, although largely re-fenestrated in the eighteenth century, has some striking brick corbelling and false machicolation (fig. 109). The brickmaker had a Flemish or Dutch name as he had at Kirby Muxloe and elsewhere.

The bishops carried out some notable brick construction in the last decades of the fifteenth century. It was a period when tower-building was

69 Kirby Muxloe Castle, a close-up view of the gunports on the gatehouse showing sighting slits above.

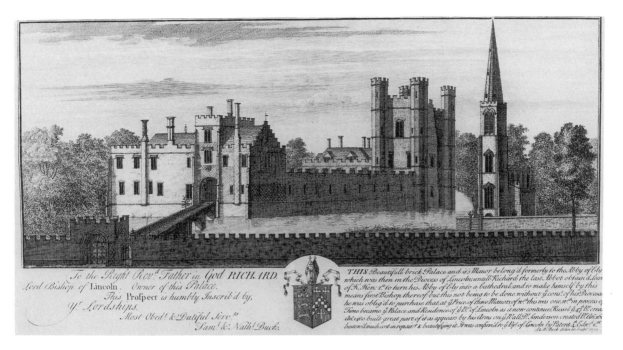

Within the engraving:

To the Right Revd. Father in God RICHARD. Lord Bishop of Lincoln. Owner of this Palace. This Prospect is humbly Inscrib'd by, Yr. Lordships. Most Obedt. & Dutiful Servts. Saml. & Nathl. Buck.

THIS Beautifull brick Palace and its Mannor belong'd formerly to the Abby of Ely which was then in the Diocess of Lincoln: unto Richard the last Abbot obtain'd leave of K. Hen: 1st to turn his Abby of Ely into a Cathedral and to make himself by this means first Bishop thereof but this not being to be done without ye consent of his Diocesan he was oblig'd to purchase that at ye true ofthree Mannors of wch this was one & in process of Time became ye Palace and Residence of ye Bp of Lincoln as it now continues: Russel ye 47 Bp. erected the two built great part of it as appears by his Arms on ye Wall Dr Anderson created Bp therein bestow'd much cost in repairs & beautifying it. It was confirm'd to ye Bp of Lincoln by Patent ye 4 Edw: 6th.

70 An eighteenth-century view of the late-fifteenth-century palace of the bishops of Lincoln at Buckden, Cambridgeshire (Huntingdonshire) showing gatehouse, great tower and parish church. Note the resemblance of tower to those at Kirby Muxloe and Warwick and the apparently seriously defensible looped wall between gatehouse and tower.

very popular, not only in parish churches but also in monasteries (e.g. Prior Overton's brick tower at Repton Priory – at the lower end of hall). At the bishop's palace at Lincoln the two ancient halls were linked by a stone gate-tower by Bishop Alnwick (1436–49). His successors Bishop Rotherham (1472–80) and Bishop Russell (1480–94) made the impressive additions to the Palace of Buckden in Huntingdonshire which must figure among the 'show-castles' of this chapter.

There had been a group of buildings at Buckden since the thirteenth century[29] comprising an aisled hall and various ancillary structures including the chapel at the upper end of the hall. The alterations made in 1470–90 recall those made at Ashby de la Zouch by Hastings: a military air was given to what had been purely domestic by the addition of a great tower and a length of curtain wall with a double tier of loops linking it to a new gatehouse, the whole being enclosed by a moat, itself spanned by a two-arched brick bridge (figs. 70, 72). The looped curtain looks as if it meant business. Brick was used throughout the new work entirely in the gatehouses but with detail in stone in the tower. The tower is an elongated rectangle with octagonal corner turrets recalling the Kirby gatehouse. It formerly had a vaulted basement, perhaps a servants' hall, while the ground floor room called a parlour in later accounts may always have been such in view of its close proximity to the upper end of the hall. Possibly the two upper floors were used by the bishop.

Bishop William Wayneflete of Winchester, who was a great builder, was the principal executor for Lord Cromwell, responsible for the erection of the parish church and college at Tattershall after Cromwell's death; it is reasonable to presume that the great brick tower he built in front of the hall at Farnham Castle, Surrey, was directly inspired by Cromwell's brick tower at Tattershall.[30] Indeed, owing to its position on top of a hill, the Farnham tower dominates the town in a most striking way, no doubt the intention of the builder. It is a square tower with a rectangular projection on one side containing the staircase and with octagonal turrets on the external corners (fig. 71). It acts as a colossal porch to the hall, its archway with grooves for portcullis and external half-label, as if for drawbridge recess when raised, opening into a passage in the ground floor leading direct into the screens passage. Like the tower at Hertford it has been re-fenestrated, the new sash windows considerably detracting from its intended martial air. String courses had been suppressed to give full play to the diaper work that covers the whole building. There are moulded brick machicolations between the turrets carried round them with decorative brick corbelling. The stair extension has its own little brick octagonal corner turret corbelled out at the top, and above the battlements there are decorated brick chimneys. The time

71 Great brick entry tower added to the hall at Farnham Castle, Surrey, by Bishop Waynflete in 1470–5, and clearly intended to provide prime accommodation at lower end of hall; note decorative moulded brick, bartisan on annex and portcullis groove.

72 Exterior face of great tower at Buckden; note massive octagonal corner turrets and central stepped flue.

of erection is closely dated from the Winchester manorial accounts, being started in 1470 and completed in 1475. The bricks were made locally and brickmakers with Low Countries names were employed. There are in fact no stone dressings, brick being used throughout – a major difference from Tattershall.

The question of function is an intriguing one. The tower clearly provided grand accommodation at the lower end of the hall, as at Tattershall, with perhaps audience chamber and bedroom for the bishop in the two storeys over the entry. This would have freed accommodation at the upper end of the hall for the senior parlour. It was a tower with a way-through at ground level, not a tall slender tower over a porch as we shall see at Hatfield. One might have been suggested by the other, but the small rooms in a porch tower could never have had the same function as the large rooms in a keep-like structure such as that at Farnham.

John Morton (1420–1500), before he became Cardinal Morton and Archbishop of Canterbury, was Bishop of Ely (1479–86). Like Wayneflete he was a considerable builder, and seems to have initiated the reconstruction of the bishop's palace at Hatfield as a courtyard house in brick. Only one range of this now survives in the grounds of the Jacobean mansion, the others being visible merely as mounds in an ornamental garden. However, a plan made before their demolition shows the original lay-out with the internal division of the hall range, the two towered porches being at either end of the screens passage (fig. 73). The whole range with its splendid roof has now been thrown into one, but originally it was hall on one side of the passage and offices, pantry, buttery, etc. on the other. It is extremely interesting that this had been designed as one continuous building, not with offices in a cross-wing, the time-honoured medieval form. The brick towers, particularly the external one, endow the building with a little seigneurial dignity and point the way to later development (fig. 74).

Finally, mention may be made of the brick gateway, added by the Cardinal to Lambeth Palace: Morton's Tower, its flanking towers peculiarly asymmetrical, confers a certain martial air on the remarkably heterogeneous group of buildings that constitute the palace.

With the bishops' palaces of the late fifteenth century we have left castles behind, but the builders no doubt saw themselves in a continuing tradition; they did not see matters in a functional light, what was defensive and what pretence. That is the modern view; the tree of knowledge and its forbidden fruit came with the Renaissance. What had been spontaneous

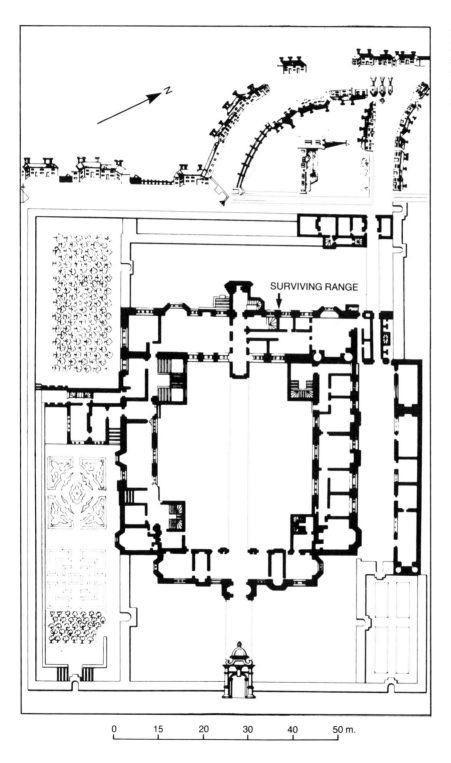

SURVIVING RANGE

73 Plan of palace erected by Bishop Morton of Ely at Hatfield, Hertfordshire, in late fifteenth century; only the hall range (at top) now survives but with its internal divisions removed.

0   15   20   30   40   50 m.

74 Tower over porch of hall of Bishop Morton's palace at Hatfield (all in brick). Unlike the keep-like structure at Farnham it was probably not for the bishop's use.

75 Brick gatehouse at Oxburgh Hall, Norfolk erected in 1480s; note the highly ornate panelled decoration and stepped merlons demonstrating excellence of East Anglian workmanship.

became self-conscious imitation; chivalry became a pose, not a part of life.

This chapter may be concluded by reference to a house constructed just before the Tudor period which illustrates by its gatehouse that preoccupation with grandiose gatehouses that lasted until the seventeenth century, a kind of sublimated desire for a true castle. Edmund Bedingfield received a licence to fortify his manor at Oxburgh Hall, Norfolk, in July 1482.[31] The construction of the handsome brick moated manor house presumably followed from this. The social status of Bedingfield might not have entitled him to build a castle, but he certainly erected a very impressive manor house.

The area enclosed is almost exactly 160 feet square. The splendid gatehouse is just off-centre in the north side, an attempt to line up with the porch of the hall on the other side of the court which it does not quite do (fig. 75). The ranges have been largely rebuilt but an eighteenth-century plan shows their original disposition. The hall with opposing oriels has a doorway facing north into the court but the main aspect was probably south looking over the moat where the small intervening space was probably a garden. The rest of the plan calls for no comment. Brick was used throughout for walls and dressings. The main surviving feature is the magnificent gatehouse approached over a bridge of three arches. It consists of a rectangular structure of three storeys straddling the gate passage in its ground floor, and fine rooms with four- and three-light windows above. Two octagonal turrets, covered with tiers of decorative brick panelling project either side of the gate, one with the spiral staircase inside lit by quatrefoil openings, the other with cross loops at the base and single-light windows above. The loops suggest a minimal defence purpose. The turrets terminate in ornamental corbelling and crenellations, and there are ornamental battlements on the front and back of the building. The back is plainer with projecting semi-octagonal turrets with three windows at each stage, the corners terminating in corbelled out turrets. Even in East Anglia where decorative brickwork reaches a very high level (witness the fifteenth-century brick gatehouse of the Deanery at Hadleigh, Suffolk) the Oxburgh gatehouse is something of a *tour de force*.

Chapter 6

Accelerating decay

> As for nobility in particular persons: it is a reverend thing to see
> an ancient castle or building not in decay . . .

Sir Francis Bacon's remark in his essay 'Of Nobility' is that much better
understood when we appreciate that by early Stuart times the great
majority of castles were in decay. The vivid simile of Spenser (*Faerie
Queene* 1, ii, 20) 'The Lady when she saw her champion fall – like the old
ruins of a broken tower', or the 'stately palace' (1, iv, 5) so ill-provided
with foundations that 'all the hinder parts, that few could spy – were
ruinous and old, but painted cunningly' are reminders of the pervasive
nature of ruins in Elizabethan England. The countryside was strewn with
ruined or derelict structures, hundreds of them, secular and monastic.

This chapter will be concerned with tracing the acceleration of decay in
the period up to the outbreak of the Civil War with some reference to the
new fortifications which were still being erected in this period.

In 1523, Fitzherbert in *The Boke of Surveying and Improvements* (fol. p.),
in his advice on valuation of the castle and other buildings, drew a distinction between structures in repair and in use, worth twice the value
of the materials in them, and those where realisation of the materials was
desirable. In this case it was more profitable to sell off items separately
rather than in gross. This was clearly better done before dereliction had
gone too far. The whole attitude is only understandable on the assumption of very widespread abandonment, contemplated or carried out, and
it may be that the thought had passed through not a few minds – if castles
why not monasteries?

One of the besetting difficulties in the study of castles is to know how
far events at a particular place were peculiar to it or whether they reflect
more widespread changes over large areas. This is to some extent inescap-
able since the contemporary source was written by a clerk, chronicler or
surveyor who was not interested in trends or comparisons but in particular conditions or events experienced by the building with which he was

concerned. The early Tudor period is especially fortunate in that it possesses an account by an authorised traveller who rode over England and Wales in 1535–45 noting the condition of the several hundred castles that he saw, thus providing a unique record of their condition at the end of the Middle Ages.

The difficulties of using Leland's *Itinerary* are well known: the confused state of the manuscripts, the difficulty in reconstructing the routes taken by Leland, the ambiguities of the laconic statements, and so on. These are factors that have to be borne in mind when reading the work but they should not deter us from recognising its value and its inherent merits. Castles and bridges were Leland's main interests, ecclesiastical structures such as churches or chapels coming a long way behind. His concern was by no means purely antiquarian; it was castles and stone bridges in active use that particularly aroused his admiration, for he had no romantic interest in ruins. He was not concerned with estates of particular owners (although understandably he was not very critical of Crown properties), but was simply interested in the appearance of the buildings as he saw them. His visits were no doubt brief but the strength and weakness of his observations are precisely their pungent immediacy, often more telling than the long-winded report or survey. Although he occasionally mistook prehistoric or Roman remains for medieval castles, he never had any doubt about their character and identity, and importance, in the town and countryside that he visited.

Leland makes references to some 500–600 castles in England and Wales, although he had not seen all of them. In Appendix 2 (p. 171) I have listed some 258 names of castles in the *Itinerary* where the mentions are sufficient to justify some inference about their condition. This may be little more than in indication that the structure was still in use implying reasonable condition, or more specific references saying it was 'clean down' or 'ruinous'. The phrases used can be very ambiguous, and not everyone may agree with the interpretation placed upon them in the Appendix.

It would be difficult to classify degrees of dereliction or ruin in buildings that one has seen oneself,[1] but with the laconic remarks of Leland they are even more elusive. Nevertheless, if the information is to be reduced to some kind of intelligible order, such a classification has to be attempted. Three divisions have been made: castles apparently in good enough condition to be in normal use (N), those in partial dereliction (D) and those where the structures were wholly ruinous (R). On this basis the 258 castles have been broken down into 91 in normal use, 30 partially derelict and 137 ruinous.

258 is a fairly sizeable sample for statistical purposes and if only 35% of the individual castles were in normal use the implication is that the institution was itself in a very unhealthy state. Even allowing for sites of early abandonment in the twelfth and thirteenth centuries, such a low proportion of structures functioning normally cannot be attributed to wastage and disuse; we are dealing with something that was in severe decline. It is a case of decline, not yet death, as the recent reconstruction work mentioned by Leland shows (at Belvoir, Brancepeth, Carew, Castle Hedingham, Chirk, Montgomery, Newcastle Emlyn, Rose, Tong), although much of this had a domestic rather than a military character. In at least two cases, Belvoir and Castle Hedingham, the reconstruction had been of a ruin or derelict structure and not the alteration of a building in active use.

As with villages that had been deserted in the same period, it was often the smaller castles that were abandoned first. Nevertheless, although there are a good many of these, large castles also feature in the list of those in a ruinous condition at the time of Leland's journeys in 1535–45; Barnstaple, Berkhamsted, Caerphilly, Devizes, Hereford, Marlborough, Shrewsbury. Continuity of ownership with the resources to maintain the fabric was no doubt a key factor, so that one has a distinct impression that castles owned by bishops (Maidstone, Hartlebury, Durham etc.) or by Crown or Duchy (Bolingbroke, Warwick, Carlisle etc.) had fared better than others. It is indeed for this reason that the history of royal castles in the period is not necessarily a typical experience.

It was possible, indeed common, for part of a castle to be ruinous while another part was in active use. The most striking case was Warwick, which so excited the enthusiasm of Leland, where the keep on top of the motte was ruinous, while the buildings on the other side of the court were in active use, reconstruction work by the king actually being in progress at the time of Leland's visit. On the other hand, at Tamworth the situation was reversed and the keep was occupied but the rest of the castle was in ruin. Other examples of partial ruin are Nottingham, Plympton, Totnes and Rockingham. Undoubtedly what Leland meant by 'ruinous' – in many cases – was that the internal domestic buildings were in decay, not necessarily the defences. Pickering, where the chantry chapel was still in use, is probably an example.

The sites mentioned by Leland where most or all the masonry had vanished may have been abandoned at any time during the previous 400 years. Sometimes this may have been due to atrophy, or in other cases to deliberate demolition, as at Bedford and Malton, previously mentioned (p. 13). The failure to reconstruct is of no little significance in itself, understandable in the case of a conquered Welsh castle like Dinas Bran, but not so readily explicable in the middle of an English town. In four cases (Dursley, Elmley, Fulbrook and Hanley) Leland was either an eye-witness or had reports of stone being removed from the ruin for another purpose such as repairing a bridge or building a house. At a certain point of dereliction and decay the temptation to apply the stone to another purpose was a strong one. The whole of Edward I's castle at Builth Wells, Powys, was reported to have been removed in this way in Elizabethan times,[2] and it was no doubt the fate of many others. The stone suddenly available from the dissolved and ruined monasteries may have stimulated an appetite for more.

Careful analysis of Leland's comments suggest very marked regional variations in the extent of abandonment. To demonstrate this the country has been divided into five areas: the south (the Home Counties and southern coastal counties as far west as Hampshire), the south-west (Wiltshire and Gloucestershire westwards), the Midlands (as far north as Staffordshire and Lincolnshire but omitting East Anglia since we have no information for Norfolk, Suffolk and Cambridgeshire), the North, and Wales (virtually no information for modern Gwynedd). Taking the regions in this order and using our three categories some interesting results emerge.

In the south we have information on nineteen castles (excluding Henry VIII's coastal forts) although we lack information on some important ones like the Tower and Windsor which were clearly in active use. Of these, seven remained in normal or full use, that is 37%. The continuing threat on the coast not only led to the construction of the new forts of Henry VIII but also no doubt prolonged the life of older castles, like Arundel.

In the south-west the story is very different: out of forty-five castles, eleven were in normal use, that is 24% or less than a quarter. William Worcester had already drawn attention to the ruinous condition of the castles in Cornwall and Wiltshire (p. 19), so Leland's comments are less surprising, the two being in particular accord on these two counties.

In the Midlands (excluding East Anglia), out of seventy castles mentioned, twenty or 29% were in normal use. This is the lowest proportion after the south-west and is probably due to the high rate of abandonment in the March area adjoining Wales. The two great castles of Hereford and Shrewsbury were in a bad way, and Shropshire with the highest number of abandonments was only surpassed on the Welsh side by Glamorgan and Powys.

In the north, out of fifty-two castles, twenty-six were in normal use, that is 50%. Leland mentions many castles in Northumberland and Cumbria with no information about their condition although it is clear that some of them must have been in normal use. This was a still flourishing period for the tower-house or castle in the Border area, although an almost exactly contemporary survey of castles, peels and bastels in Northumberland in 1541, revealed widespread decay and damage and destruction by the Scots.[3] Apart from Yorkshire, the number of abandonments mentioned by Leland in other counties is small. Yorkshire, on the borders of the peel or tower-house zone, maintained a vigorous castle culture acting as country seats, often of recent construction in a local style. It was indeed the royal castles that seem to have suffered from neglect in this area; York was in ruins and Pickering and Scarborough were showing signs of decay. Leland described the Yorkshire castles with some enthusiasm: Bolton, Crayke, Hinderskelf (destroyed, near Castle Howard), Hornby, Knaresborough, Middleham, Mulgrave, Nappa, Pontefract, Ravensworth, Sandal, Scarborough, Sheriff Hutton, Snape, Thorne, West Tanfield, Wressell.

The last area is Wales, south and east Wales, for the *Itinerary* has little to say of north Wales. Out of seventy-two castles, twenty-seven or 37.5% remained in normal use, roughly the same as in south-east England. Abandonment seems to have been extensive on the east side: Glamorgan with seventeen ruined and two partially derelict castles heads the list of all counties both in England and Wales. The Yorkshire castles in use and those in ruin in Glamorgan are the two most striking features of the *Itinerary*. There were still not a few castles in active use, both in Dyfed and Powys, as indeed in Glamorgan itself. Nevertheless the survey of the fifty-five castles in Glamorgan by Rice Merrick only thirty to forty years later revealed very nearly universal abandonment.[4]

Can we draw any general conclusions from this regional analysis? There was clearly a marked difference between the Scottish and Welsh borders in terms of survival. There was evidently something of an Indian summer for castles in Yorkshire and some of the Tudor problems in this area (Pilgrimage of Grace, Rising of the Northern Earls) may have some common connection with the social background responsible for these. In the rest of the country, abandonment was widespread but more extensive in the Welsh Marches and south-west. Events during the Glyndŵr revolt (incidentally causing much destruction among castles, e.g. Criccieth, which was abandoned at this time) suggest that the functional aspect of the castle, because of ethnic differences, assumed greater importance in

Wales. As the open hostility disappeared, so castles themselves tended to become superfluous in the principality, while in the Midlands and south-east they still perhaps retained prestige and ceremonial value.

Between the time of Leland and the Civil War there was a century of almost unremitting decay and abandonment of castles, well chronicled in the endless surveys of them by the Crown and Duchy of Lancaster.[5] After the Battle of Bosworth (1485) the Tudor monarchy acquired a number of castles, not perhaps intentionally as in the twelfth century, but fortuitously by attainder or other forms of forfeiture and sequestration. Surveys in 1561 and 1609 showed the extent of the problem of decay and attempts to combat it were both half-hearted and ineffective.

Other sources tell the same story. One of the most striking is in the *Abridgement* by John Speed of his larger work and Atlas of 1611[6] where he lists market towns, castles and parish churches by counties in his descriptions. There is a marked discrepancy between the number of castles he gives in the description and in the overall table. Taking those counties where he specifies the numbers we have 186 castles but in the table the same counties have only 68 castles, about a third, evidently on the grounds that the others were so ruinous that they did not count!

From a distant part of Wales, Pembrokeshire, we have our closest observation in the remarkable description of the county by George Owen,[7] written in *c.* 1600 and published at the end of the last century. Of the nineteen ancient castles in the county only three were in use: Carew, Picton and Stackpole. The remaining 85% were by this time abandoned and ruinous, although they still had a defensive capability. Owen was concerned about coastal defence and the risks of the sites being seized by an invading enemy, for the mere collapse of domestic buildings did not mean that a castle was unusable as events of forty years later amply demonstrated. As Owen said:

> . . . all the buildings of the ancient castles were of lime and stone,
> very strong and substantially built, such as our masons of this age
> cannot do the like; for though all or most of the castles are ruin-
> ated and remain uncovered, some for diverse hundred years past,
> yet are all the walls firm and strong, and nothing impaired, but
> seem as if the lime and stone did incorporate the one with the
> other and became one substance inseparable . . . [8]

It must not however be supposed all was ruin on the eve of the Civil War, since travellers writing in 1634–5 show this was not so.[9] There were marked variations as might be expected: ruin widespread and general in the south but much less so in the north. Among castles in active use were: Arundel, Dover, Carisbrooke, Pontefract, Winchester, Carlisle, Greystoke, Chester, Eccleshall, Warwick, Berkeley, Lumley, Morpeth and Alnwick (in part). Among those in ruin were Fotheringhay, Northampton, Taunton, Exeter, Southampton, Lewes, Canterbury, Rochester, Orford, Bristol, Hereford, Nottingham, Stafford, York and Warkworth.

There is a quite perceptible change in attitude towards the subject noticeable already among Tudor writers. There remained, it is true, some who felt that the decay and ruin of the national strongholds (the change in seeing them as national, not private, strongholds is in itself significant) as an affront to patriotic pride and a loss of part of the country's military resources.[10] There was however a latent hostility felt by others, undoubtedly stimulated by the interminable sieges in the Low Countries that occupied so much of the latter part of the century. Two Elizabethan writers with very different views may be mentioned.

William Harrison, in the section 'Description of England' in Holinshed's *Chronicles*[11] written in 1575, took a decidedly jaundiced view, more or less writing off castles except for coastal defence:

> It hath been of long time in controversy and not yet determined whether holds and castles near cities or in the heart of commonwealths are more profitable or hurtful for the benefit of the country. Nevertheless it seemith by our experience that we here in England suppose them altogether unneedful . . . since that time [of Henry II] also not few of those which remained have decayed, partly by commandment of Henry the Third and partly of themselves, or by the conversion of them into dwelling houses of noblemen, their martial fronts being removed, so that at this present there are very few or no castles at all maintained within England, saving only upon the coasts and marches of the country, for the better keeping back of the foreign enemy whensoever he shall attempt to enter and annoy us . . .

The second account is probably fairly close to an official view of policy because the writer, Sir Thomas Wilson, born about 1560 had been translator, judge and diplomat ending up as the head of a Cambridge college.[12] He was familiar with the Continent and the account is thought to have been written to an Italian friend. He is trying to justify the absence of fortifications in this country; we have seen that the neglect of fortification had surprised Italian visitors in the fifteenth century but by the following century the contrast was even greater. The extent to which Wilson was influenced by the wars in the Low Countries and France is evident; the reasons for the lack of fortification adduced by him are certainly ingenious.

> It is true that in England there is no great reckoning made of castles and fortresses, for they do willingly let them go to ruin and instead thereof build them stately pleasant houses and palaces. The reasons they allege are these, that if there should be any invasion the enemy should have no hold but such as they be forced to make themselves, and within that time will find means enough to be disturbed therein; and besides they think the courage of the people would be the greater knowing they have no retiring places, but must needs fight it out at the first brunt; for when there were places of defence it was the cause of a lingering war which was the greatest woe that ever any country endured. Yet castles there be which are these . . . [13]

This is followed by a list of ninety-three castles starting with the Tower. Allowance is made to some privately owned castles if on the coast or Scottish Border, otherwise castles:

> which be inland are suffered to decay, as is a great pity to behold. But upon the borders of Scotland are well maintained both with soldiers and ammunition, as well for the jealousy of Scotland, as also to withstand the incursion of the Scots . . . Those castles and forts in the West Country are also well fortified and kept for fear of the Spaniard, the capital enemy of England. But those toward Ireland, France and the Low Countries (except the River Thames) are but weakly provided by reason the former 2 are known not to have any navy . . . And thus the occasion of these castles and forts and the state of them ministreth knowledge in what terms England standeth with her neighbouring princes . . . [14]

The great difference between England and the Continent in the sixteenth century was the massive urban fortification with angled bastions that had taken place in the latter. England's insular position had spared it the necessity of this heavy expenditure; it is interesting to hear Wilson's justification even if we are not entirely convinced. He is referring to the secrecy of affairs of state:

> They are persuaded, according to the opinion of the Lacedemonians, that fortifying towns doth more hurt than good

to their preservation, in that it make the people either cowardly or revolting, and besides if the enemy land and gain them nothing more damageable; it is true that before these new devices of artillery and such like of that kind, sanpices, petards, rams and such like, there were many strong towns in England after the manner of strength we accounted in those days, but since no force is found able to withstand the subtility of man's invention they are not of the opinion that walls and fortifications can help them, but that the best fortification is on the fortitude and faithfulness of subjects' hearts.[15]

In the Welsh Marches a transfer of authority from the marcher castles to the new council at Ludlow has already been mentioned (p. 20) and in Tudor times this new administrative responsibility gave that castle a new lease of life.[16] Such transfer of authority to the Crown was a general Tudor phenomenon. In the Middle Ages the Crown had only accepted a limited liability for coastal defence. Thus ancient royal castles along the coasts like Scarborough or Dover or Carisbrooke were a Crown responsibility, and perhaps the foundation of Winchelsea by Edward I or certainly that of Queenborough by Edward III would fall into this category, but on the other hand at Bodiam or Cooling it was a private responsibility and at Southampton a municipal one. In the fifteenth century the citadel at Plymouth or the advanced artillery work at Dartmouth at the end of the century were municipal works. In the sixteenth century the Crown suddenly displayed a willingness to take responsibility for coastal defence on a quite unprecedented scale; large numbers of the fortifications erected by Henry VIII on the south coast still survive in the form of circular forts or blockhouses, but others like those at Hull have long since disappeared. Before briefly discussing the works of Henry VIII it may not be inappropriate to look at the relations between private castle and state.

There is strong contrast between France and England. There is fairly general agreement that licences to crenellate were not a method of control of construction (some of the most important fortifications never had licences to crenellate or at least licences that were enrolled) and as legislation against castles is unknown and punitive demolition rarely recorded in the fifteenth century there is very little evidence that the government saw them as a threat to its authority; the accelerating decay that has been described was not as a consequence of official policy. It might be indeed that the strength of the monarchy since the twelfth century promoted an unfavourable ambience for castles, as Harrison thought, but there was no overt hostility. A very different situation obtained in France where the centralising monarchy of the later Middle Ages was confronted by too many fortifications and castles. From the time of Louis XI, the monarchy took a jaundiced view of castles, but it was Cardinal Richelieu who, extending legislation that Henry IV had applied to Brittany to the whole of France, carried out demolition on a really intensive scale.[17] This might be regarded as something of a precedent for this country twenty years later when, as a result of the Civil War, castles did become a threat to central government and were extensively demolished.

The building works of Henry VIII[18] very well illustrate the dominant position of the state and also, as a corollary of this, the end of the medieval idea of a castle as a seat or home. Unlike Edward I or Henry II, he built coastal forts for defence and palaces (courtyard houses) to live in. The division between a seigneurial dwelling and fortification was complete; it was as much an indication of the end of the Middle Ages as the Dissolution of the Monasteries itself.

A description of Henry VIII's coastal forts would be inappropriate in a work on castles, although their shapes give them a special fascination. No two are alike but they have certain features in common. The tall towers and the machicolations, the bartisans and pointed roofs of the late medieval castle have gone, to be replaced by squat shapes, low parapets with receding merlons, vaults and thick walls with casemates for guns firing through square apertures. The only surviving medieval feature is a central tower or keep (fig. 76). Unlike the polygonal shapes preferred in the fifteenth century, curved surfaces were now in favour but presumably on the same assumption that this was likely to deflect enemy shot. The south coast forts for this reason tend to be round or shaped like the petals of a flower.

Kingston upon Hull had been founded by Edward I on the west bank of the river Hull in the estuary of the Humber, the part of the river below the bridge serving as its port. The original walls of the town had frequent square towers rising above them with six tall gateways. The vulnerability of such structures to artillery needs no elaboration. To strengthen its defences, Henry VIII added the three lobate (brick) forts on the east, undefended side of the river Hull, linked by a wall and ditch and what in Hollar's view looks like a *fausse braie* (fig. 77). The forts, really *bastilles*, which provided fire in all directions against an enemy who had already landed or against enemy ships trying to enter the harbour, were so arranged that they supported each other.

Description of the defences at Hull is a reminder that the whole emphasis on the Continent had shifted away from private defence to town defences. This was partly a question of cost; the size of the defences required against artillery and the number of men and guns needed to man them demanded resources beyond the reach of an individual and only

Calshot Castle or rather Caldshore from the Ancient Name of the Place where it stands, was built by K. Hen. 8ᵗʰ about the same Time with Netley Castle for the Defence of the Entrance into Southampton River.

1. Southampton.
2. Netley Abby and Castle.

S.& N. Buck delin et sculp. 1733.

76 One of Henry VIII's coastal artillery forts, Calshot Castle, Hampshire, shows gun embrasures and receding merlons (no machicolations!) but reveals its medieval ancestry in 'keep', moat and drawbridge – a view of 1733.

77 Mid-seventeenth-century view of Hull showing town with medieval fortifications in fore-ground and the row of artillery blockhouses added by Henry VIII on the other side of the river.

within the means of a town or the state. Furthermore the structures by their shape and appearance lacked all the attraction and glamour of a traditional castle. Engineers had devised a formidable form of fortification which made a town, if not impregnable, certainly very difficult to take: the angled bastion, a discovery in Italy of the beginning of the sixteenth century which was adopted all over Europe. The fortifications of Henry VIII were indeed obsolete at their time of construction. The angled bastion was roughly of arrowhead shape, and was intended to be used not alone but in a continuous series (a trace) since the fire from each bastion was designed to support its neighbours, guns in the neck of the bastion enfilading the intervening wall face and firing across the inclined face of the adjoining bastion. The concentration of fire attainable in this way removed one of the main disadvantages hitherto suffered by defenders, and meant that for 250 years defence and attack were evenly matched; particularly if the defenders had water defences as in the Netherlands.[19] It was this protracted type of warfare that Wilson believed could be avoided in England if continental-style defences were not constructed around the towns.

In fact, at the time Wilson wrote, one English town had a set of defences based on angled bastions, Berwick upon Tweed. There had been repeated taking and re-taking by Scots and English during the Middle Ages, but after 1482 the town remained in English hands.[20] The medieval castle in

KYNGES

HV

RIVER

North
gate

the Bridge ouer Hull

Scale of 600 foote

VPON
L

This Humbre is broad against this
Towne 2 miles or better.

THE RIVER

HVMBER

A. the olde ferye place
B. Salters ftaires
C. Hornefey ftaires
D. Chapell ftaires
E. Bifhops ftaire
F. Scalelane ftaires
G. Kyngs ftaires
H. heringe ftires
I. Horfe ftaires
K. Bruer lane
L. the bocherie
M. Finkell ftreete
N. Ogger lane

Easte

PART OF NORFOLK

the NORTH SEA

Flamborough head   The Sparshead

Waxham

Brillington

Carnabye

Tibthorp

Ratfey

PART OF HULL

YORKE

Welton

Wighton

Bodington

SHIRE

YORKE   Wrefle

Bishopstorp

Cowed

Humber

Redon

Hull R.

Barton

Clarfton

Burton

Belton

N. Trent

Haxley

Owfton

Sober

Thorne

Whitthorp

Cranthorp

Tofney

Grymfly

Lymbergh

Thornton

Kirton

Wefte

Fiskotoft

LYNCOLNE

Meltonbye

Stanton

Bofton

Kirk

Dunnington

Karnworth

LYNCOLNE

Somerton Caf

Thirf

Barton

Grenham

PART

Trickfey

Ludbury

OF NOTTIN

GAM

SHIRE

Nottingham

Southe

English miles

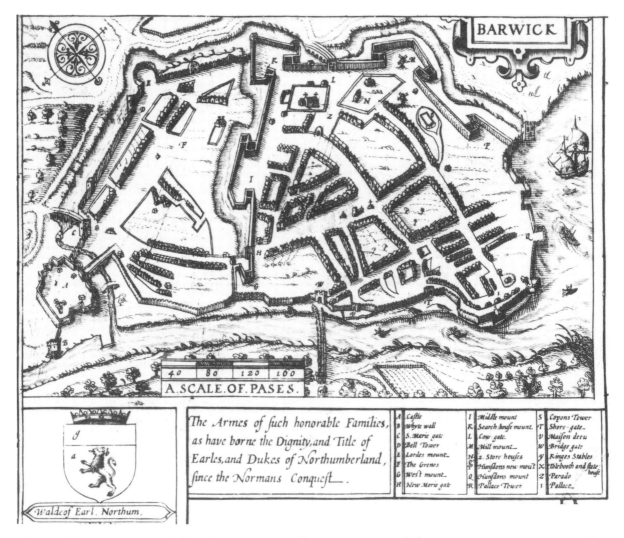

78 Plan of Berwick upon Tweed in 1611 showing the Elizabethan artillery fortifications (with angled bastions) on the right which exclude part of the medieval wall, as well as the castle, on the left.

the south-west corner and the existing town walls were not regarded as sufficient defence and so after an experiment in the reign of Edward VI with a fort with angled bastions at the corners, about two-thirds of the eastern part were enclosed with bastioned defences in Elizabethan times as shown by Speed in 1611 (fig. 78). Sir William Brereton writing in 1635 was enthusiastic: 'the strongest fortification I have met with in England . . . with bulwarks conveniently placed to guard one another like unto Buss (Bris le Duc), Bergen, Antwerp or Gravelin'.[21] By this time the medieval castle was ruinous, a fair indication of the contemporary view of the efficacy of the Elizabethan defences compared to those of the Middle Ages, and a telling illustration of the inadequacy of the latter in the face of the new arm.

Chapter 7

A continuing theme

79 Viollet-le-Duc's reconstruction of Renaissance windows being inserted into a broad vertical incision made in the side of a medieval mural tower to save the cost of demolition and reconstruction.

The foreign tourist who has visited the *son-et-lumière* at Chenonceaux leaves with an overwhelming admiration for the builders who chose to erect the château in the middle of the river, confirming his belief in the innate aesthetic sense of the French. It is something of an anti-climax therefore to learn that the prime consideration of the builders was defence, although the later bridge was certainly not erected without appreciation of the beauty of the result. Thanks to the drawings of the French architect Du Cerceau[1] which were made in the 1560s we have a great deal of knowledge on the original appearance of the great French châteaux of the Renaissance period; water defences were a normal feature (Chantilly, St Germain, Verneuil).

These sixteenth-century châteaux cannot be called castles since the defences were minimal. The most striking feature indeed is the enormous formal garden that was attached to them, geometrically laid-out parterres covering several acres. This decidedly unmedieval adjunct of the house was later copied in England. The construction of seriously-defended castles ceased in *c.* 1500 or soon after but the ground plan with corner towers and so on is clearly a direct continuation of the previous century. The enormous steep roofs also recall the tall conical roofs of the previous period; the whole transition is smoother than in England with a deeper medieval survival, so that one can well understand that it was not felt necessary to change the name from *château*.

The moats and drawbridges look decidedly incongruous separating the house from the gardens; to what extent were they seriously intended? Boorde had recognised a moat as an optional extra[2] and Hampton Court for example had one, but in France they continued into the first half of the seventeenth century when their construction was regarded as a sport in this country.[3] Before attributing the French defences to fantasy it is worth considering Du Cerceau's plan of the vaulted semi-basement of the château designed by Serlio at Ancy-le-Franc (Yonne) over which the building has been erected (figs. 80, 81). The bird-like openings are clearly intended to give the marksmen (using cross-bow and small arms) room to

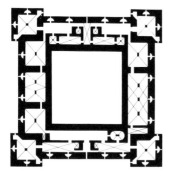

80 The plan of the mid-sixteenth-century château of Ancy-le-Franc shows its castle ancestry in the corner towers, while the birdlike openings in the vaulted basement were for the discharge of crossbows or smallarms across a broad moat.

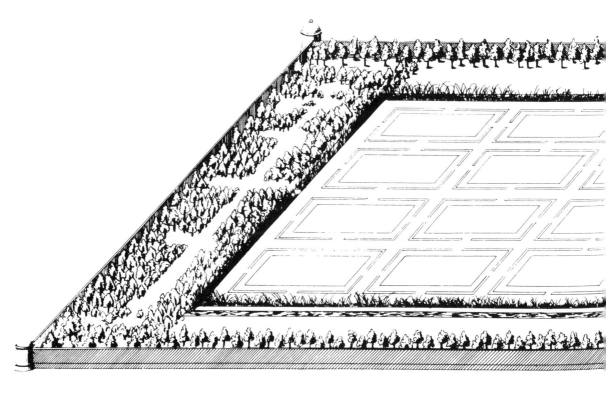

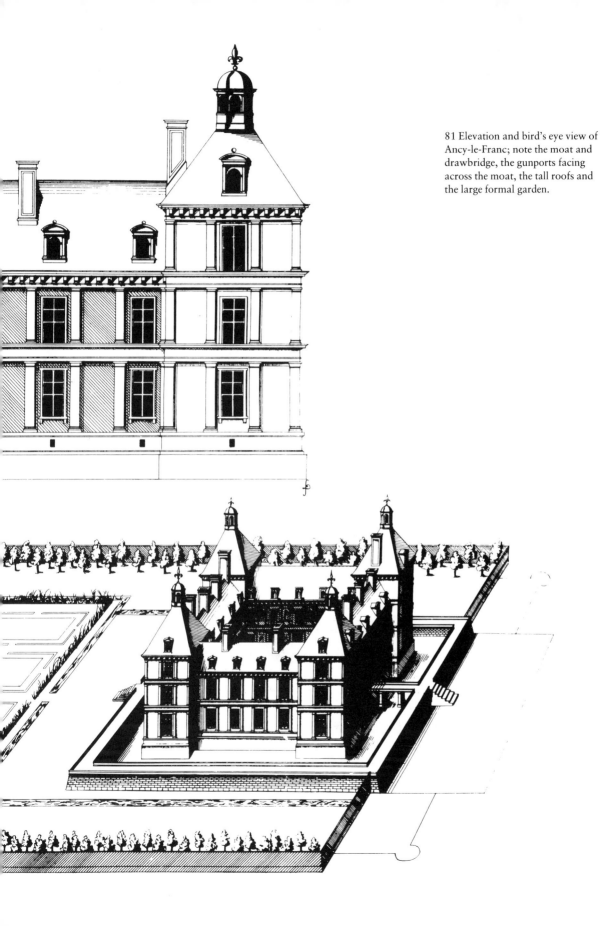

81 Elevation and bird's eye view of Ancy-le-Franc; note the moat and drawbridge, the gunports facing across the moat, the tall roofs and the large formal garden.

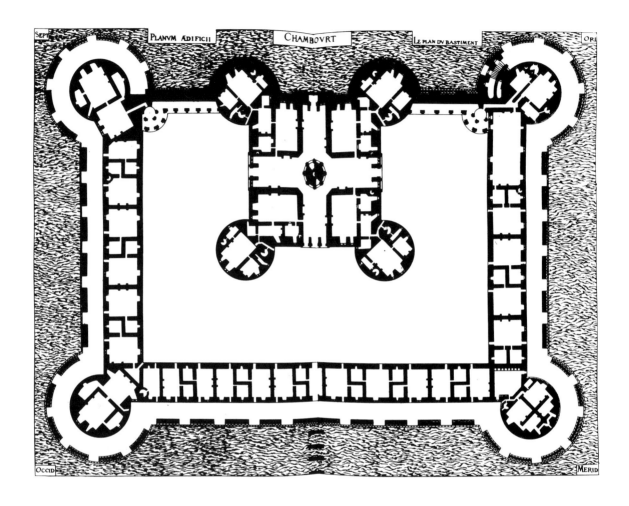

manipulate their weapons; the apertures allowed fire at a man's height across a sixty-foot wide moat as well as enfilading the walls from the corner towers. The building was entered by a drawbridge. These are not incidental features but part of the original design, and can leave no doubt that defence, at least against a small body of attackers, was an important consideration.

More fantastic was the great château of Chambord (Loir et Cher) constructed by Francis I from 1519 (figs. 82, 84). The ground plan shows a keep with corner turrets placed on one side of a rectangular court with round corner towers all set in a broad moat with entry by a bridge facing the 'keep'. The latter had a most extraordinary central staircase, while the terrace outside had corbelled-out projections apparently for cannon! One thinks instinctively of the extravaganza of the Field of the Cloth of Gold. The description of it by Viollet-le-Duc as a Rabelaisian parody of a castle

82 The château of Francis I at Chambord has a plan entirely derived from the castle.

is perhaps not far short of the mark. The point about this remarkable structure is that it demonstrates how much deeper the castle concept had penetrated into French, in contrast to English, design, as indeed we might reasonably have expected.

From the second half of the sixteenth century the new form of defence, the angle bastion, was introduced as a new feature at the corners of the terrace that surrounded the *château*. They did not form a complete trace and no doubt were often ornamental, giving a modern military air to the house, or at the most allowed enfilading fire by small arms along the moat. This was perhaps the case with the projections that Cardinal Richelieu had at his new château,[4] but the house built by Louis XIII at Versailles had defences of a more serious nature. It was built as little more than a hunting lodge, although his son by adding vast wings created the palace that we know today. As can be seen in the figure (83) it was a fairly modest building occupying one side of a courtyard with service wings on the others. It was entered by a bridge across a broad star-shaped moat that enclosed the whole courtyard, which had in its turn a projecting square tower at each corner that could enfilade all sides of the structure. There cannot be much doubt about the serious nature of these defences which were erected in the second quarter of the seventeenth century.

The French Wars of Religion and the consequent disturbed state of the

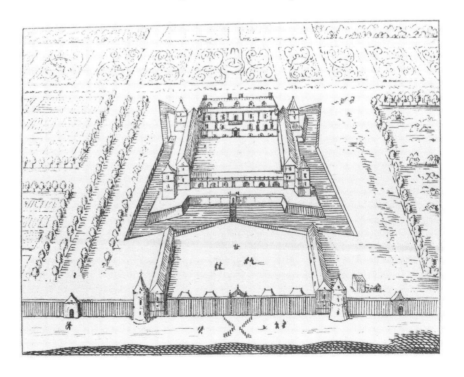

83 The original château of Versailles as built by Louis XIII was decidedly defensible but was transformed by his son into the palace we know today.

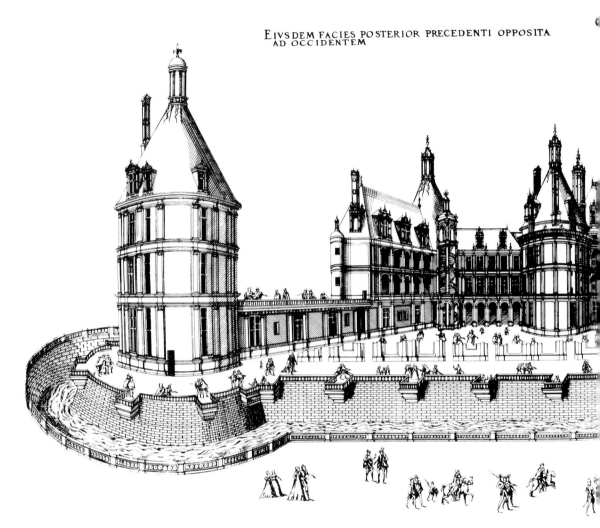

EIVSDEM FACIES POSTERIOR PRECEDENTI OPPOSITA
AD OCCIDENTEM

SCENOGRAPHVM

country are no doubt sufficient explanation of the need for at least some minimal defence for a house at that time in France. This combined with the form and plan of the buildings themselves provided a measure of continuity with the true castle of the Middle Ages that is quite lacking in this country. Most noteworthy is the complete absence of the massive gatehouses that so dominated early Tudor palaces and mansions in England; the French château wore a quite sufficiently seigneurial guise without requiring a symbol of that kind.

It is time to look northwards if only briefly. The tower-houses discussed

84 A sixteenth-century view of Chambord, the château erected earlier in the century by Francis I. The borrowings from castle design – keep, corner towers, moat, cannon embrasures – have caused it to be described as a Rabelaisian parody of a castle!

G

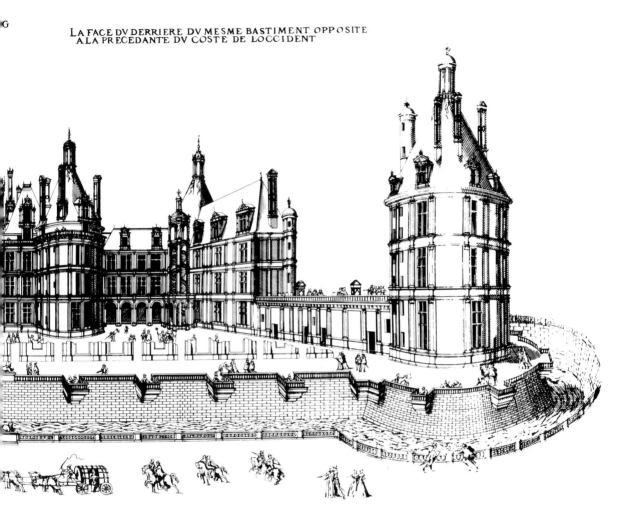

LA FACE DV DERRIERE DV MESME BASTIMENT OPPOSITE
ALA PRECEDANTE DV COSTE DE LOCCIDENT

ELEVATION OV PORTRAICT EN PERSPECTIVE

above (p. 22) continued to be the normal dwelling for the well-to-do in
the Border Area, Scotland and Ireland up to the middle of the seventeenth
century. In Scotland they were still being constructed in the first half of the
seventeenth century, not only adopting L- and Z-shape plans, but also
achieving a high degree of sophistication in their construction, particularly in the corbelling-out of various projections as bartisans, flues etc.

Figures 85 and 86 show views by MacGibbon and Ross of what is
regarded as one of the finest of these tower-houses, Craigievar in
Aberdeenshire, which had been started before 1610 but then acquired by
William Forbes, and was completed inside and out by 1626.[5] It is

L-shaped with a square turret in the angle containing the doorway which was closed by a grill or *yett*, as can be seen in the drawing. The lavish use of corbelling on the outside for bartisans and turrets may be noted, the conical caps on them, as well as the Renaissance balustrading on the square turrets. On the ground floor are the vaulted service rooms with hall and kitchen at principal first-floor level, the building rising no less than four storeys higher. The hall is luxuriously appointed with elaborately decorated plaster ceiling, fine fireplace and panelling. The rooms are not impossibly large so that they provided convenient accommodation for the laird until a few years ago. Now in the hands of the Scottish National Trust the tower has recently been *harled* (rendered over) and painted so that it offers a splendid spectacle to the visitor.

This noble structure is so different from anything to which we are accustomed in England that it must prompt thoughts as to why William

85–6 Craigievar, Grampian, is perhaps the finest of the early seventeenth-century Scottish tower-houses; note the bartisans and stepped gables, and the door closed with its 'yett' in the left-hand view.

Forbes in particular and his compatriots in general felt it necessary to live in towers of this kind at this date. It was a cultural tradition that was now 300 years old, but it may be suspected that the insecurity of life that presumably gave rise to it continued, and still persisted indeed up to at least the Act of Union of 1707.

It is fitting that, if the origin of keeps in this country should be sought in eleventh-century gatehouses like Ludlow or Richmond (Yorkshire) which by blocking the gate-passage were turned into independent towers, then, what came in as a gatehouse equally in the sixteenth century left it as one. It is time to take up the story which had been left with the gatehouse at Oxburgh Hall, Norfolk (p. 101).

The great gatehouse became a necessary part of every courtyard building whether it was house, palace or institution. One of the most striking cases is Leez Priory, Essex, where at the dissolution of the Augustinian priory Lord Rich when he acquired the site promptly set about building himself a mansion that incorporated much of the conventual buildings.[6] The church nave became the hall, and the cloister, which was on the north side, the inner court, while the great court of the monastery on the west became the outer court of the new house. The west range was severed for the construction of an enormous brick gatehouse, while the south side of the great court was treated similarly for the construction of another brick gatehouse of slightly smaller size (fig. 87). The alterations are very revealing of what modifications were felt necessary to make a monastic lay-out suitable for a secular Tudor owner. One thinks of the Holbein Gate in Whitehall or Wolsey's great gatehouse at Hampton Court inherited by Henry VIII. To judge by Speed's illustration of Nonsuch Palace (fig. 88), built by Henry VIII, its elaborate corner towers and panelled decoration in plaster recall some French work of the period (even Chambord), but what most emphatically is not French is the great dominating gatehouse with polygonal corner turrets.[8] The tallest of the Tudor gatehouses, at Layer Marney, Essex (Fig. 89) has Renaissance detail in its decoration in the form of scallop shells, but it is an extremely interesting commentary on Tudor gatehouses in general that its construction had top priority, being built first by Lord Marney on the site when his death prevented the main house from being erected at all! It was a statement by the owner on his status before he began his house.

Although the early Tudor period was very much the age of the gatehouse, their occurrence varied geographically. Brick gave the gaudy impression that was required, an effect that was largely lost in grey or brown stone, so in the districts where stone was the natural building

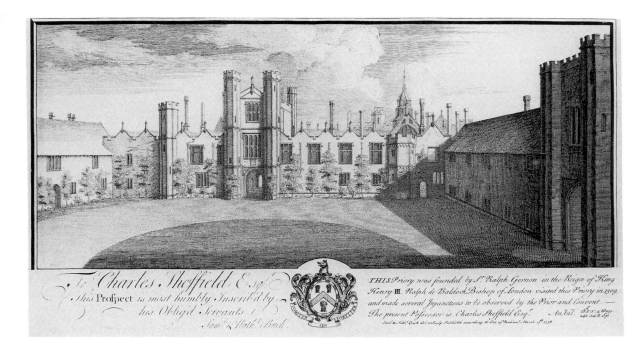

To Charles Sheffield Esq.
This Prospect is most humbly Inscrib'd by
his Obligd Servants
Sam & Nath: Buck.

THIS Priory was founded by S.' Ralph Gernon in the Reign of King
Henry III. Ralph de Baldock Bishop of London visited this Priory in 1309.
and made several Injunctions to be observed by the Prior and Convent.—
The present Possessor is Charles Sheffield Esq.'   An.Val.

material it was adopted with much less enthusiasm. The point can be well
demonstrated by comparing the entrances to the Cambridge colleges on
the one hand (Trinity, St John's, Christ's) with those of Oxford on the
other.

The long lodging ranges of the late medieval courtyard houses provided
accommodation for people of a social status either equal to, or only a step
or two lower down the scale than the owner himself; where there was an
evident need for cellular lodgings in a college or inn the form has
continued almost to the present day, but for the house it was rendered
obsolete by social changes brought about with the Renaissance. The great
staircases or the long galleries for portraits of ancestors were not com-
patible with the old plan. A house became not a dwelling for a large
household but an extension of the owner's personality, something to
display like one's clothes. No doubt the 'progresses' of Queen Elizabeth,
with their strong incentive to owners to show off, accelerated this process.

The rambling and decidedly uninspiring appearance of a courtyard
house was unable to satisfy this new requirement: aesthetically lacking in
drama, the lodgings in addition detracted from the importance of the
owner who remained cooped up at one end of the hall. The fifteenth-
century towers may indeed represent a first show of resentment against
this; in Elizabethan times this situation could be reversed and the owner

87 At Leez Priory, Essex, the
conversion of the monastic layout
to secular use entailed the erection
of large brick gatehouses over the
entries to the former outer court
and the cloister, symbols of the
status of the new lay owner.

also become full occupier. The courtyard survived in some cases into the seventeenth century – Audley End, Essex, built in Jacobean times had a great courtyard, since pulled down – but the Elizabethan 'prodigy houses' built *en bloc* gave new opportunities for dramatisation into which, as we might expect, the castle theme was soon introduced, for it had of course never disappeared.

The simplest way of giving a castle feel to a building without too great an interference with its symmetry or plan was to endow it with towers, especially at the corners. The earliest of the great Elizabethan houses, Longleat, does not have them but it is not long before they appear at, for example, Barlborough, Heath Old Hall and so on.[8] They could be created by carrying oriel windows up above roof level. In Hardwick New Hall, generally considered the finest, there are six towers, two at the front and two at the back with one at each end. The most dramatic and explicit allusion is at Wollaton Hall, Nottingham, where not only are there

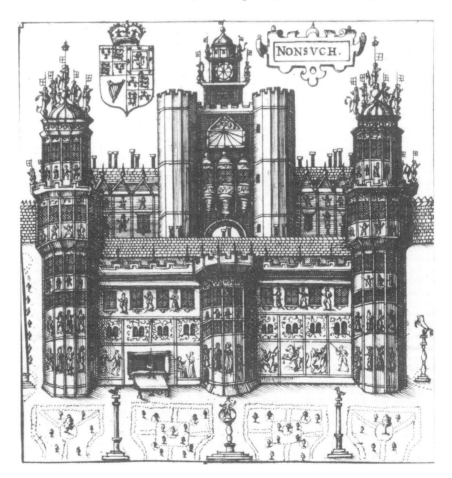

88 Nonsuch Palace (built by Henry VIII) in 1611 showing the domination of the inner court by the great gatehouse.

89 The great gatehouse, with eight storeys in the turrets, at Layer Marney, Essex, a gateway leading to a house that was apparently never built.

90 The Elizabethan Wollaton Hall at Nottingham with corner towers and central, tall, keep-like hall as evident castle allusions.

corner towers but the hall is put in the middle rising up like a keep above the surrounding buildings and lit by great clear-story windows (fig. 90).

Whether any influence reached England from the areas where tower-houses were still in active use and being constructed it is difficult to say. Presumably this must have been the case in the northern counties although it is not a subject on which information is readily available. In Wales there are three cases, widely separated, at Aberlleiniog, Anglesey,[9] Plas-teg, Flintshire[10] and Rupperra (Rhiwperra) Castle, Glamorgan[11] of square tower-like structures with round towers at the corners (square in the case of Plas-teg) of early seventeenth-century date which it is tempting to relate to similar contemporary buildings in Ireland. However that may be, there certainly appear in England at that time several buildings consciously adopting a castle form and usually called a castle.

Lulworth Castle, Dorset, was built in about 1608 by Thomas Bindon, 3rd Viscount Bindon, not as his principal seat but as a hunting lodge.[12] It

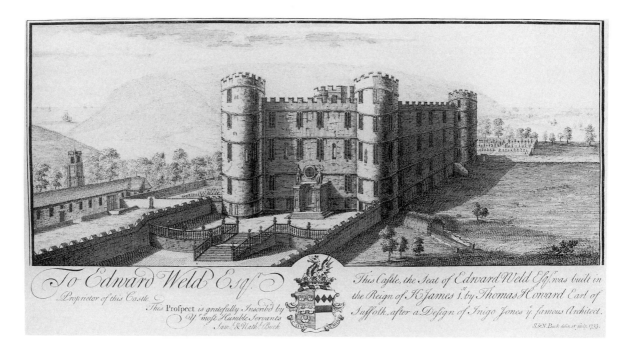

To Edward Weld Esq.

Proprietor of this Castle.

This Prospect is gratefully Inscrib'd by
Y.ʳ most Humble Servants
Sam.ˡ & Nath.ˡ Buck.

This Castle, the Seat of Edward Weld Esq. was built in
the Reign of K. James 1.ˢᵗ by Thomas Howard Earl of
Suffolk, after a Design of Inigo Jones y.ᵉ famous Architect.

S. & N. Buck delin. et sculp. 1733.

consisted of a central block about eighty feet square with towers at the corners, circular on the outside, polygonal on the inside (fig. 91). It was three-storeyed with the kitchen in the basement. The battlements and forms of the windows gave it a medieval air. It had been preceded in the same county by Sir Walter Raleigh's Sherborne Castle, the new castle, not the medieval one.[13] It started life as a plain rectangle but the addition, first of hexagonal corner turrets which gave it a ground plan similar to a Tudor gatehouse, and secondly of wings extending from each corner flanking courtyards, gave it a ground plan of decidedly idiosyncratic form (fig. 92). Even more aberrant is the triangular 'castle' built by Sir Thomas Gorges at Longford Castle, Wiltshire, which has circular towers at each apex (fig. 93). It recalls the Triangular Lodge of Sir Thomas Tresham in Northamptonshire, although much larger, but like it must be regarded as the work of an eccentric, so may be treated as marginal to our story. Other Elizabethan 'castles' might be mentioned although the name has been attached to what are houses with castle allusions, like Slingsby Castle in Yorkshire. Sufficient has been said to show the *genre* and the rest of the chapter can be devoted to the most remarkable of them all which does indeed fall into a category of its own, Bolsover Castle, Derbyshire.

Reference has been made to the 'progresses' of Queen Elizabeth of which descriptions in some cases survive. A particularly detailed account sur-

91 A Jacobean house at Lulworth Castle, Dorset, with castle features.

92 Sir Walter Raleigh's 'castle' at Sherborne, Dorset, with Jacobean extensions.

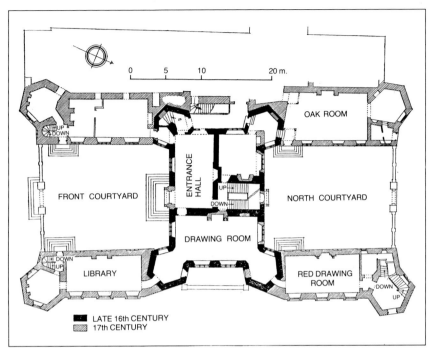

93 The triangular 'castle' at Longford, Wiltshire, an idiosyncratic Jacobean design.

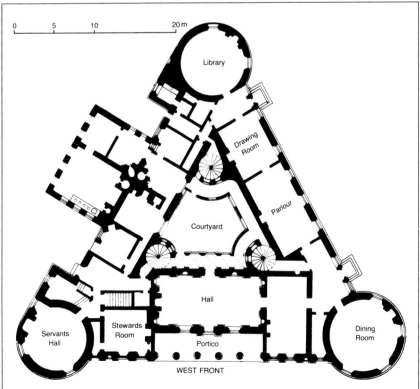

vives of her arrival and the entertainments provided by her favourite, Robert, Earl of Leicester, in July, 1575, when she came to Kenilworth Castle.[14] It was not her only visit there but certainly the most famous. The entertainments were mixed, partly fairly bucolic like the bear-baiting, but mainly allegorical, masque-like performances, partly on the adjoining lake. The earl had carried out certain alterations to the castle, building a gatehouse at the northern end, modifying the keep and constructing a long stable block with decorative timber-framing on its first floor within the castle (probably a consciously rustic feature). The alterations were made as if the theatrical part played by the castle in these masques held a prominent place in the earl's mind. Masques assumed an even more sophisticated and mature form at her successor's court where preparations for their performance occupied a great deal of the time of no less a person than Inigo Jones. What is suggested is that the massive reconstruction of Bolsover Castle was undertaken with a view to it serving as a background for such performances. Ben Jonson indeed wrote a masque entitled 'Love's Welcome to Bolsover' that was performed at the castle in 1634 on the occasion of a visit by Charles I and Henrietta Maria.[15]

There had been an amply documented medieval castle at Bolsover, erected there in the twelfth century by William Peveril; the shape of the present seventeenth-century castle must correspond more or less in outline with the earlier one although that has vanished without trace. Even the position of the original keep is in dispute, but it is inferred from its shape and thickness that the core of wall around Fountain Court must be the medieval curtain wall. The sequence of building started in about 1608 with the keep or little castle and went anti-clockwise, the terrace range and Fountain Court and finally the riding-school range (1630–4; the date is disputed). The owners responsible for the construction were Sir Charles Cavendish and his son Sir William Cavendish, later Duke of Newcastle, while the mason–architects were the three generations of Smythson, mainly John, but also Huntingdon.

Ignoring the riding school (possibly post-Restoration) especially remarkable for its great timber roof with tie beams and queen-posts, collars and kingposts, curved braces and pendants, the terrace range of roofless buildings down the west side of the great court deserves attention (figs. 94, 95). It was designed as a house, elongated to conform with the shape of the earlier castle. Owing to the length of time over which it was erected, thirty years or so, it underwent some changes of plan. The northern end, two storeys over a basement, contained the service rooms for an adjoining hall, but later an enormous single-storey gallery extended the outside front southward and later still state rooms were added behind this. The impressive front facing the valley has uniformity imposed upon it by the two-light transomed windows with pediments, as well as the pilaster buttresses shaped like cannon pointing upwards that occupy the middle part of the elevation. These give an appropriately martial air to the whole range. The precipitous slopes on three sides of the castle, valuable for defence in medieval times, but very inconvenient for an eighteenth-century mansion, were no doubt responsible for its early abandonment in favour of Welbeck Abbey.

The main centre of interest at Bolsover, however, is the 'Little Castle' or 'Keep', the first building erected by Sir Charles Cavendish, probably to the design of John Smythson. It was a domestic unit quite independent of the rest of the castle, recalling in its original form more an Italian villa than a castle keep or Jacobean mansion. It was approached from the west through a gate flanked by small lodges, across a courtyard flanked by two more lodges, up steps through a porch to the ground floor that rests on the vaults of a semi-basement. It is a rectangular building, seventy by fifty-five feet with square turrets at three corners and a large square turret for the staircase which rises above the main structure at the north-east corner. The semi-basement, which contained kitchen, offices and servants' hall, has three storeys over it. The ground floor, beyond a decorated waiting room with paintings, contains a vaulted, aisled hall, and, reached from its upper end, the 'pillar-chamber', a highly ornate room with central pillar, also vaulted. By medieval analogy this would be the senior parlour or mess-room. At the lower end of the hall two staircases give access down to the kitchens and one also goes up to the first and second floors. This is a recognisable medieval arrangement. The upper floors must have been bedrooms except for the 'Star Chamber', given this name because its ceiling was decorated with stars, perhaps best interpreted as audience or presence chamber. Most of the rooms have highly decorative panelling and extremely ornate hooded overmantels over the fireplaces of a kind not found elsewhere. Several rooms have wall paintings representing either pagan Classical scenes or Christian ones, not mixed but in separate rooms. The building was rent and riven by mining subsidence but years of patient restoration and cleaning have left the internal decoration, if not as original, certainly quite dazzling.

It is very tempting to compare the Little Castle at Bolsover with the tower at Tattershall and the Victorian castle erected by the Marquess of Bute at Castell Coch near Cardiff (p. 165). Built at intervals of roughly 200 years, each was on the site of an earlier castle; at Tattershall and Bolsover the earlier remains were demolished (although the shape retained at the latter), but characteristically, preserved as a base for the

94 A perspective view in the early eighteenth century of the Jacobean 'castle' of Bolsover, keep on the left, terrace range on the right.

The Castle of Bolsover in Darbyshire one of the Seats of the most Noble and
Earle of Clare Baron Haughton of Haughton, Lord L of y County of
Knight of y Most

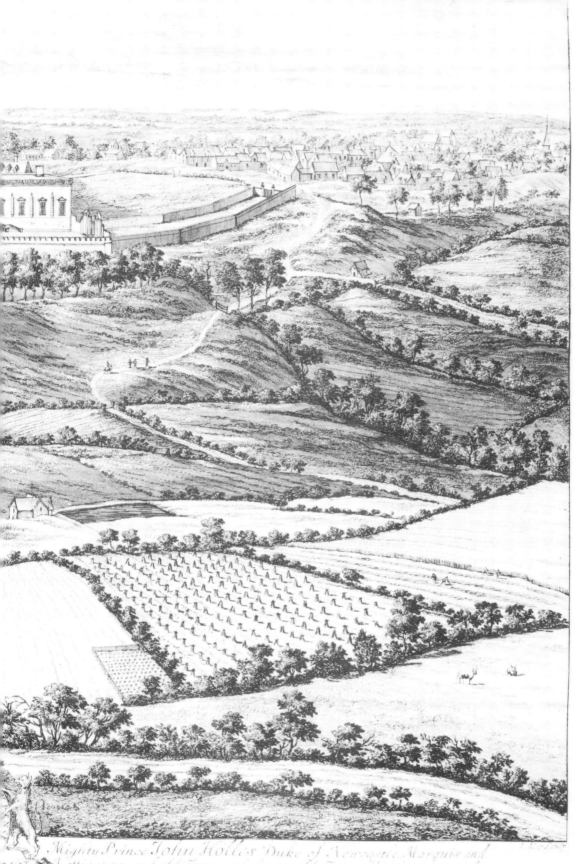

The Mighty Prince John Holles Duke of Newcastle Marquis and
Earl of Cottingham and of the Town and County of the Town of Nottingham and
Knight of the order of ye Garter.

new work at Castell Coch. Resplendent overmantels on the fireplaces are common to all three, but it is the degree of fantasy in the inspiration of the building that is the common denominator. 'Chivalry' has been invoked as the motive in the first two, while Roman Catholic revivalism in a very romantic form was one of the chief influences on the Marquess of Bute. The madonna over the door, the figure of St Lucius, the religious scenes on the walls all emphasise this, although there are pagan elements (in the Fates over the fireplace in the drawing room). I am by no means sure that the word 'chivalry' or searching for it cannot be applied to describe the Marquess's motives.

'Chivalry' can indeed be something of a portmanteau term for the varied fantasies of individuals in many periods. Masques which could be held perfectly well in the Banqueting House at Whitehall did not require a mock castle for their performance. The concept of a castle with the authority and importance it conferred on the owner is one that has

95 The terrace range at Bolsover Castle; note pilasters in the shape of cannon and the distinct change at the far end of the range, which is earlier in date.

entered deeply into European consciousness since the Middle Ages. The idiosyncratic element in a construction like that at Bolsover should never be overlooked.

Let us extend the comparison 150 years earlier, to Caernarfon in North Wales. The fantasy element at Caernarfon, the walls of Constantinople, is unmistakable, but the castle is a formidable fortress: function predominates over fantasy. At Tattershall, fantasy predominates over function, although in an authentic medieval context. At Bolsover, we are in the realm of pure fantasy, theatre one might say. At Castell Coch there is an element of self delusion: by erecting the castle as it might have been one could in some measure live in it the idealised form of life that it was assumed had then been lived. There was a moral element present (not the unbalanced delusions of Ludwig of Bavaria). The patrons (Edward I, Cromwell, Cavendish, Bute) were confined within the cultural bounds of the time in which they lived, but it was their fantasies that were transmuted into buildings; the modern dominant rule of the architect misleads us as to where responsibility lay in the past. Burges was indifferent to religion, while it seems highly unlikely that Smythson, Baldwin or James of St George shared the feelings of their clients.

Chapter 8

Destruction

The outbreak of the Civil War in 1642 suddenly altered the whole situation producing a state that was endemic on the Continent but which England had been spared for a century and a half or indeed for much longer; not a dynastic struggle between York and Lancaster but a basic challenge to the authority of central government itself. Fortification which had been despised as a continental vice now became a necessity; ancient castles and towns walls suddenly acquired a value and function that had been almost forgotten. The number of towns, castles, country houses, cathedral closes and so on that were now garrisoned must have run to several hundreds, recalling indeed the multitude of fortified places of the early Norman period.[1]

The extent of the destruction that took place during the fighting or, more importantly, by demolition afterwards, is not always appreciated. The alterations produced in the landscape or townscape recall those of the Dissolution of the Monasteries a hundred years before. It differed from the Dissolution in that a large number of the structures were already ruinous, and it was not associated with a massive transference of property, and in any case what had been transferred was returned at the Restoration. Nevertheless the destruction constitutes a part of the background to the great change in mental outlook that divides the seventeenth century into two such distinct halves, changes that we see in the coinage, writing, architecture or in the new intellectual outlook revealed in the creation of the Royal Society, and so on.

Not all castles were fit for use at this time; indeed the majority had undoubtedly passed beyond that stage. Some were little more than humps in the ground, while others which had been so breached by collapse due to instability or earth movement had been rendered incapable of defence.[2] In many others extensive rehabilitation was required. At Ruthin Castle, Clwyd, described by the Parliamentary commander as 'ruinous' the Royalist garrison were busily occupied in carrying out repairs.[3] At Nottingham Castle, Mrs Hutchinson, the wife of the Parliamentary commander, tells us ' . . . the buildings were very ruinous and uninhabitable neither affording room to lodge soldiers or provisions'.[4] So long as the massive defensive walls were intact, infantry assault could be resisted, but the requirements of artillery and small arms made it essential to construct earthwork bastions and redoubts outside them to confront the enemy's siegeworks beyond. As the Governor of Cambridge (whose castle had been abandoned in the fifteenth century) wrote early in 1643: 'our town and castle are now very strongly fortified being encompassed with breast-works and bulwarks'.[5] Very few of such earthworks now survive but the familiar angled bastions can be recognised, for instance, as a continuous trace on the eighteenth-century plan of the earthworks at Donnington Castle, Berkshire (fig. 96).

Our concern here is to describe how the fabric of ancient castles suffered in the course of hostilities from enemy action, and subsequently, and far more importantly, from the deliberate demolition that in many cases followed. Sometimes the two are not easily distinguished, particularly if the place was taken by storm.

The fabric could be attacked by fire, mining or bombardment. Internal buildings or country houses with their wooden floors and roofs were very vulnerable to fire by which they could be largely destroyed. Burning the houses of the enemy was carried out by both sides: around the Parliamentary stronghold of Lyme Regis all the great houses of the vicinity were reported to have been burnt by one side or the other.[6] The Parliamentary commander recorded after taking the house at Abbey Cwmhir in Radnorshire (Powys) that he was 'forced to burn the house, otherwise we could not render it unserviceable for the future'.[7]

The massive defences of a medieval castle were, however, largely impervious to fire so that more violent methods of assault were required to breach them: mining or artillery bombardment or, quite often, both means were employed. Clearly serious damage was inflicted in a number of cases; one thinks of Wardour and Sherborne Castles as examples that were mined with devastating effect. It is quite impossible to quantify the damage, particularly as successful assault might have been associated with partial demolition as at Basing House, Donnington or Sherborne Castle. What however is clear is that the damage inflicted by assault was only a small fraction of that inflicted over a period of years by deliberate demolition, or 'slighting' as it was called, which deserves closer study than it has usually received.

For obvious reasons the Royalists were normally the besieged party, often in the owner's house or castle, and because they were the losers in the war they were usually the victims of 'slighting' by the other side; but it was in fact regarded by both sides as a normal practice from the beginning of the war. In May 1644 for example the King's forces at Reading slighted the newly-constructed fortifications before abandoning the town to the enemy, who upon recapturing it set about reconstructing them.[8] In December 1645 the King, now in desperate straits, ordered the governors of Worcester, Exeter, Chester and Oxford to destroy their fortifications and concentrate their forces at Worcester.[9] Colonel Ludlow chose to defend Wardour Castle, an act of considerable bravery because he had been authorised by Parliament to slight the castle and withdraw if he

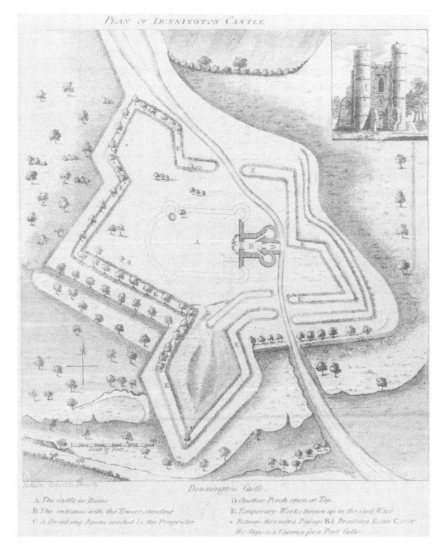

96 An eighteenth-century plan of the Civil War earthen bastions around the demolished castle at Donnington, Berkshire.

wished.[10] The result of the Royalist mining was not only to cause him to surrender but also effectively to slight the castle.

There was a school of thought, particularly among Parliamentary military commanders, that held fortifications to be evil in themselves, encouraging unrest and civil commotion, recalling the views of Wilson in Elizabethan times (p. 109). Sir John Meldrum, a Parliamentary commander killed at Scarborough in 1645, wrote a report to the Committee of Both Kingdoms in November in 1644 justifying his action at Gainsborough which neatly expresses the point:

> I cannot forbear that accustomed freedom I have taken to acquaint your Lordships with what, in my apprehension, I conceive may be both dangerous and unprofitable to this state, which is to keep up forts and garrisons which may rather foment than finish a war. France, Italy and the Low Countries have found by experience during these three hundred years what losses are entailed by places being fortified, while the subjects of the Isle of Britain, through absence thereof, have lived in more tranquillity. If Gainsborough had not been razed by my order the enemy might have found a nest to have hatched much mischief at this time. Reading might have produced the same effects if the fortifications had not been demolished. If there be a garrison kept at Liverpool there must be at least 300 men, which will make the jealousies and emulations among these gentlemen endless and chargeable . . . [11]

So long as the fighting was in progress the motive for 'slighting' was clear: to deny the use of the fortifications to the enemy. Thus the demolition carried out on the orders of Parliament at Sherborne Castle at the beginning of the war in 1642 was intended to deny the use of the fortifications to the Cavaliers (apparently not with much success), a kind of 'scorched earth' policy. If you captured the enemy's strongpoint there was a choice between garrisoning or slighting. While the outcome of the war was uncertain the sensible course no doubt was to garrison, but if you were winning, or had won, it was a very different matter, and particularly if a large number of strong points had been captured; the desire to avoid the costs of garrisoning could be an overriding consideration. The reduction of costs was the main argument advanced for this action from 1647 onwards.

It could be argued that places held by Royalists previously were likely to be re-occupied by them again in the event of a further rising and so were suitable to be slighted. No doubt this weighed in the minds of members of the House of Commons, but equally there was a certain punitive element or desire for revenge in the choice of structures to be slighted, both while the fighting was in progress and afterwards. The threat by the besiegers of Donnington Castle not to leave a stone standing in order to intimidate the garrison[12] may not have been carried out (although apart from the gatehouse the whole castle does seem to have been demolished after the siege), but in a large number of cases in the list in Appendix 3 (see p. 179) the slighted structure had withstood Parliamentary siege (Basing House, Corfe, Belvoir, Pontefract and Scarborough Castles, Lichfield Close . . . etc.).

The true extent of demolition in the years 1642–59 can never be fully known but it certainly went well beyond the places listed in the Appendix. The work was carried out as a rule by the County Committees or Deputy Lieutenants whose records have not survived. Normally they acted under instructions from the Derby House Committee or Council of State acting on behalf of Parliament, but they were sometimes given blanket authority (Leicestershire, Shropshire, Isle of Ely . . . etc.) and no doubt in any case occasionally acted on their own account. Even during the fighting, demolition without authority could lead in the long run to a claim in the courts by the owner which was a deterrent to some extent from unauthorised action. The Parliamentary Records, Commons' Journal and actions of its Committee recorded in the State Papers, allow us to form a general picture of the extent and nature of the demolition that took place between 1646 and 1659 which tallies reasonably well with the remains that are visible today.

Soon after the Battle of Naseby, as the Royalist strongholds passed in increasing numbers into the hands of Parliament, the problem of which were to be preserved and maintained as garrisons and which disgarrisoned and slighted exercised the minds of members of the House of Commons more and more. As early as August 1645 the Committee of Oxfordshire, Buckinghamshire and Berkshire was asked to consider 'what garrisons are fit to be continued, and what are fit to be slighted'.[13] By October the Commons had decided to refer the same question to the Committee of Both Kingdoms,[14] and subsequently in 1646 the same matter was put to the Committees on a request from Hereford.[15] By early 1647 sufficient information was available to furnish a long list of places, discussed between 23 February and 3 March, distinguishing between those where a garrison was to be maintained and those that were to be disgarrisoned and slighted.[16]

It might have been thought that this ended the matter but the list was sent to the House of Lords with whom a conference was held.[17] It is quite apparent – although no record of the conference survives – that the two houses did not agree on the degree of demolition required, the Lords wishing for much milder treatment of the older structures; since, when the cases were returned to the Commons, either they 'adhered' to their original vote, or, more usually, agreed with the Lords that only new works, those constructed since the troubles, should be slighted or in a few cases omitted slighting altogether. It can be seen in the Appendix that the second resolution in the Commons in July is normally milder than the initial one in January, February or March.

It is unfortunate that the records of the Committee for Both Kingdoms, the seat of executive government and the body that dealt directly with the County Committees, have not survived for 1647, so we do not know what work was actually carried out. The amount of demolition of ancient fabric that took place must have been limited, since it was precisely in some of the castles where slighting had been decided on that the major demolition was not carried out until late in 1648 after the Second Civil War (e.g. Helmsley, Mulgrave, Bolton, Pontefract). It must indeed have been particularly galling that in some cases where the Lords had reduced the severity of the measures in 1647 the Royalists used the castles as strongholds in 1648. The same mistake was not made again.

The main decisions in July 1647 had concerned disgarrisoning and slighting the new works made since the troubles. This refers to the extensive bastions, forts and trenches outside the ancient walls intended primarily for the operation of artillery and muskets. There was no masonry to pick so it was a question of shovelling back the soil into the holes that had been dug. It may be likened to a great tidying up exercise, returning the situation to what it had been in 1642, leaving the masonry fabric of the ancient fortifications largely intact. It had also the effect that the few traces of these Civil War earthworks, so conspicuous in drawings of the period, survive for the modern visitor to see.

The Second Civil War, really a series of risings in South Wales, Kent and elsewhere, for the King was a prisoner in the hands of Parliament, transformed the situation, leading as it did to the execution of the King and the abolition of the House of Lords, no longer able to restrain the Commons, as well as to a much harder attitude towards demolition. It was no longer sufficient to level earthworks: substantial areas of masonry had to be brought down. Some of the most severe demolition was carried out in the period 1648–51 at, for example, Pontefract, Belvoir, Nottingham,

Bolingbroke, Montgomery, Aberystwyth and so on (see figs. 97, 99 and 103).

There were continual Royalist conspiracies from 1649 to the Restoration but it was an actual rising or Scottish invasion that caused Parliament to reconsider the question of garrisons. Thus in November 1648 a Committee was set up to consider 'all the castles, garrisons and places of strength in the kingdom, what are fit to be kept up and what to be slighted

97 The site of Nottingham Castle, demolished in 1651 and replaced after the Restoration by the Duke of Newcastle's mansion. A fragment survives in the foreground.

98 Chirk Castle, Powys, from the air, the far end demolished in 1659 with the truncated part closed by a cross range.

and made untenable'.[18] In March 1651 the Council of State was asked to consider 'what castles and garrisons are fit to be demolished and disgarrisoned, and how and when; what walled towns are fit to be dismantled; and report their opinion therein to the house'.[19] The matter of town walls had been given a special relevance by the Battle of Worcester after which it was ordered that the defences of the city be made untenable (the Lords had prevented the execution of earlier proposals). Whether there was further demolition of other town walls before the Restoration is not known to me.

As late as the Summer of 1659, after the death of Oliver Cromwell, the defeat of Sir George Booth's premature rising in Cheshire and Lancashire led to orders being given to Major General Lambert to demolish Chirk Castle, Clwyd, whose owner, Sir Thomas Myddleton, had supported the rising and held the castle against Lambert.[20] The Council of State was further asked to consider 'what inland garrisons and castles within this Commonwealth are fit to be demolished'. Chirk Castle, built at the time of the conquest by Edward I, not by the king himself but by Roger

Mortimer, was a splendid rectangular structure with round towers at the corners and semi-circular ones in the centre of each side. The southern third comprising three towers (or gatehouse) has been removed, the open side created by the demolition being filled after the Restoration by a new range, some of which had perhaps already existed at this time. Some £30,000-worth of damage on castle and park is said to have been done so that after the Restoration Myddleton and his family had to live in another house, Cefn-y-wern, until rehabilitation of the castle had been carried out.

The executive arm of the Commons was now the Council of State, not the Derby House Committee, but its position relative to the army had undergone great change. In 1647 they had been rivals; one of the motives behind the slighting and disgarrisoning was to expedite the disbanding of the army and so reduce its authority. As we know the army came out on top and this was reflected in the new method of working, still through the counties, but now through the intermediary of the Commissions of Militia rather than the Committees. Sometimes indeed the Council acted directly through local officers, the governors of castles or towns. A new development was to employ private owners to pull down their own castles in return for compensation. Thus the Earl of Rutland was paid £1,500 for demolishing Belvoir Castle, and Lord Herbert allowed £1,600 deducted from his delinquency fine as compensation for the demolition of Montgomery Castle (see Appendix 4, p. 186). The question of compensation for the Countess of Kent was also raised as recompense for the much less extensive demolition at Goodrich Castle.

A bizarre case involved the owner of Tattershall Castle, Lincolnshire (see p. 87). The great fifteenth-century brick tower that was re-roofed, re-floored and glazed by Lord Curzon in the present century is the most remarkable structure on the site.[21] The Council of State asked the owner, the Earl of Lincoln, to demolish it. The Earl replied that he felt it was only necessary to remove the floors and roof, but the Council retorted that their experience in the recent war had convinced them that this was insufficient and demolition was necessary. Nothing happened so the Council ordered the Governor of Boston to do the work. Still nothing happened so the aid of local JPs was enlisted, and voluntary labour was invited. The Council had wanted the work done free but eventually had to offer £60. As the tower still stands it is clear that only the floors and roof can have been removed, although the eighteenth-century view by the Buck brothers must raise doubts about even this because they show the conical roofs on the corner turrets still there (fig. 60). The amusing point is that the question of compensation to the Earl came up two years later!

The case of Tattershall is a reminder of the extraordinary difficulty that Parliament had in transmuting its orders and resolutions into effective action on the ground. At Winchester the orders were repeatedly ignored (although ultimately demolition was very thorough), while at Lancaster the obstructive attitude of the Governor amounted almost to mutiny and the Deputy Governor had to be instructed to carry out the slighting. Several other examples could be cited. No doubt after a year or so when the heat of battle had passed away enthusiasm for demoliton was likely to wane. There might be fear of the owner or future claims by legal action, or there might be a personal interest involved; the Parliamentary commander at Kenilworth, Major Hawkesworth, had constructed himself a dwelling in the Elizabethan gatehouse of the castle.[22] These explanations have to be weighed but surely the underlying cause was that the Commons entirely underestimated the scale of expenditure and labour that extensive demolition of these medieval fortifications required. Walls five to twenty feet thick and up to seventy feet high are not easily demolished without the assistance of modern machinery.

A telling case is Banbury Castle. It had been agreed to disgarrison and slight new works in 1647 (it had surrendered after a fierce siege in 1646) but demolition which had evidently been decided in 1648 was delayed for lack of money so the adjoining counties of Northamptonshire and Warwickshire were authorised to assist.[23] At Ashby de la Zouch the surrender terms allowed three months for demolition, although evidently for new works and not for the tower (p. 93) which is specifically referred to later. At Scarborough a company of foot was sent from Hull to carry out the work. For substantial demolition we are thinking perhaps in terms of fifty or a hundred men for six or twelve months; it is not surprising that voluntary recruits were not easy to come by!

In three cases there is detailed information on the costs of demolition. At Wallingford there is a specific figure of £450/5/8 for demolition and £516/17/11 produced by the sale of materials, leaving an appreciable profit of over £66.[24] At Pontefract the sale of materials was even more worthwhile: £1,540/7/2 for lead and £201/7/10 for timber of £1,779/17/4 altogether against £777/4/6 for wages of 16 men for 10 weeks.[25] Provided the lead still survived on the site it could be a profitable business, although we are not here talking of demolition so much as thorough stripping. A very interesting account survives of the work of demolition at Montgomery Castle in Powis from June to October 1649 which is transcribed in Appendix 4 (p. 186).[26] It only gives the wages, and the possibly greater profits from the sale of materials are not recorded. The scale

99 The recently-exposed remains of Montgomery Castle, Powys, demolished in June to October 1649.

of the work was very large with up to 140 labourers on the site at a time, together with three kinds of craftsmen: masons, miners and carpenters, up to 180 men at work. The function of the miners was no doubt to undermine and bring down tall upstanding masonry, while presumably the masons and carpenters were there to retrieve as much as possible of the materials for re-use or sale. The costs were £675/18/2, all but a small part for wages. Quite probably further work was done later, or perhaps the surviving lumps of masonry became a quarry for years to come; the diarist Evelyn records seeing men at Pontefract dismantling, presumably taking stone, as late as 1654.

The proposal in 1642 that Sherborne be 'razed to the ground' is no doubt parliamentary rhetoric. In later years a distinction was clearly made in the Commons between demolition or total demolition on the one hand, and slighting or making untenable on the other. The proposal at Kenilworth Castle for demolition was rapidly scaled down to making untenable, no doubt due to the impracticability of the former and protests by the County Committee at the scale of work involved; the removal of the north side of the keep and north curtain wall skilfully rendered the castle indefensible (fig. 101). Similarly at Wressell, Humberside, the question was raised while the work was in progress whether demolition was necessary rather than making untenable; the remains show two square corner towers surviving of the square castle, recalling the sort of partial

100 Daily expenditure, 27 July to 1 August 1649, on demolition at Montgomery Castle. Four groups were employed: carpenters at 2/6 a day, masons at 1/6 a day, miners at 2/– a day and labourers at 1/– a day. The first two were engaged in recovering material for re-use, the last two in demolition. The 130–40 labourers at work indicate the large scale of the operation (see Appendix 4).

demolition seen at Chirk (fig. 102). The nearest to total demolition was achieved perhaps at Greenhalgh Castle and Lathom House in Lancashire, Banbury, Wallingford, Winchester, Nottingham (fig. 97), Belvoir, Bolingbroke (fig. 103), Pontefract, Montgomery (fig. 99) and Aberystwyth and even in these cases substantial fragments usually survived. Recent excavations at Montgomery and Bolingbroke castles have shown that walls that stand to first floor level survive below the grass.[27] Inevitably much of the lower parts of the walls were buried by material knocked off the upper parts.

At Winchester, where the castle (except the hall) was thoroughly demolished, the advice of an engineer was required on how to proceed and at Dover, where demolition never took place, a surveyor was sent as a first step when it was envisaged. A certificate was required to certify that sufficient work had been carried out, but the gentlemen appointed to view at Belvoir said they had not sufficient military knowledge to know whether the work was adequate. Some expertise in this work was clearly

101 At Kenilworth Castle the north side of the keep and whole north curtain wall were demolished in 1649 on the orders of Parliament to render the castle untenable.

desirable. Today the most distinctive features of the remains of castles slighted in the period are walls reduced to uniformly low level by picking, as at Flint, Bolingbroke, Kenilworth (north side) etc. or large vertical exposures of ragged masonry where tall blocks have been toppled by undermining, particularly in the case of keeps or towers, as at Scarborough (fig. 104), South Wingfield (fig. 105), Ashby de la Zouch (see fig. 66), Raglan (see fig. 51) etc. One of the most drastic examples, showing a thorough treatment of the fabric, is at Helmsley, North Yorkshire. The huge fallen piece of masonry from undermining the keep lies in the ditch, while all the wall round the curtain has been planed off leaving the living accommodation on one side sticking up like an island (fig. 106). It was extremely expensive to use gunpowder, which in any case did not produce the tidy results of picking by hand (quite apart from making retrieval for re-sale impossible); at Aberystwyth where it is known to have been used on Edward I's castle the remains are decidedly ragged.

If there was sometimes difficulty in persuading local agents to carry out the work of demolition, equally, particularly during the fighting, it was sometimes necessary for London to exercise a restraining hand on the over-zealous, especially where what we might term 'cultural monuments' were concerned. In January 1645 the Derbyshire Committee were told that Hardwick and Chatsworth being of so 'goodly and costly a structure' were not to be demolished as intended.[28] The Shropshire Committee were told in April 1646 that at High Ercall House only the new works

102 Wressel Castle, Humberside, showing the two corners left after Parliamentary demolition had been halted.

were to be demolished and the moat drained leaving the house intact: 'neither do we think it fit that all houses whose situation or strength render them capable of being garrisons should be pulled down. There would be then too many sad marks left of the calamity of this war . . .'.[29] The Parliamentary troops stationed at Sudeley Castle were ordered to stop tearing down the wainscotting to use it for firewood,[30] although this edifice was later thoroughly slighted. Perhaps the most interesting case was the instruction given for slighting the great Jacobean 'castle' at Bolsover (p. 132): ' . . . that so much only be done to it as to make it untenable as a garrison and that it may not be unnecessarily spoiled and defaced . . .' Later the Derbyshire Committee was instructed to demolish outworks, garden walls with turrets and walls of frontier court, remove doors and window bars. It is difficult to judge what was done from the surviving remains, especially as there is some disagreement about the

103 Bolingbroke Castle, Lincolnshire, was demolished by orders of Parliament in 1649; the aerial view shows the formerly completely overgrown site after the recent exposure of the surviving lower parts of the walls.

104 The keep at Scarborough Castle, North Yorkshire, showing one side brought down by demolition in 1651.

105 The 'slighted' great tower at South Wingfield, Derbyshire.

dates of the riding-school range. It is surprising that the military threat of this seventeenth-century mock castle was put so high although it should be remembered that it had been held earlier in the war. Protected by a steep hill on three sides, no doubt bastions on the level approach would have made it difficult to assault.

Where did the demolition take place? Are the slighted castles to be found anywhere? As there was a punitive element involved in the choice, the areas of slighting correspond to some degree with the areas of the earlier conflict, particularly its sieges. There are examples which had been held by a Parliamentary garrison throughout the Civil War, like Nottingham Castle commanded by Colonel Hutchinson, where clearly there was no punitive intention in later demolition. It was seen primarily as an economy measure, to save the cost of a garrison while denying it to a watchful enemy who might seize it. We have then to be thinking in terms of economies: where could garrisons be reasonably dispensed with?

From 1646 to 1659 the word that was used to justify slighting of a

castle was 'inland': 'being inland castles' these ten Yorkshire castles should be made untenable.[31] The risks of attack from overseas, by foreigners or foreign-supported Royalists were felt to be greater than risings inland. It was indeed very much a continuation of Tudor policy on coastal defence when 'inland' castles had been allowed to fall into decay (p. 110). As a result, coastal castles and forts usually remained garrisoned and were not slighted. Demolition was carried out mainly in the Midlands and Yorkshire, east and south Wales, the Thames Valley, and, particularly after the Second Civil War, in Essex, Surrey and Hampshire. The Scottish Border was for obvious reasons hardly affected. The new earthworks for artillery constructed since 1642 could be levelled anywhere, and it was indeed the House of Lords, in an unusual role, that gave orders for the demolition of the extensive fortifications around London.

It is worth looking at the coasts to see what happened on the different sides of the island, starting on the east. As a result of treaty negotiations with the Scots, Berwick, like Carlisle, was to be disgarrisoned and its fortifications slighted. Some demolition evidently took place in 1646 but

106 Helmsley Castle, North Yorkshire; its curtain wall has been planed off and half the keep brought down by demolition in 1649.

a changed relationship with Scotland led to re-garrisoning and no doubt a strengthening of its fortifications. Right down the coast garrisons were maintained and fortifications sometimes strengthened: Berwick, Newcastle and Tynemouth, Hull, King's Lynn, Yarmouth. Boston was apparently too far up river to be garrisoned. Even Queenborough in Sheppey was considered for re-fortification with artillery.[32] Scarborough was an unusual case in that a Royalist garrison had been besieged there; it was intended to abandon the castle and replace it with a small battery to protect the harbour. There is clear evidence of demolition on the keep (see fig. 104) but owing to a change of mind a garrison was retained and it remained in use until the present century.

On the south coast from Kent to Cornwall garrisons were maintained in the forts erected by Henry VIII, in the Isle of Wight and the naval stations. Arundel, Bodiam and Herstmonceux were not slighted. There was some reduction of forts around Plymouth and Dartmouth. Southampton Castle was already in an advanced state of decay, but Christchurch and Winchester Castles were demolished except for their halls. Kent had played little part in the First Civil War but a very prominent one in the Second Civil War;[33] doubts about its loyalty may have led to the survey of Dover Castle in 1651 with the intention of demolition, possibly dropped on account of the scale of the estimated work revealed in the report.

On the west coast it is a very different story, particularly after the Irish threat had been eliminated by military action and Charles II's reliance was placed on the Scottish Presbyterians. There were garrisons in the great Edwardian castles of the north-west, Caernarfon, Conwy and Beaumaris, as well as on the north side of the Severn estuary at Chepstow, Cardiff, and Carmarthen (for a period). Otherwise the 'inland rule' did not apply on the west coast: Cardigan, Aberystwyth and perhaps Harlech were slighted on the coast of Cardigan Bay and Flint castle on Deeside. At a later date Bristol Castle was demolished and there was an 'Act' to do the same at Liverpool. The Welsh Marches were never viewed as a frontier like the Scottish Border area: Raglan and Chirk were regarded as slightable in a way that would never have been considered at Carlisle or Newcastle.

In East Anglia, Kent, Devon, Cornwall, Cumbria and Northumberland, evidence of slighting is not common; in Yorkshire (Scarborough, Helmsley, Middleham, Wressel, Pontefract, etc.), the Midlands (Bolingbroke, Nottingham, Belvoir, Kenilworth, Tutbury etc.) and much of Wales (Hawarden, Flint, Montgomery, Aberystwyth etc.) it is the rule rather than the exception. The testimony of Leland on the large number of Yorkshire castles in use (p. 107) may have meant that more were capable of defence in 1642, and so required slighting after the war. Survivals of structures that were already ruinous at the time, like Clifford's Tower at York or the keep at Conisborough, or had Parliamentary use, like Warwick castle, point the contrast. Some survivals were due to payment by the owner of an indemnity to Parliament for his good conduct in not using it against them, Maxstoke Castle in Warwickshire being a case in point.

Destruction did not cease with Restoration. Demolition, ordered by General Monk, started at Denbigh Castle on 27 March 1660 and went on for six weeks, while after the Restoration two towns which had been particularly loyal to Parliament, Coventry and Gloucester, were humiliated by having part of their town walls pulled down.[34] The authorised demolition that had been so widespread encouraged self-help; in May 1660 a number of gentlemen in the region of Caernarfon banded themselves together to raise £500 'conceiving it to be for the great advantage of ourselves and posterity to have the castle of Carnarvon and the strength thereof demolished'.[35] Happily not much was done. At Conwy in the same county the lead, iron and timber were removed from the castle by the order of Lord Conway in the autumn of 1665 leaving it a roofless ruin.[36] It was not formal destruction that followed the Restoration so much as the removal of psychological barriers by the example of earlier events that made it so much easier both to covet the materials and at the same time satisfy this desire without offending local opinion or that of relatives.

The extent to which slighted castles were brought back into use after the Restoration depended of course on the degree of destruction that had been carried out. Where it had been partial, as at Chirk, Berkeley, Powis or Dunster, normal occupation could be resumed. At Kenilworth, where the gatehouse had been converted into a dwelling during the Commonwealth period, limited re-occupation could take place. At Bolsover the restricted nature of the slighting allowed full occupation again, while at Farnham large sums were spent over a number of years by Bishop Morley to re-habilitate the castle, although parts of it like the keep went permanently out of use.[37] Alternatively a completely new building in the current Classical style could be built on the former site of the castle: Nottingham, Belvoir, Wolvesey at Winchester, or Hartlebury are examples that come to mind. In the majority of cases, demolition was followed by abandonment not only of the fabric but of the site also.

Two and a half centuries or more of decay and decline came thus to a dramatic conclusion. From the Restoration the castle really disappears as a major element in the English countryside. Very few still remained in private occupation. The situation may be contrasted with that described by Leland when he had seen 500 or so (p. 104). About two thirds were ruinous, it is true, but in some areas like Yorkshire it probably still constituted the principal form of country seat. It is interesting to compare the views of eighty country seats by Kip in the early eighteenth century which were predominantly post-Restoration Classical structures (not half a dozen castles), with the seats described by Leland soon to be shown as ruins in the views of the Buck brothers.

Comparisons with neighbours help to bring out certain features. The demolition of fortifications by Cardinal Richelieu has already been mentioned (p. 112) although the wording of the law suggests that it was fortified towns, rather than private castles unprotected from artillery, that had been the cause for concern. At all events, lists of French *châteaux* suggest a far greater measure of continuity of use from later medieval times than in this country.[38] Viollet-le-Duc's drawing of Renaissance windows being inserted into a great vertical incision made into a medieval tower shows a greater determination to convert rather than abandon as in England; the loss of face that transfer to a courtyard house entailed could not be endured in France (fig. 79). The demolitions in England created something of a *tabula rasa* that allowed Classical styles like Palladianism to sweep the board; there is a smoother continuity about the course of French architecture rather than the abruptness and jerkiness on this side of the Channel.

There is again a contrast with Scotland and Ireland. There was no comparable demolition of Scottish tower-houses, some of which remained in use until the eighteenth century and later. There was therefore a greater overlap of 'survival' and 'revival'. We can see this in the 'castle style' of the eighteenth century and even more in the 'Scottish baronial' style of the nineteenth century. The contrast between the Italianate house built by Queen Victoria at Osborne, Isle of Wight, and the 'castle' built by her at Balmoral is revealing.

In English literary convention the reduction of castles to jagged fragments and shapeless lumps also had its influence. Since Horace Walpole, through the Picturesque and Romantic movements, the attitude towards castles has been basically sentimental, a feeling aroused by seeing them only as ruins. On the Continent their connotations were more sinister, epitomised perhaps by the storming of the Bastille, and continuing to the present day in central Europe as for example in the decidedly unpleasant castle in Kafka's novel, *The Castle*.

Chapter 9

Nostalgia

> As to the outside I thought 'twas absolutely best to give it some-
> thing of the castle air tho' at the same time to make it regular. And
> by this means too all the old stone is serviceable again; which to
> have had new would have run to a very great expence; this
> method was practiced at Windsor in King Charles's time and has
> been universally approved. So I hope your Lordship wont be so
> discouraged if any Italians you may shew it to should find fault
> that tis not Roman, for to have built a front with pilasters and
> what the Orders require could never have been born with the rest
> of the castle. I am sure this will make a very noble and masculine
> show and is of as warrantable a kind of building as any.[1]

So wrote Sir John Vanbrugh to the Earl of Manchester in July 1707 referring to the replacement of the early Tudor house at Kimbolton Castle,
Huntingdonshire (now Cambridgeshire) by the present mansion in the
construction of which Vanbrugh was then engaged. The word 'masculine'
reveals the continuity of thinking: the seat of the landowner should reflect
the robust authority of its occupier, and a 'castle air' did this better than
too great an adherence to the Classical Orders. Vanbrugh was particularly involved at Nottingham, Grimsthorpe and Kimbolton with the
reconstruction of medieval seats, and his experience as a dramatist no
doubt made him especially conscious of appearances. Features of the
'castle air' are present in most of his buildings: Castle Howard, even
Blenheim, the tower at Claremont, his own house at Greenwich and so
on.

The view that a 'castle air' for his seat enhanced the authority of a landowner gained ground in the latter part of the eighteenth century and was
certainly very important in the nineteenth century. However at the time
of Vanbrugh's death it ran quite against the flood tide of Palladianism. A
castellated structure might be acceptable as a folly or garden ornament
closing a prospect but it was not suitable for a major seat or building
(fig. 107). The lone champion of the Gothic style, Batty Langley, signifi-

cantly was a gardener, and his writings tended to make the style an object of ridicule, and treated as a frivolity. The alterations made by William Kent to Bishop Wayneflete's gatehouse at Esher, a genuine Gothic building titivated to make it more evocative of the Middle Ages, express this attitude (fig. 108).

A far stronger impulse came from Horace Walpole (1717–97), MP, author, connoisseur. In 1746 he rented a house in Windsor Castle,[2] which may have prompted ideas of creating his own castle, and in 1747 he leased premises further downstream at Strawberry Hill north-west of Twickenham and 300 yards west of the river. It was a fashionable area at that time for a rural retreat for London society. He acquired the freehold in 1749 and then extended the property north and south to provide land for pleasure gardens, at the same time as, over a period of 20 years, he reconstructed the house. Strawberry Hill in its completed form was a range of two-storeyed buildings running east–west for some 220 feet with

107 A folly castle erected in 1772 (to the earlier design of Sanderson Miller) to close a prospect at Wimpole Hall, Cambridgeshire.

a round tower at the west end, linked by a gallery over a 'loggia' ('cloister') with the entry and main living rooms at the east end.[3] It was designed to house the large collection of pictures, curios, antiques etc. of the bachelor aesthete who owned it,[4] in whose catalogue of his collection it is referred to as a villa. The only hint of anything castle-like about it is the tower, for as Walpole said: 'I did not mean to make my house so Gothic as to exclude convenience and modern refinements'.[5] The most striking things about the building are the fittings, bookcases in the library, staircase and the ceilings imitating vaults (fig. 110). The windows with their pointed heads are more redolent of a church than a castle! Nevertheless the large number of Walpole's guests (apart from the public to whom the house was opened in the afternoons) spread familiarity with the new 'Gothic style' far and wide.

More important in some ways was the Gothic story of Walpole, 'The Castle of Otranto', published in 1764, inspired so the author said by a dream he had in Strawberry Hill.[6] The story itself is 'chivalric', stilted in style like a contemporary opera, but it introduces those elements of terror (apparitions, giants, subterranean passages etc.) which were taken up by later writers (Mrs Radcliffe, Lewis, Scott etc.) to change the image of the castle in the public's mind.[7] Hitherto only the owner got satisfaction from his castle, but now almost anyone could be thrilled by the terror elements

108 Erected in the 1480s by Bishop Waynflete the gatehouse at Esher Place, Surrey, was altered by Kent in the early eighteenth century to look more 'Gothic'.

109 Hertford Castle, with a brick gatehouse of the 1460s, and inserted eighteenth-century windows.

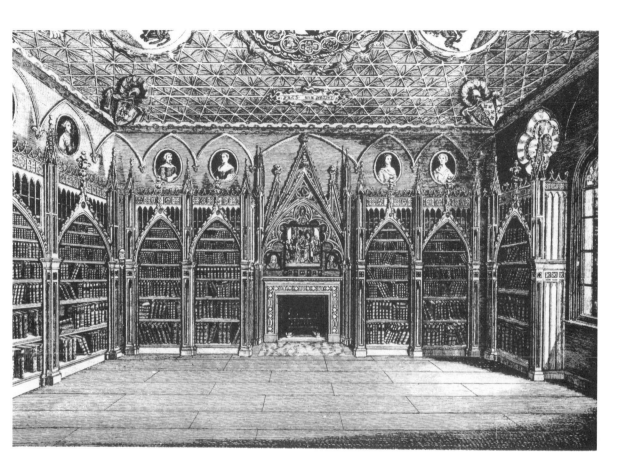

110 Horace Walpole's library at Strawberry Hill, Twickenham.

in it; thus a different attitude was created with the public at large, arousing curiosity and interest, which the modern marketing man has been so adroitly able to exploit.

Strawberry Hill established, or at all events, consolidated the 'Gothic Style'. It could be applied successfully to a church (Shobdon in Herefordshire comes to mind) but the weakness of Walpole's creation was that there was no seigneurial estate to go with it; the true successor of the castle was the country house not the Thames-side villa. In the second half of the eighteenth and the early decades of the nineteenth century, large country houses in the 'castle style' were erected in England and Wales, as well as in Scotland and Ireland. Some of the most notable were indeed erected in the last two countries where, as we have seen, there was a far more vigorous survival of castles, and where indeed the disturbed conditions (the '15 and '45 risings) were leading to the contemporary construction of massive fortifications, as at Fort George.[8] As the title implies the Gothic was one of two or three styles that could be chosen for the house, and most of the leading architects, Carr, Wyatt, Nash, Adam, carried out work in it. The object was to model the exterior with pointed windows, corner towers, battlements and so on, in such a way that the association of ideas at once suggested a castle. The disposition of the rooms inside remained unaffected. The building was of course set in elaborately land-scaped park to harmonise with and yet at the same time to accentuate this impression. The building could be basically a classical one with Gothic detail as favoured by Robert Adam in Scotland, but as realism crept in with the nineteenth century so there was a tendency to adopt a more medieval shape and plan. The style culminated or rather terminated with the 'Norman style' in which a gigantic 'keep' was a dominating feature, as at Penrhyn Castle, near Bangor, north Wales. Unfortunately the best account of this fascinating subject still remains an unpublished thesis in Cambridge University Library.[9]

The background to the 'castle style' is the Picturesque, an aesthetic stance towards the landscape developed in the eighteenth century, identified by Christopher Hussey and now considered as a peculiarly English mode.[10] Originally an attitude derived from seeking in the real landscape certain features expressed in painting by Poussin, Salvator Rosa and so on it soon became an all-embracing feeling covering land-scape and buildings. The 'castle style' did not escape and asymmetrical, elongated buildings with round towers at the end (recalling the Straw-berry Hill villa) represent the 'picturesque castle style'. Downton Castle in Shropshire erected by Richard Payne Knight to his own design is of particular importance, since he was one of the chief exponents of the Picturesque. The intensity of feeling on this subject may be illustrated by quotation from the Journal of Sir Richard Colt Hoare, the Wiltshire antiquary who went frequently to Wales over the twenty years 1793–1813 in search of the picturesque and antiquities (which were *ipso facto* picturesque), first on Downton Castle and then on his favourite medieval castle at Conwy, Gwynedd.

> Whoever views these grounds must consider that the owner here intended that nature should have no ornament but those peculiar to herself, no trappings borrowed from her rival, art. View Downton with these ideas and no one will be disappointed. If criticism can anywhere be well founded it is on the house which I do not think quite adapted to the genius of the place. Too great a variety of different architecture of different aera – it is neither an

ancient castle nor a modern house but a mixture of modern and antique.[11]

Hoare judged Downton as an antiquary and his antiquarian interests are even clearer in the description of Conwy:

> For a short interval the road becomes uninteresting – when Conway's proud towers burst suddenly on the sight. I envy the traveller (if such there be) who not knowing such a castle existed should be thus unexpectedly and pleasingly surprised . . . The castle itself is a most noble structure and of the most picturesque form and in a much less dilapidated state than most of baronial and royal castles with which this country abounds . . . In short the whole is so beautiful in all its parts and so judiciously situated that I could almost suppose the artist, not the engineer, had directed its construction.[12]

The *floruit* of the 'castle style' corresponded with the era of the Industrial Revolution, not of great importance for rural seats, but productive of major alterations in towns, to castles but far more important to town walls, which since medieval times had been their companions. Many had fallen into decay in Tudor times but had often met a renewed need during the Civil War. The fact that at the Restoration they could be demolished for punishment, as at Gloucester (p. 156), suggests that they were still a source of considerable civic pride. The city walls of York were manned at the time of the invasion by the Young Pretender in 1745.[13] Narrow town gates constricted the rising traffic flow while walls were a constraint on growth at a time of rapid expansion of industrial towns, so there was extensive demolition between 1760 and 1840. All the gates and most of the walls of Hereford were swept away in this period,[14] while in Wales the industrial towns of the south-east (Newport, Cardiff, Swansea) lost their walls but many rural towns (Conwy, Caernarfon, Tenby, Chepstow) kept them.

Mention has been made of the Hanoverian fortifications in Scotland. In England, coastal fortification did not cease at the Restoration. The Dutch attack on the Medway in 1667 indeed stimulated it; Tilbury Fort was built in response to this.[15] There are eighteenth-century artillery works on the chalk hills on either side of Dover. The early years of the nineteenth century saw the erection of the strange, stubby Martello towers on the south and east coasts to resist the feared invasion of Napoleon I, while the same fear of Napoleon III led to the construction of the gigantic fortified batteries and barracks along the south coast and in Milford Haven. These structures form no part of the story that is being unfolded here but deserve mention as a sequel to earlier references to coastal defences.

The Victorian period saw the construction of many huge country houses which have been so ably and graphically described by Mark Girouard.[16] It might have been thought that the Gothic Revival with its emphasis on faithful and accurate copying of medieval buildings would have produced a crop of extremely accurate representations of medieval castles. Why is that not so?

A church that was only used for worship three or four hours a week could be a perfect facsimile of a medieval church without much inconvenience to worshippers. A building lived in 24 hours a day for 365 days a year was quite a different matter. The communal life of the medieval hall; the wholly different relationships within the medieval, as opposed to Victorian, household; the absence of carpets, window-glass and most furniture (compared to its profusion in Victorian rooms); the absence of gas lighting, of billiard and smoking rooms, of pictures and fine china – of indeed all those elements of luxury essential to a wealthy family – made it quite impossible to substitute medieval castle life for that of the Victorian country house, however desirable for the moralists and revivalists that might be. The passionate dedication to thirteenth-century church architecture which did not allow the cavalier inaccuracies of the 'castle style', that had treated Gothic forms as decorative not intrinsic features of the building, killed the older style. The dilemma of how to replace it with a mode of building that was not a mere style but something imbued with the real essence of the Gothic spirit was not easy to resolve. Pugin in his *Examples* chose mainly late medieval or Tudor domestic architecture which could be followed, while Scott offered a similar solution, pinning his hopes on the late medieval vernacular.[17] This was not very satisfying for the railway or industrial tycoon, who wanted a house to display his wealth and power, although it was in fact the direction taken by domestic architecture in the final decades of the century (Webb, Lutyens, Voysey).

In France, where the Gothic Revival took a less evangelistic form than in England, the patriotic element was stronger. At all events Viollet-le-Duc, the great *Inspecteur-Général* to Napoleon III, thought the science of restoration had reached a point where not only a replica but even an improvement on the original could be made.[18] His restorations, perhaps more successful at Carcassone than at Pierrefonds (the former not inhabited of course) need not concern us except in so far as to say that his studies undoubtedly enormously advanced our knowledge of the nuts and bolts of medieval architecture. It is a blending of this French attitude with English evangelism in an attempt to recreate a thirteenth-century castle at Castell Coch, about five miles north of Cardiff, that deserves our attention.[19]

As an infant the third Marquess of Bute had inherited great wealth from his father including much of Cardiff with its docks as well as coal mines in the valleys. He was converted to Roman Catholicism during youth and soon afterwards became a client of the architect William Burges. Burges was not a man of strong religious conviction but he had designed the Protestant cathedral at Cork in Ireland in a French Gothic style. He was at first concerned with the reconstructions of Cardiff Castle where his splendid interiors and exteriors do not cease to astonish us. He had started work there in the 1860s, but the proposal to reconstruct Castell Coch arose in the early 1870s. A volume of drawings by Burges made in 1875, after the extensive clearance by contractors of the fallen rubble that had buried the remains, survives with his proposals for reconstruction, which correspond reasonably closely to what was actually built.[20]

Castell Coch (Red Castle, referring to the stone colour) had been a triangular structure with a round tower at each apex, erected in *c.* 1300 but with no recorded history. It had been ruinous when Leland visited it in *c.* 1540, and legend has it that Owain Glyndŵr's supporters had destroyed it in *c.* 1405. In many ways it was an ideal choice for restoration. It was small, which minimised costs, and, just as important, made it more feasible to design it for modern occupation. One of the main snags at Peckforton Castle, Cheshire, a massive new structure by Salvin put up twenty years before, which had tried to reproduce the shape of a medieval castle, was that such a dispersed design made modern occupation difficult. At Castell Coch the medieval walls stood to varying heights and the new structure was raised upon them, so that there could be no doubt about the authenticity of the groundplan (fig. 111). The exterior aspect with its bleak round towers has a decidedly thirteenth-century feel about it. Conical roofs were normal in late medieval France but their employment in this country must be open to doubt; Burges was at great pains in his written proposals to defend his decision. The shutters and fittings owe much to Viollet-le-Duc. The small inner court with external staircase to hall and gallery carries considerable conviction.

Problems arose in the interior, not perhaps with the actual disposition of the rooms which follows a not-improbable pattern, but in the decoration, furniture and fireplaces where the inventive genius of Burges was given free rein. The butterflies on the ceiling of the drawing room rising to the point of suspension of the chandelier, the three Fates over the fireplace, the extraordinary bed and chairs and cupboard in the bedroom emphatically jar on the medieval ambience! It tries much harder than the Bolsover keep (p. 133) to recapture the secular atmosphere of the High Middle Ages, a formidable task, and is most impressive. Unfortunately the discomfort of the building combined with its limited accommodation gave it only a very short life as a dwelling; it virtually passed out of use with the beginning of the First World War.

The last building to be discussed represents perhaps the last of the neo-castles, its construction spanning the 1914–18 war, the terminal point of the erection of large country houses. Castle Drogo in Devonshire, west of Exeter on the edge of Dartmoor, was erected between 1911 and 1930 for Julius Drewe (1856–1931) by Sir Edwin Lutyens.[22] Drewe as a young man had been in China working for Francis Peek and Winch, but realising the opportunities launched out for himself and made a fortune in the grocery business. Sir Henry Peek (of Peek Freane biscuits, also in the grocery business) had erected a colossal neo-Tudor mansion from 1874 at

111 Castell Coch, Glamorgan, view towards the entry of Burges' castle of the 1880s.

112 The castle at
Castell Coch,
Glamorgan, shown in
section by Burges,
below as it existed in
ruin and above as he
proposed to recon-
struct it. The actual
reconstruction
corresponds fairly
closely with this.

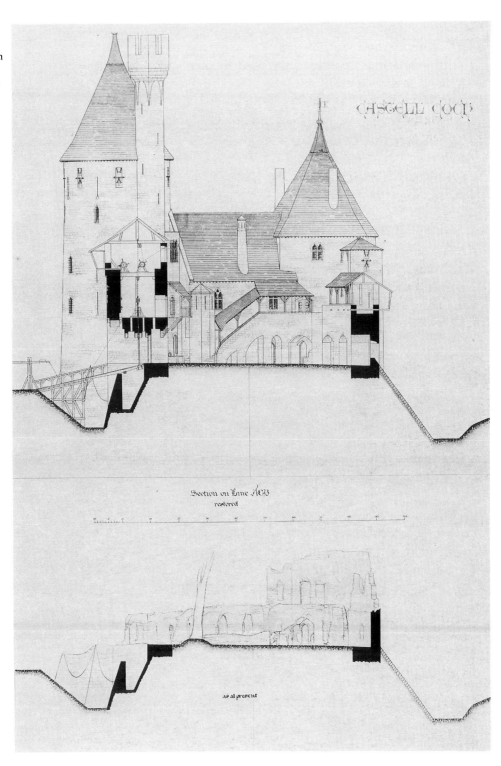

CASTELL COCH

Section on Line ACB
restored

as at present

Rousdon in south-east Devon, near Lyme Regis,[23] his architect being Ernest George, in whose office Lutyens worked as a young man. The idea of erecting a castle in Devonshire may have been suggested by experience at Rousdon. Drogo was a Norman who had come over at the Conquest and from whom Drewe believed he was descended. A high granite ridge overlooking the River Teign was the chosen site and by extensive purchasing an estate of some 1,500 acres was built up around it.

The first proposals of Lutyens for a courtyard and huge hall with hammerbeam roof had to be abandoned for the sake of economy, but the altered design is most successful. The plan is dog-legged, each part of the leg being 120 feet long with transepts in the middle. Owing to the differences of ground level, the four floor levels on the two sides of the transepts do not match up. The north-east limb (the shin) was the service wing, while the south limb (the thigh) contained the principal living rooms. There is no attempt to reproduce a medieval plan in the internal layout, and yet there is a decided 'castle air' about the building externally. This is partly due to the harshness of the material employed, the local granite, but mainly due to the severity of the treatment. The windows are uniformly rectangular with no dripstone, severely plain mullions and transoms, demarcating rectangles (not diamonds) of square leaded panes. The walls

113 North end of Castle Drogo, the great granite structure erected on the edge of Dartmoor by Lutyens in this century (National Trust).

have no string course, or plinth or decoration except at the octagonal turrets of the entry (which has a small portcullis), while the top, so important for the silhouette, is either flat with undifferentiated parapet or has widely spaced merlons. The ends and the centre which rise above the wings give a suggestion of towers. It is a masterly exercise, suggesting the dourness of a thirteenth-century castle without actually imitating it.

In Castle Drogo a room is dedicated to Adrian Drewe, the eldest son of the builder, sadly killed in 1917, which might indeed be regarded as a shrine to the construction of great buildings of this kind. That is a subject to which we must now turn attention.

None of the buildings discussed in this chapter could be described as *châteaux forts* although many, perhaps most, could be described at *châteaux* in the status sense of seigneurial seats. Territorial authority was very much in the minds of the builders, a large estate and a large house being inseparable; to that extent they were non-functional 'castles', true heirs of the medieval fortresses, which as we have seen had not been constructed since about 1400. If it was possible to construct mock castles up to 1914: why is it not possible to do so today?

The great agricultural depression of the last decades of the nineteenth century due to the import of cheap overseas food certainly reduced the available capital derived from land-ownership to be spent on such large-scale building.[24] This did not prevent money from industry or commerce being so employed, as we have seen at Rousdon and Castle Drogo (fig. 113), but it made an unattractive investment, if indeed investment it could be called. The depression lasted up to 1939. Death duties introduced at the beginning of the century were a discouragement to any attempt to create a permanent patrimony of this kind. The profound social changes of the war undermined the social base on which such an establishment rested, while increased wages made it more costly to maintain the army of servants required to support it. Many of such buildings were in serious difficulties between the wars (Rousdon for example was sold together with its estate to a school in 1938). The Second World War acted as a *coup de grâce*: the relative increase in costs of fuel, wages, materials meant that only the most determined owner could resist partial or total demolition or sale for institutional use. The changes in social ethos had gone too far for the reversal in the fortunes of agriculture since the war to alter the situation. 'Heritage' and 'tourism' are the two rather chilly words we associate with such surviving buildings today.

Appendix 1

Derelict or abandoned castles in the fifteenth century

The following list has been compiled merely from references in printed sources that have come to my attention; it is not in any sense exhaustive and must indeed represent only a fraction of castles to be found in that condition at that time. The information that is available from the contemporary sources is not sufficient to compile a full list, but this sample is probably a fair indication of how widespread disuse was at that time.

Barton Seagrave (Northamptonshire) 24/4/1401 – castle and manor: 'much waste, strip, ruin, dilapidation, trespass and other damage' *CIM* vii, 1399–1422, p. 82.

Bedford 1224 – after demolition never rebuilt. *VCH, Beds.* iii. Cf. Speed's map (fig. 8).

Beeston (Cheshire) 'completely neglected'. *KW*, ii, 560.

Berkhamsted (Hertfordshire) 1495 – 'ceased to be inhabited'. *KW*, ii, 563.

Bolsover (Derbyshire) *KW*, ii, 573.

Bridgnorth (Salop, now Shropshire) 'completely neglected'. *KW*, ii, 577.

Bristol 'totam ad ruinam'. *WW*, 399–406.

Cambridge Hall demolished to use materials in King's College. *KW*, ii, 587.

Canterbury (Kent) *KW*, ii, 590.

Carreg Cannen (Dyfed) 1462 – demolished. *KW*, ii, 602.

(Castle) Combe (Wiltshire) 1480 – 'dirutum'. *WW*, 140.

Criccieth (Gwynedd) Destroyed by forces of Glyndŵr. *KW*, i, 367.

Deganwy (Gwynedd) Demolished by Llewelyn in 1263. *KW*, ii. 626.

Devizes (Wiltshire) *KW*, ii, 628; *VCH, Wilts.*, x, 245.

Dorchester (Dorset) Demolished and site used for friary. *KW*, ii, 629.

Dyserth (Clwyd) Demolished by Llewelyn in 1263. *KW*, ii, 645.

Exeter (Devon) *KW*, ii, 649.

Fenny (Somerset) 1480 – 'dirutum'. *WW*, 292–3.

Hedingham (Essex) Later rebuilt, *Leland*, ii, 25.

Helston (Cornwall) 1480 – 'dirutum'. *WW*, 20.

Hereford *KW*, ii, 677.

Lincoln *KW*, ii, 705.

Malton (Yorkshire) 1430 – 'scitus castri'. *CIPM* (1828), iv, 131.

Marlborough (Wiltshire) 1391 – needs 'complete rebuilding'. *CIM*, v, 167; *KW*, ii, 738.

Miserden (Gloucestershire) *c.* 1275 abandoned. *VCH, Glos.*, xi, 50.

Norwich (Norfolk) *KW*, ii, 755.

Oxford *KW*, ii, 774.

Peak (Castleton) (Derbyshire) *KW*, ii, 777.

Porchester (Hampshire) *KW*, ii, 792.

Reigate (Surrey) 1441 – buildings within described as ruinous. *VCH, Surrey*, iii, 231.

Rhayader (Powys) 1425 – 'scitus castri veteris'. *CIPM* (1828), iv, 94.

Salisbury (Old Sarum) *KW*, ii, 828.

Sauvey (Leicestershire) *KW*, ii, 829.

Shrewsbury (Salop) *KW*, ii, 837.

Somerton (Lincolnshire) *KW*, ii, 839.

Tintagel (Cornwall) 1480 – 'fortissimum dirutum'. *WW*, 21.

Trowbridge (Wiltshire) 1480 – 'dirutum'. *WW*, 140.

Truro (Cornwall) 1480 – 'dirutum'. *WW*, 20.

Worcester 1459, stones used for repairing town walls and gates. *CPR*, 26/11/1459; *KW*, ii, 888–9.

York *KW*, ii, 894.

Condition of castles mentioned in Leland's *Itinerary*

Only those castles are listed where either Leland refers to the condition or it can be reasonably inferred from the mention; in a great many cases that are omitted no inference is possible about the condition. All references are to the edition of L. Toulmin-Smith (published in London in 1910 by E. Bell and Sons Ltd in five volumes, used here by permission of their modern successors, Bell and Hyman), the spelling being modernised. A very rough classification is made: normal use (N), partially derelict (D), and a ruin (R).

Abergavenny(Gwent) 'a fair castle' – iii, 45 (fair refers to appearance rather than the condition). (N?)

Alberbury (Salop, now Shropshire) 'ruins' – iv, 1. (R)

Aldbrough (Yorkshire) 'great ruins' – iv, 27. (R)

Ampthill (Bedfordshire) 'standing stately on an hill, with 4 or 5 fair towers of stone' – i, 102–3. (N)

Appleby (Cumbria) 'ruinous castle wherein the prisoners be kept' – v, 47. (R)

Baginton (Warwickshire) 'now desolated' – v, 11. (R)

Bagworth Park (Lincolnshire) 'within a ditch ruins of a manor place, like castle building' – i, 20. (R)

Banbury (Oxfordshire) '2 wards . . . in the outer a terrible prison . . . In the north part of the inner ward is a fair piece of new building of stone' – ii, 39. (D)

Barnard (Durham) 'standith stately upon Tees' – i, 77. (N)

Barnstaple(Devon) 'manifest ruins of a great castle . . . and a piece of the dungeon yet standith' – i, 169. (R)

Barnwell (Northamptonshire) 'remain yet 4 strong towers . . . Within the ruins of the castle is now a mean house for a farmer . . .' – i, 3. (R)

Barry (Glamorgan) 'most of it is in ruin' – iii, 23–4. (R)

Bedford 'now clean down' – v. 8. (R)

Belvoir (Leicestershire) ' . . . The Lord Hastings carried much of this lead to Ashby de la Zouch where he much built. Then fell all the castle to ruin, and the timber of the roofs uncovered rotted away, and the soil between the walls at the last grew full of elders, and no habitation was there till that of late days the Earl of Rutland hath made it fairer than ever it was . . .' – i, 97–8. (N)

Benefield (Northamptonshire) 'the ditch and ruins of an old castle' – i, 12; 'clean fallen down to the ground' – iv, 123. (R)

Berkeley (Gloucestershire) ' . . . no great thing. Divers towers . . . ' – v, 101. (N)

Berkhamsted (Hertfordshire) 'to my sight it is much in ruin' – i, 104. (R)

Beverstone (Gloucestershire) Good condition implied – iv, 132, 133. (N)

Birdsall (**Mount Ferrant**) (Yorkshire, North Riding) 'now clearly defaced, and bushes grow where it stood' – i, 58. (R)

Bishop's Castle (Salop, now Shropshire) 'well maintained' – v, 15. (N)

Bishop's Stortford (Hertfordshire) 'the ruins of a few pieces of the walls . . . and the dungeon hill . . . ' – iv, 117. (R)

Blaen Llyfni (Powys) 'shape of a fair castle, now decaying' – iii, 107. (D)

Bolingbroke (Lincolnshire) 'meetly well maintained' – v, 36. (N)

Bolton (Yorkshire) 'all compacted in 4 or 5 towers' – i, 79; 'chiefest house of Lord Scrope' – iv, 27. (N)

Bourne (Lincolnshire) 'There appear great ditches and the dungeon hill of an ancient castle' – i, 25. (R)

Brackley (Buckinghamshire) 'There was a fair castle . . . the site and hill where it stood is yet evidently seen . . . but there is not seen any piece of a wall standing' – ii, 36; 'hath been a castle' – v, 224. (R)

Brancepeth (Durham) 'The earl that is now hath set a new piece of work to it' – i, 71 (N)

Brandon (Warwickshire) ' . . . now desolated . . . ' – v, 11. (R)

Brecon (Brecknock) 'very large, strong, well maintained' – iii, 105. (N)

Bridgwater (Somerset) 'sometime a right fair and strong piece of work, but now all going to mere ruin . . . ' – i, 162. (R)

Bridgnorth (Salop, now Shropshire) 'There were 2 or 3 strong wards in the castle that now go totally to ruin' – ii, 85. (R)

Brinklow (Warwickshire) 'now desolated' – v, 11. (R)

Bristol (Somerset) 'many towers yet standing . . . but all tendith to ruin' – v, 87. (R)

Broncroft (Salop, now Shropshire) 'a very goodly place like a castle' – v, 15. (N)

Bronllys (Powys) 'great ruins' – iii, 111. (R)

Bronsill (Herefordshire) 'a castle having fair towers . . . Sir John Talbot of Grafton by Bromsgrove bought it' – iv, 133. (N)

Brougham (Cumbria) 'an old castle that the common people there sayeth doth sink' – v, 47. (R)

Builth Wells (Powys) 'a fair castle of the kings' – iii, 109. (N?)

Burgh (Cumbria) 'old castle' – v, 47. (R?)

Bury (Lancashire) 'a ruin' – v, 43. (R)

Bwlch y Ddinas (Powys) 'now ruinous almost to the hard ground. There be manifest tokens of iii wards walled about' – iii, 108. (R)

Caerleon (Gwent) 'the ruins of the walls of the town yet remain, and also of the castle . . . ', iii, 44. (R)

Caerphilly (Glamorgan) 'ruinous walls of a wonderful thickness, and tower kept up for prisoners . . . ' – iii, 18. (R)

Cardiff (Glamorgan) 'now in some ruin' – iii, 34. (R)

Carew (Dyfed) 'repaired or magnificently builded by Sir Rhys ap Thomas' – iii, 115. (N)

Carlisle (Cumbria) 'being within the town is in some part as a closer of the wall' – v, 52. (N?)

Carmarthen (Dyfed) 'very fair and double walled' – iii, 59. (N)

Carreg Cennen (Dyfed) '50 or 60 years since almost totally defaced by men of Kidwelly, finding the country vexed with resort of thieves thither' – iv, 179. (R)

Castell Coch (Glamorgan) 'all in ruin, no big thing but high' – iii, 18. (R)

Castle Bytham (Lincolnshire) 'yet remain great walls of building' – i, 23. (R)

Castle Eaton (Wiltshire) 'great ruins of a building' – i, 127. (R)

Castle Hedingham (Essex) 'Mr Sheffield told me that afore the old Earl of Oxford's time, that came in with King Henry VII the castle of Hedingham was in much ruin, so that all the building that now is there was in a manner of this old Earl's building, except the gatehouse and the great dungeon tower' – ii, 25. (N)

Castle Hewin (Cumbria) 'ruins' – v, 56. (R)

Castlemartin (Dyfed) *'vestigia'* – iii, 63. (R)

Castle Troggy (Gwent) 'very notable ruins' – iii, 42. (R)

Caverswall (Staffordshire) 'now somewhat in decay' – iv, 129; 'pretty pile' – v, 19. (D)

Cawood (Yorkshire) 'a very fair castle' – iv, 12. (N)

Cefnllys (Powys) 'now down' – iii, 11. (R)

Chartley (Staffordshire) 'now in ruin' – v, 24. (R)

Chepstow (Gwent) 'fair and strong' – iii, 43. (N)

Chilham (Kent) 'now almost down' – iv, 55. (R)

Chirk (Powys) 'a mighty large and strong castle . . . a late well repaired by Sir William Standeley' – iii, 72. (N)

Cleobury Mortimer (Salop, now Shropshire) 'There was a castle . . . ' – v, 189. (R)

Clun (Salop, now Shropshire) 'somewhat ruinous' – iii, 53. (D)

Codnor (Derbyshire) 'now all ruinous' – v, 31. (R)

Coity (Glamorgan) 'is maintained . . . Gamage is lord of it and it is his principal house' – iii, 33. (N)

Colwyn (Powys) 'ruins' – iii, 11. (R)

Conisborough (Yorkshire) 'The walls of it hath been strong and full of towers' – i, 36. (D?)

Cottingham (**Stuteville's**) (Yorkshire) 'double ditched . . . nothing now remainith' – i, 47. (R)

Crayke (Yorkshire) 'The great square tower that is thereby, as in the top of the hill and supplement of lodgings is very fair . . . ' – i, 66. (D?)

Dartmouth (**Stoke Fleming**)(Devon) ' . . . one of these towers standith by Sir George Carew's castle called Stoke Fleming at the haven mouth.' – i, 221. (N)

Denbigh (Clwyd) 'very large thing and hath many towers in it. But the body of the work was never finished.' – iii, 97. (D?)

Devizes (Wiltshire) 'now in ruin, and part of the front of the towers of the gate of the keep and the chapel in it were carried full unprofitably to the building of Master Bainton's place at Bromham scant 3 miles off. There remain divers goodly towers yet in the outer wall of the castle, but all going to ruin.' – v, 82. (R)

Dinas Bran (Clwyd) 'now all in ruin' – iii, 90. (R)

Dinas Powys (Glamorgan) 'all in ruin' – iii, 23. (R)

Dolforwyn (Powys) 'ruinous' – iii, 54. (R)

Dover (Kent) 'The main, strong and famous castle' – iv, 50. (N)

Drayton (Northamptonshire) '. . . the prettiest place in these quarters . . . most built by Grene that was so great a man in Richard the Second's days . . . ' – i, 6. (N)

Drumburgh (Cumbria) 'Lord Dacre's father built upon old ruins a pretty pile for defence of the country' – v, 51. (N)

Dunstanburgh (Northumberland) 'hath been great building in it' – v, 64. (D)

Dunster (Somerset) 'The dungeon of the castle of Dunster hath been full of goodly building. But now there is but only a chapel in good case . . . The fairest part of the castle well-maintained is in the north-east of the court of it.' – i, 166. (D)

Durham 'The castle standith stately on the north-east side of the Minster . . . Bishop Fox did much reparation of this dungeon . . . ' – i, 73. (N)

Dursley (Gloucestershire) 'Part of Dursley Castle brought to make the new house of Dodington' – iv, 130; 'fell to decay and is clean taken down' – v, 96. (R)

Dynevor (Dyfed) 'ruinous' – iii, 57. (R)

Eaton Socon (Bedfordshire) *vestigia castelli* . . . The ruines . . . belong to Lord Vaux' – iv, 22. (R)

Elmley (Worcestershire) 'There standith now but one tower and that partly broken. As I went by I saw carts carrying stone thence to amend Pershore Bridge about 11 miles off.' – v, 9. (R)

Ewloe (Clwyd) 'ruinous castelet' – iii. 93. (R)

Ewyas Harold (Herefordshire) 'It hath been a notable thing' – ii, 69. (R)

Exeter (Devon) 'standith stately on a high ground' – i, 227. (N?)

Farleigh Hungerford (Somerset) '. . . diverse pretty towers . . . the gatehouse of the inner court of the castle is fair . . . The hall and 3 chambers within the second court be stately' – i, 137, 138. (N)

Fenny Castle (Somerset) '. . . castle on an hill . . . *cuius ruinas adhuc apparent.*' – i, 147. (R)

Folkingham (Lincolnshire) 'fallith all to ruin' – i, 25. (R)

Fonmon (Glamorgan) 'yet standith and belongith to Sir John St John' – iii, 24. (D?)

Ford (Cumbria) 'in decay' – v, 64. (D)

Fotheringhay (Northamptonshire) '. . . fair and meetly strong . . . There be very fair lodgings in the castle. And as I heard Catharine of Spain did great works in late time of refreshing it' – i, 5. (N)

Fowey (Cornwall) '. . . Thomas Treury built a right fair and strong embattled tower in his house: and embattling all the walls of the house in a manner made it a castle; and on to this day it is the glory of the town building in Fowey' – i, 204. (N)

Fulbrook (Warwickshire) 'Sir William Compton . . . seeing it going to ruin helped it forward, taking part of it, as some say, for the buildings of his house at Compton . . . ' – ii, 48; 'a castelet of stone and brick stood *bremlye* in the sight of Warwick Castle and was cause of heartburning. Compton of late days razed much of it, bringing part to Compton toward building of his house and some part he gave away'. – v, 155. (R)

Gleaston (Lancashire) 'a ruin and walls of a castle' – v, 222. (R)

Gloucester No reference to decay; 'of an wonderful old building'. – iii, 100. (N?)

Goldington (**Risinghoe**) (Bedfordshire) 'tokens where a large castle hath been . . . there appearith no manner of part of building, but it is easy to see where the area of castle was . . . ' – i, 101; iv, 22. (R)

Greenhalgh (Lancashire) 'a pretty castle of the Lord of Derby's' – iv, 9. (N)

Groby (Leicestershire) 'few tokens of the old castle . . . hill that the keep of the castle stood on very notable, but there is now no stonework upon it . . . newer works . . . foundations and walls of a great gatehouse of brick and a tower, but that was left half unfinished . . . ' – i, 17, 18. (R)

Grosmont (Gwent) 'Most part of the castle walls stand' – ii, 71. (R)

Hanley (Worcestershire) 'Mr Cometon clean defaced it in his time . . . ' – iv, 135; ' . . . ruins . . . ' – v, 9; 'ruins of a castle . . . ' – v, 154. (R)

Haringworth (Northamptonshire) ' . . . a right goodly manor place . . . built castle-like. The first court whereof is clean down saving that a great piece of the gatehouse . . . yet standith. The inner part of this place is meetly well maintained and hath a ditch about it . . . ' – i, 13. (D)

Harptree (Richmont) (Somerset) ' . . . clean down . . . There standith yet a piece of the dungeon . . . ' – v, 85; ' . . . was a goodly castle . . . now defaced to the hard ground . . . ' – v, 107. (R)

Hartlebury (Worcestershire) Good condition implied – ii, 89. (N)

Hay on Wye (Powys) 'sometime hath been right stately . . . ' – iii, 111. (D?)

Hedon (Yorkshire) 'tokens of a pile or castle . . . ' – i, 61. (R)

Heighley (Staffordshire) 'The tenants of Audeley come to this castle' – v, 20. (N?)

Helston (Cornwall) 'There hath been a castle' – i, 194; '*vestigia castelli*' – i, 321. (R)

Hemyock (Devon) 'is down saving a 2 or 3 towers . . . ' – iv, 74. (R)

Hereford 'now the whole castle tendith towards ruin. It hath been one of the fairest, largest and strongest castles of England . . . There was a great bridge of stone arches . . . now clean down . . . ' – ii, 64–5. (D)

Higham Ferrers (Northamptonshire) 'now of late clean fallen and taken down . . . ' – iv, 22. (R)

Hinckley (Leicestershire) 'ruins of the castle' – i, 21. (R)

Hinderskelfe (Yorkshire) [A vanished village nr Castle Howard; see M. Beresford and J. Hurst, *Deserted Medieval Villages* (London, 1971) 46, 47, 210.] 'a fair quadrant of stone having 4 towers built castle-like but it is no ample thing' – i, 65. (N)

Holt (Clwyd) 'a goodly castle' – iii, 69. (N)

Hope (Clwyd) 'There stand yet great walls of a castle set on a hill . . . ' – iii, 73. (R)

Hornby (Yorkshire) 'chiefest house of Lord Conyers' – iv, 26; 'there is his usual dwelling' – iv, 33. (N)

Kenfig (Glamorgan) 'in ruin and almost choked and devoured with the sands that the Severn Sea there castith up . . . ' – iii, 29. (R)

Kenilworth (Warwickshire) 'King Henry 8 did of late years great cost in repairing the castle of Kenilworth' – ii, 109. (N)

Kidwelly (Dyfed) 'meetly well kept up' – iii, 59. (N)

Killerby (Yorkshire, North Riding) 'ruin' – iv, 26. (R)

Kilpeck (Herefordshire) 'some ruins of the walls yet stand' – v, 185. (R)

Kimbolton (Cambridgeshire) 'double dyked, and the building of it meetly strong . . . new fair lodgings and galleries upon the old foundations of the castle' – i, 2. (N)

Kingsland (Herefordshire) 'the ditches whereof and a part of the keep be yet seen' – ii, 75. (R)

Knaresborough (Yorkshire) 'the castle standith magnificently and strongly on a rock'. – i, 86. (N?)

Knockin (Salop, now Shropshire) 'a ruinous thing' – v, 14. (R)

Lancaster 'strongly built and well repaired' – iv, 11. (N)

Launceston (Cornwall) 'Much of this castle yet standith . . . ' – i, 174. (D?)

Leicester 'at this time a thing of small estimation: and there is no appearance either of high walls or dikes. So that I think that the lodgings that now be there were made since the time of the Barons' War in Henry the 3's time . . . ' – i, 15. (N?)

Lichfield (Staffordshire) 'There hath been a castle of ancient time . . . but no part of it standith . . . ' – ii, 99; 'in old time had a castle. There is a causeway through the pool to the castle . . . ' – v, 19. (R)

Liskeard (Cornwall) 'There was a castle . . . It is now all in ruin. Fragments and pieces of walls yet stand . . . ' – i, 208. (R)

Little Harle (Northumberland) 'a fair castle' – v, 65. (N?)

Llanblethian (Glamorgan) 'yet partly standing . . . kept as a prison' – iii, 31. (D)

Llanmaes (Glamorgan) 'almost all down' – iii, 27. (R)

Llantrisant (Glamorgan) 'is in ruin . . . It hath been a fair castle . . . and at this castle is the prison' – iii, 21. (R)

Ludgershall (Wiltshire) 'sometime a castle in Wiltshire . . . stood in a park, now clean down . . . a pretty lodge made by ruins of it' – v, 6. (R)

Ludlow (Shropshire) 'a fair castle' – iii, 50. (N)

Maidstone (Kent) 'Well maintained by the Archbishop of Canterbury' – iv, 47. (N)

Malton (Yorkshire) 'hath been large, as it appearith by the ruin. There is at this time no habitation in it, but a mean house for a farmer' – i, 57. (R)

Manorbier (Dyfed) 'ruins . . . many walls yet standing whole do openly appear' – iii, 61. (R)

Marlborough (Wiltshire) 'The dungeon half standith' – iv, 130; 'ruin of a great castle . . . whereof the dungeon tower partly yet standith . . . ' – v, 80. (R)

Maxey (Northamptonshire) 'the ruin of a castle' – v, 32. (R)

Melbourne (Derbyshire) ' . . . pretty and in meetly good reparation . . . ' – i, 21. (N)

Merdon (Hampshire) 'some small ruins or tokens yet remain . . . ' – i, 275. (R)

Mere (Cheshire) 'The ditches and the plot where the castle of Mere stood . . . ' – v, 223. (R)

Middleham (Yorkshire) 'All the outer part of the castle was of the very new setting of Lord Neville . . . The inner part . . . of an ancient building of the FitzRandolf' – i, 79; 'the fairest castle of Richmondshire next Bolton' – iv, 26. (N)

Middleton Stoney (Oxfordshire) 'Some pieces of the walls of it yet a little appear; but almost the whole site of it is overgrown with bushes' – ii, 35. (R)

Mitford (Northumberland) 'Ruins' – v, 63. (R)

Montgomery (Powys) 'now a late re-edified' – iii, 11. (N)

Morlais (Glamorgan) 'in ruin' – iii, 18. (R)

Moreton Corbet (Salop, now Shropshire) 'a fair castle of Mr Corbet's – iv, 1. (N)

Morpeth (Northumberland) 'fair castle . . . well maintained' – v, 63. (N)

Moulton (**Quapelode**) (Lincolnshire) 'castle in the fen . . . whereof some small part yet standith' – ii, 147. (R)

Mulgrave (Yorkshire) Good condition implied – i, 59. (N?)

Myddle (Salop, now Shropshire) 'very ruinous' – v, 13. (R)

Nappa (**Hall or Castle**) (Yorkshire) 'goodly house' – iv, 27; 'the head house of the Metcalfs' – iv, 33; 'in the which building 2 towers be very fair, besides other lodgings' – iv, 86. (N)

Narberth (Dyfed) 'a little pretty pile of old Sir Rhys's' – iii, 62. (N)

Newcastle Emlyn (Dyfed) 'repaired or new built by Sir Rhys ap Thomas' – iii, 57. (N)

Newcastle under Lyme (Staffordshire) 'All the castle is down save one great tower' – v, 19. (R)

Newhall Tower (Cheshire) 'now down' – v, 25. (R)

Newport (Gwent) 'A very fair castle' – iii, 45. (N)

New Radnor (Powys) 'in ruin, but that a piece of the gate was late amended. The town was defaced in Henry the fourth's days by Owain Glyndwr' – iii, 10. (R)

Northallerton (Yorkshire) 'Bishop of Durham's Palace . . . 2 flight shots west north west from it be ditches where the castle of Alverton sometime stood. No part of the walls thereof now appearith' – i, 67. (R)

Northampton 'The castle standith hard by the West gate and hath a large keep. The area of the residue is very large . . . ' – i, 7. (N?)

Nottingham 'much part of the west side of this inner ward as the hall and other things be in ruins. The east side is strong and well towered, and so is the south side. But the most beautifullest part and gallant building for lodging is on the north side, where Edward the 4 began a right sumptuous piece of stonework, of which he clearly finished one excellent goodly tower . . . ' – i, 95. (D)

Nunney (Somerset) 'pretty castle . . . the walls be very strong and thick, the stairs narrow, the lodging within somewhat dark . . . ' – v, 97. (N)

Odell (Bedfordshire) 'now nothing but strange ruins' – v, 8. (R)

Ogmore (Glamorgan) 'is meetly well maintained' – iii, 28. (N)

Old Sarum (Wiltshire) 'There was a right fair and strong castle within Old Salisbury . . . Much notable ruinous building of this castle yet there remainith' – i, 261. (R)

Owston (Lincolnshire) 'There was a castle at the south side of the church garth' – i, 37. (R)

Oystermouth (Glamorgan) 'remain ruins of a castle destroyed by Prince Llywelyn' – iii, 127. (R)

Pembroke (Dyfed) 'large and strong' – iii, 116. (N)

Pendragon (Westmorland) 'there standith yet much of this castle' – v, 146. (R)

Penllyn (Glamorgan) 'yet standith' – iii, 32. (R)

Penrith (Cumbria) 'a strong castle of the king's' – v, 54. (N)

Pentyrch (Glamorgan) 'some tokens of buildings yet remained' – iii, 21. (R)

Peterston (Glamorgan) 'almost all in ruin' – iii, 26. (R)

Pickering (Yorkshire) 'The castle walls and towers be meetly well, the lodgings in the inner court that be of timber be in ruin; in this inner court is a chapel and a chantry priest' – i, 63. (D)

Plymouth (Devon) 'on a rocky hill hard by it is a strong castle quadrate having at each corner a great round tower. It seemith to be no very old piece of work' – i, 214. (N)

Plympton (Devon) 'a fair large castle and dungeon in it, whereof the walls yet stand, but the lodgings within be decayed' – i, 216. (D)

Pontefract (Yorkshire) 'containith 8 towers of which the dungeon cast into 6 roundels, 3 big and 3 small, is very fair . . .' – i, 39; 'a very fair castle' – iv, 13. (N)

Pontesbury (Salop, now Shropshire) 'certain ruins of a castle' – ii, 26. (R)

Powderham (Devon) 'it is strong and hath a barbican' – i, 232. (N)

Quatford (Salop, now Shropshire) 'great tokens' – ii, 86. (R)

Raby (Durham) 'Raby is the largest castle of lodgings in all the north country . . .' – i, 75. (N)

Raglan (Gwent) 'a very fair and pleasant castle' – iii, 45. (N)

Ravensworth (Yorkshire) 'excepting 2 or 3 square towers . . . nothing memorable in it' – i, 79; 'the Lord Parr is owner thereof . . .' – iv, 27. (N?)

Red Castle (Salop, now Shropshire) 'now all ruinous' – v, 13. (R)

Restormel (Cornwall) ' . . . the base court is sore defaced. The fair, large dungeon yet standith. A chapel cast out of it, a newer work than it, and now unroofed' – i, 205. (R)

Richard's Castle (Herefordshire) 'The keep, the walls and towers of it yet stand but going to ruin. There is a poor house of timber in the castle garth for a farmer' – ii, 76. (R)

Richmond (Yorkshire) 'in mere ruin' – iv, 25. (R)

Rochester (Kent) No comment on condition – good? – iv, 45. (N?)

Rockingham (Northamptonshire) 'The outer walls of it yet stand. The keep is exceeding fair . . . The lodgings . . . be discovered and fall to ruin' – i, 12; 'fallith to ruin' – iv, 21. (D)

Rose (Cumbria) 'a castle of the Bishops of Carlisle . . . Bishop Knight made it fresh' – v, 56. (N)

Rotherfield Grey (Oxfordshire) 'entering into the manor place on the right hand 3 or 4 very old towers of stone, a manifest token that it was sometime a castle. There is a very large court built about with timber and spaced with brick; but this is of later work . . . by attainder it came by gift to Knolls' – v, 72. (N)

Ruan Lanihorne (Cornwall) 'a castle of 7 towers, now decaying for lack of coverture . . .' – i, 99. (D)

St Clears (Dyfed) 'ruins' – iii, 57. (R(

St Donats (Glamorgan) Active use implied – iii, 27. (N)

St Fagans (Glamorgan) 'a part of it yet standith' – iii, 25. (R)

St Georges (Glamorgan) 'The castle is now the king's: and one Roger Herbert a bastard dwellith in it' – iii, 26. (N?)

Sandal (Yorkshire) 'a very pretty castelet on an hilling ground with a ditch about it . . .' – i, 40. (N)

Scarborough (Yorkshire) ' . . . an exceedingly goodly, large and strong castle . . . Without the first area is a great green . . . and in it is a chapel, and, beside, old walls of houses of office that stood there . . .' – i, 60. (N)

Sherborne (Dorset) 'There be few pieces of work in England of the antiquity of this that standith so whole and so well couched' – i, 154. (N)

Sherriff Hutton (Yorkshire) ' . . . I saw no house in the north so like a princely lodgings . . . The castle was well maintained by reason that the late Duke of Norfolk lay there x years, and since the Duke of Richmond' – i, 65. (N)

Shrewsbury (Salop, now Shropshire) 'now much in ruin' – ii, 82. (R)

Skenfrith (Gwent) 'Much of the outer ward of this castle yet standith' – ii, 70. (R)

Sleaford (Lincolnshire) 'very well main-tained' – i, 26; 'The ornament of it is the Bishop of Lincoln's castle . . .' – v, 32. (N)

Snape (Yorkshire) 'a goodly castle' – iv, 26. (N)

Snodhill (Herefordshire) 'somewhat in ruin' – v, 176. (R)

Southampton (Hampshire) 'The glory of the castle is in the dungeon, that is both large, fair and very strong, both by work and the site of it' – i, 277. (N?)

Stoke under Hambdon (Somerset) 'very notable ruins of a great manor place or castle . . .' – i, 158; v, 84–5. (R)

Sturminster Newton (Dorset) 'The castle since clearly decayed and the Abbots of Glastonbury made there a fair manor place' – v, 107. (D)

Sudeley (Gloucestershire) 'Now it goith to ruin, more pity' – ii, 56. (D)

Tadcaster (Yorkshire) 'A mighty great hill, ditches and garth of this castle on Wharfe be yet seen' – i, 44. (R)

Talyfan (Glamorgan) 'clearly in ruin' – iii, 33. (R)

Tamworth (Staffordshire) 'The base court and great ward of the castle is clean decayed and the walls fallen down, therein be now but houses of office of no notable building. The dungeon hill yet standith, and a great round tower of stone on it, wherein Mr Ferrars dwellith, and now repairith' – ii, 105. (D)

Tarsett (Cumbria) 'ruins' – v, 58. (R)

Tetbury (Gloucestershire) 'It is now over-grown with trees and bushes of juniper' – iv, 135. (R)

Tewkesbury (**Holm**) (Gloucestershire) 'some ruins of the bottoms of walls appear' – iv, 137. (R)

Thirsk (Yorkshire) 'At Thirsk was a great castle' – i, 67. (R)

Thornbury (Gloucestershire) 'Edward, late Duke of Buckingham . . . pulled down a great part of the old house and set up magnificently in good square stone the south side of it . . . in the year of our Lord God 1511 . . . The foundation of a very spacious base court was there begun and certain gates and towers in it castle-like. It is of a iiii or v yards high, and so remainith a token of a noble piece of work purposed' – v, 100. (D)

Thorne (Yorkshire) 'a pretty pile or castelet well ditched . . .' – i, 36. (N)

Thorpe Waterville (Northamptonshire) 'the ruins of the outer wall of Waterville's castle' – i, 6. (R)

Thurnam (**Goddard's Castle**) (Kent) '. . . the ruins of a castle' – ii, 30; 'now all clean in ruin' – iv, 46. (R)

Tickhill (Yorkshire) 'The dungeon is the fairest part of the castle. All the buildings within the area be down, saving an old

hall . . .' – i, 35; 'a ruinous castle' – iv, 15. (R)

Tintagel (Cornwall) '. . . hath been a marvellous strong and notable fortress . . . sheep now feed within the dungeon. The residue of the buildings of the castle be sore weatherbeaten and in ruin . . .' – i, 177. (R)

Tong (Shropshire) 'There was an old castle of stone . . . Sir Henry Vernon a late days made the castle new of brick' – v, 16. (N)

Tonge (Kent) 'the ditches and ruins of this castle yet appear' – iv, 68. (R)

Torrington (Devon) 'a fair castle . . . of the which at this present nothing remainith standing but a neglected chapel' – i, 173. (R)

Totnes (Devon) '. . . The castle wall and the strong dungeon be maintained. The lodgings of the castle be clean in ruin . . .' – i, 218. (D)

Trecastle (Powys) 'ruins' – iii, 112. (R)

Tredine (Cornwall) 'ruins . . . *manifesta adhuc exstant vestigia*' – i, 89. (R)

Tretower (Powys) 'a pretty castle longing now to the king, and thereby also in the village is a fair place of Henry Vehan Esquier' – iii, 108. (N?)

Trowbridge (Wiltshire) 'now clean down. There was in it 7 great towers, whereof pieces of 2 yet stand' – i, 137. (R)

Trematon (Cornwall) '. . . whereof great pieces yet stand and especially the dungeon. The ruins now serve for a prison.' – i, 210. (R)

Truro (Cornwall) '. . . now clean down. The site thereof is now used for a shooting and playing place' – i, 198. (R)

Tynboeth (Powys) 'great ruins' – iii, 11. (R)

Usk (Gwent) 'hath been great, strong and fair' – iii, 44. (D?)

Wakefield (Yorkshire) 'dykes and bulwarks . . . whereby it appearith that there hath been a castle' – v, 38. (R)

Wallingford (Berkshire) 'hath 3 dykes, large and deep . . . About each of the 2 first dykes as upon the crests of the ground cast out of them runnith an embattled wall now sore in ruin, and for the most part defaced. All the goodly building with the towers and dungeon be within the 3 dykes.' – i, 119. (D)

Wallington (Northumberland) 'chiefest house of the Fenwicks . . .' – v, 65. (N)

Warwick 'magnificent and strong castle' – ii, 40; 'The east front hath 3 towers. The keep standith in ruins by west . . . The king now buildith strongly on the south side, and there is all the fair lodgings of the castle. King Richard the 3 began a strong piece for artillery on the north side of the castle' – v, 154. (N)

Warkworth (Northumberland) 'well maintained' – v, 64. (N)

Wells, Bishop's Palace at (Somerset) 'strongly walled and embattled castle-like . . . the hall of the palace is exceeding fair . . .' – i, 146. (N)

Welshpool (Powys) 'The Lord Dudley's part is almost fallen down. The Lord Powys part is meetly good' – iii, 53. (R/N)

Weobley (Herefordshire) 'somewhat in decay' – ii, 69. (D)

Wenvoe (Glamorgan) 'All the buildings . . . is down saving one tower and broken walls . . .' – iii, 23. (R)

West Tanfield (Yorkshire) 'longed to the Lord Marmion, and so came to the Fitzhugh' – iv, 27. (N?)

Whitwick (Leicestershire) 'the ruins' – i, 18. (R)

Winchcomb (Gloucestershire) 'There was a fortress or castle . . .' – ii, 54. (R)

Winchester (Hampshire) No comment on condition. – i, 270. (N?)

Worcester 'clean down and half the base court or area of it is now within the wall of the close' – ii, 90. (R)

Worksop (Nottinghamshire) 'clean down and scant known where it was' – i, 89; 'the stones of castle were fetched, as some say, to make the fair lodge in Worksop Park, not yet finished . . . But I am of the opinion that the canons had the ruins of the castle stones to make the closure of their large walls' – iv, 17. (R)

Wressell (Yorkshire) 'all of very fair and great squared stone . . . the house is one of the most proper beyond Trent and seemith as newly made . . .' – i, 52–3. (N)

Wrinstone (Glamorgan) 'all in ruin save one high tower . . .' – iii, 23. (R)

York 'There be a 5 ruinous towers in it. The arx is all in ruin' – i, 54. (R)

Parliamentary demolition, proposed or executed, 1642–60

Abergavenny (Wenny) (Gwent) *CJ*, 3/3/47, disgarrison and make indefensible; 19/7/47, adhere to vote to make indefensible. (? Substantial demolition)

Aberystwyth (Dyfed) *CJ*, 3/3/47, disgarrison and demolish; 19/7/47, adhere to vote; *CSPD*, 30/7/49, slight. (Demolished – blown up, J. C. Halliwell (ed.), *A Short Relation of a Journey . . . 1652* (London, 1859), 15)

Appleby (Cumbria) *CJ*, 3/3/47, disgarrison, slight and dismantle new works; 17/10/48 consider demolition; *Rushworth* (vi, 513), 16/10/48, County Committee order slighting.

Arnside Tower (Cumbria) *CJ*, 29/6/48, make untenable.

Ashby de la Zouch – town and castle (Leicestershire) *CSPD*, 28/2/46, 3 months allowed for slighting (? new works); 6/5/48, secure great tower; *CJ*, 25/11/48, forthwith slight and make untenable (Extensive demolition on tower and castle)

Aylesbury Town (Buckinghamshire) *CJ*, 11/7/46, garrison to be slighted and fortifications demolished.

Banbury (Oxfordshire) *CJ*, 2/3/47, disgarrison and slight new works; 19/7/47 agree same with Lords; *CSPD* 15/7/48, demolition delayed for want of money, Warwickshire and Northamptonshire to assist. (Demolished)

Basing House (Hampshire) *CJ*, 15/10/45, forthwith totally slight and demolish, materials free for those who fetch them. (Demolished)

Bath (Avon) *CSPD*, 29/5/46, slight works and fortifications.

Bedford Town *CJ*, 11/7/46, slight garrison; *CSPD*, 6/8/46, slight and demolish fortifications.

Belvoir (Leicestershire) *CJ*, 1/3/47, disgarrison and slight new works; 11/6/49,

pay Earl of Rutland £1,500 for demolition; *CSPD*, 3/4/49, to be demolished for safety of Commonwealth; 21/5/49, £1,500 paid to earl; 20/7/49, those appointed to view 'professing not to be soldiers' not certain whether sufficient done; 10/5/50, inspect and see if more work required. (Largely demolished)

Berkeley (Gloucestershire) *CSPD*, 25/11/45, as Lord Berkeley had suffered so much, no demolition or slighting; *CJ*, 28/7/46, slight garrison, works and gates and some parts of walls be slighted and thrown down. (Some demolition. *5th Report Historical Manuscripts Commission* (HMSO, 1876), 356–7)

Berwick-on-Tweed *CJ*, 28/12/46, local MPs to oversee slighting of fortifications; 31/12/46, ordnance and arms to be removed to Newcastle. (Re-garrisoned in 1648)

Betham House (Cumbria) *CJ*, 29/6/48, make untenable.

Beverston (Gloucestershire) *CJ*, 28/7/46, works, gates and parts of wall to be thrown down. (? Substantial demolition)

Bolingbroke (Lincolnshire) *CJ*, 1/3/47, disgarrison and make indefensible; 25/11/48, forthwith slight and make untenable. ('Demolished' – so described in a Survey in April 1654 *MA* x (1966) 156)

Bolsover (Derbyshire) *CJ*, 23/10/48, slight and disband forces; *CSPD*, 5/9/48, make untenable without unnecessary spoiling or defacing; 2/7/49, demolish outworks, garden wall, turrets, walls of frontier court, remove doors, window bars; 13/5/50, proceed with demolition. (Limited demolition carried out)

Bolton (Yorkshire) *CJ*, 30/4/46, make untenable; 26/2/47, disgarrison and make untenable; 13/7/47, adhere to decision. (Corner tower demolished in 1648 (*Rushworth*, vi, 513))

Boston Town (Lincolnshire)   *CJ*, 1/3/47, dis-garrison and slight new works.

Bridgwater (Somerset)   *CJ*, 14/8/46, garrison to be slighted and dismantled; 2/3/47, reconsider slighting; 19/7/47, slight new works.

Bristol (Avon)   *CJ*, 2/3/47, retain garrison at castle and great fort but disgarrison forts and works; 5/4/53, forthwith dismantle and disgarrison; *CSPD*, 15/4/53, Scotch and Irish Committee to consider order for demolition; 3/10/55, speaks of demolition as past event. (Castle demolished in 1653–5)

Broncroft (Shropshire)   *CJ*, 11/7/48, County Committee authorised to demolish and make untenable. (? Substantial demolition)

Burghley House (Northamptonshire, now Cambridgeshire)   *CSPD*, 20/4/46, proposal to disgarrison and slight fortifications.

Caernarfon (Gwynedd)   *CSPD*, 22/3/53, Irish and Scottish Committee to consider how garrison may be slighted.

Cambridge   *CJ*, 11/7/46, slight garrison; 13/7/47, slight new works about town and castle. (? Some demolition)

Cambridgeshire   *CJ*, 23/2/47, dismantle and slight all garrisons.

Canon Frome (Herefordshire)   *CSPD*, 15/4/46, proposal to abandon and slight. (? Some demolition)

Cardigan (Dyfed)   *CJ*, 3/3/47, disgarrison and demolish; 19/7/47, adhere to vote. (? Extensive demolition)

Carlisle (Cumbria)   *CSPD*, 6/7/45, in proposed new treaty with Scots new works be slighted; *CJ*, 26/12/46, gentlemen of county to oversee slighting of fortifications.

Carmarthen (Dyfed)   *CJ*, 25/3/47, disgarrison, slight and make untenable; 19/7/47, keep garrison of 100 men. (Some demolition, see *RCAHM, Carmarthen*, 251)

Caversham (Berkshire)   *The Diary of John Evelyn* (ed. E. S. de Beer, London, 1955, iii, 99), 8/6/54, '... my Lord Craven's house at Causam, now in ruins, his goodly woods felling by the rebels ...'

Cawood (Yorkshire)   *CJ*, 30/4/46, disgarrison and make untenable; 26/2/47, make untenable. (? Demolished)

Chichester Town (Sussex)   *CJ*, 2/3/47, disgarrison and demolish new fortifications.

Chirk (Clwyd)   *CJ*, 3/3/47, disgarrison and slight new works; 27/8/59, demolish and

make untenable; Maj. Gen. Lambert to see castle demolished and made untenable; *CSPD*, 27/8/59, same to arrange demolition. (Missing side of castle demolished. See chap. 8, n. 20)

Christchurch (Hampshire)   *CSPD*, 29/5/50, consider what further slighting required; 30/11/50, Governor of Southampton to oversee demolition (Mostly demolished)

Clitheroe (Lancashire)   *CSPD*, 27/3/49, Committee to consider demolition with Bolsover and 'such inland castles as they shall think fit'; *CSPD*, 6/4/49, to reduce to neither a charge nor a danger. (? Some demolition)

Cockermouth (Cumbria)   *CJ*, 13/7/47, disgarrison; *Rushworth* (vi, 513), 16/10/48, order to slight to Cumberland Committee.

Colchester Town and Castle (Essex)   *CSPD*, 11/6/49, walls and strengths to be demolished; 8/5/50, local militia to demolish strengths and fortifications; 25/3/51, dismantle, not yet dismantled; 5/7/51, certified, garrison to be dismissed. ('... now wretchedly demolished by the late siege ...' *Evelyn's Diary* (ed. de Beer, iii, 176) 8/7/56)

Conwy (Gwynedd)   *CSPD*, 22/3/53, Irish and Scottish Committee to consider how garrison may be slighted. (See p. 156 above)

Corfe (Dorset)   *CJ*, 5/3/46, to be demolished forthwith. (Largely demolished)

Coventry (W. Midlands)   *CJ*, 3/3/46, disgarrison and slight new works; 19/7/47, agree with Lords to omit slighting. (See p. 156 above)

Crayke (Yorkshire)   *CJ*, 26/2/47, disgarrison and make untenable; *CSPD*, 7/3/50, partially demolished, complete work.

Crowland Abbey (Lincolnshire)   *CSPD*, 16/8/59. Complete the unfinished demolition of former fortifications.

Cwmhir Abbey (Powys)   *CWPD*, 8/12/44. Col. Barnard forced to burn house, 'otherwise we could not render it unserviceable for the future'.

Dartmouth (Devon)   *CJ*, 25/2/47, disgarrison and slight new works around; *CSPD*, 26/3/50, slight new fort; 6/5/50, demolish fort, repair two blockhouses.

Dawley (Salop, now Shropshire)   *CJ*, 11/7/48, Shropshire Committee authorised to demolish and make untenable. (? Demolished)

Denbigh Castle (Clwyd) *CJ*, 3/3/47, disgarrison, demolish and slight works; 15/4/47, materials to go to Governor; 19/7/47, adhere to decision to demolish. (Extensive demolition in 1660 (see p. 156))

Devizes (Wiltshire) *CJ*, 4/5/46, forthwith slight Castle Hill and works.

Dockray Hall (Cumbria) *CJ*, 3/3/47, disgarrison, slight and dismantle works. (? Demolished)

Donnington (Berkshire) No order, but recorded as ruins in 1647, after siege. *VCH, Berks.*, iv. 193. (See fig. 96)

Dover (Kent) *CSPD*, 29/1/51, consider if fit to be slighted; 16/4/51, survey to see what necessary to render untenable; 7/8/51, £200 on repairs. (No action)

Dudley (Staffordshire) *CJ*, 4/8/46, forthwith dismantle; *CJ*, 2/3/47, make untenable; 19/3/47, adhere to vote to make untenable.

Dunster (Somerset) *CJ*, 17/11/46, disgarrison; *CSPD*, 25/3/51, garrison before making untenable; 27/5/51, owner to give undertaking not to allow enemy use. (Some demolition – H. C. Maxwell-Lyte, *Dunster and its Lords* (Exeter, 1882), 96–8)

Eccleshall (Staffordshire) *CJ*, 4/8/46, dismantle works and fortifications; 2/3/47, make untenable; 19/7/47, adhere to vote. (Extensive demolition)

Ely, Isle of (Cambridgeshire) *CJ*, 23/2/47, disgarrison and slight all garrisons and forts.

Exeter (Devon) *CSPD*, 5/5/52, consider disgarrisoning.

Farnham (Surrey) *CSPD*, 16/10/45, County wishes to slight; 27/10/45, order to demolish if it can be done safely; *CJ*, 4/7/48, put in condition of indefensibility; *CSPD*, 4 and 10/7/48, authority to Surrey Committee to demolish so as not to be defensible or tenable. (Some demolition)

Farringdon House (Hampshire) *CJ*, 23/2/47, works about to be slighted.

Flint (Clwyd) *CJ*, 22/12/46, disgarrison and slight; 3/3/46, disgarrison and demolish except for one tower used as prison; 19/7/47, adhere to former vote, disgarrison and demolish. (Extensive demolition – J. C. Halliwell (ed.), *A Short Relation of a Journey . . . 1652* (London, 1859) 10)

Gainsborough Town (Lincolnshire) *CSPD*, 2/11/44, Sir John Meldrum 'razed' defences.

Gloucester Town and Castle *CSPD*, 11/1/53, dismantling of garrison; 22/3/53, Irish and Scottish Committee consider how it may be slighted; *Evelyn's Diary* (ed. de Beer, iii, 118), 31/7/54, ' . . . the Duke's House, Castle, works, now almost quite dismantled . . . ' (Some demolition, see also p. 156)

Goodrich (Herefordshire and Worcestershire) *CJ*, 25/8/46, need to demolish and compensate Countess of Kent; 1/3/47, totally disgarrison and slight; 19/7/47, agree with Lords to disgarrison and slight new works; *CSPD*, 6/7/49, allow £1,000 compensation to Countess of Kent. (Some demolition)

Harlech (Gwynedd) *CJ*, 3/3/47, disgarrison and demolish; 19/7/47, adhere to previous vote. (? Demolition of outer curtain and entry – E. Breeze, *Kalendars of Gwynedd* (1873) 18)

Hartlepool Town (Cleveland) *CJ*, 26/2/47, slight new works and disgarrison.

Haverfordwest (Dyfed) *CJ*, 25/3/47, disgarrison, slight works and make untenable. (Some demolition)

Hawarden (Clwyd) *CJ*, 3/3/47, disgarrison and demolish; 19/7/47, adhere to vote; *CSPD*, 30/7/49, consider demolition with Holt. (Extensive demolition)

Helmsley (Yorkshire) *CJ*, 30/4/46, make untenable; 26/2/47, disgarrison and make untenable; 13/7/47, adhere to vote; *Rushworth* (vi, 513), Oct. 1648, Committee of York order to be slighted. (Demolition on keep and curtain)

Herbert's Isle (**Derwentwater**) (Cumbria) *CJ*, 23/2/47, disgarrison and slight new works.

Hereford *CJ*, 1/3/47, disgarrison town, slight new works but maintain garrison of 160 men in castle. (? Some demolition – J. Price, *An Historical Account of the City of Hereford* (1798), 51–4)

High Ercall House (Salop, now Shropshire) *CSPD*, 6/4/46, instruction to County Committee not to demolish but slight and drain moat. ' . . . neither do we think fit that all houses whose situation or strength render them capable of being garrisons should be pulled down. There would be then too many sad marks left of the calamity of this war . . . ' (? Some demolition)

Highworth House (Wiltshire) *CJ*, 14/8/46, slight and dismantle.

Hillesden House (Buckinghamshire) *CJ*, 7/3/44, should they slight or garrison after capture?

Holmsdale (Surrey) *CSPD*, 17/7/48, no need for garrison if they make indefensible which they should execute.

Holt (Clwyd) *CJ*, 3/3/47, disgarrison and totally demolish; 19/7/47, adhere to decision; *CSPD*, 15/3/52, Earl of Bridgewater to give surety of £4,000 that neither he nor purchaser will use it to prejudice of Parliament, or he can demolish and retain materials. (Not demolished then)

Huntingdon Town (Cambridgeshire) *CJ*, 11/7/46, slight garrison; *CSPD*, 6/8/46, slight and demolish fortifications and disgarrison.

Kenilworth (Warwickshire) *CSPD*, 13/7/49, forthwith demolish; 21/7/49, make untenable with as little harm to dwelling house as possible; 24/7/49, take down Caesar's Tower and outer ward, but greatness of windows makes it unnecessary to harm house; 28/8/49, petition of Earl of Monmouth for materials; 16/10/49, County Committee to carry out work with all expedition. (N. side of keep and N. curtain demolished)

King's Lynn (Norfolk) *CJ*, 1/3/47, maintain garrison of 500 men; *CSPD*, 15/4/53, petition not to demolish blockhouse at Douce Hills.

Knaresborough (Yorkshire) *CJ*, 30/4/46, 'being inland castle be made untenable'; 26/2/47, disgarrison and make untenable; *Rushworth* (vi, 513), 16/10/48, County Committeee order slighting. (Substantial demolition)

Lancaster *CJ*, 1/3/47, disgarrison and slight new works; 1/7/48, gentlemen of county to consider what garrison necessary; *CSPD*, 18/6/49, demolish except parts used as gaol; 10/7/49, no obedience from Governor; 24/7/49, order to Deputy Governor after obstruction by Governor; 15/3/51, not yet untenable; 3/6/51, view to see if untenable.

Langford House (Wiltshire) *CJ*, 4/5/56, works about it to be slighted.

Lathom House (Lancashire) *CJ*, 4/5/56, House approve what County has done to demolish; 19/7/47, adhere to former vote. (Demolished)

Lechlade (Gloucestershire) *CJ*, 28/7/46, slight garrison.

Leeds (Castle) (Kent) *CSPD*, 8/5/50, if not used for magazine, should it be made untenable? (? Some demolition)

Leicester *CJ*, 19/7/47, disgarrison and slight new works.

Leicestershire *CJ*, 1/3/47, garrisons of county to be disgarrisoned and slighted.

Lichfield Close (Staffordshire) *CJ*, 4/8/46, works and walls to be demolished; 2/3/47, make untenable forthwith; 19/7/47, dismantle walls.

Liverpool (Merseyside) *CJ*, 1/3/47, keep garrison of 600 men; 4/7/59, the castle of Liverpool and the walls thereof be demolished and towers made untenable; 19/7/59, a 'Bill' for demolishing Liverpool Castle receives first and second reading; 22/7/59, 'Bill' read third time and passed. (? Demolished)

London *LJ*, 2/9/47, Ordinance to slight works and lines of communication around London; 6/9/47, militia to put order into execution; 9/9/47, slight and demolish forts and lines of communication, adjoining householders to assist, materials being sold to contribute towards cost.

Ludlow (Salop, now Shropshire) *CJ*, 25/2/47, castle to be disgarrisoned and new works slighted. County Committee to make certain that castle and town are untenable; *CSPD*, 22/3/53, Irish and Scottish Committee to consider how garrison may be slighted.

Lulworth (Dorset) *CSPD*, 21/6/49, consider whether fit to be demolished.

Lyme Regis Town (Dorset) *CJ*, 14/8/46, forthwith slight and dismantle works; 26/2/47, disgarrison and slight; 13/7/47, dismantle new works and disgarrison.

Malmesbury Town (Wiltshire) *CJ*, 14/8/46, forthwith slight and dismantle.

Martin Abbey (Surrey) *CJ*, 4/7/48, make indefensible; *CSPD*, 10/7/48, render indefensible.

Matchfield House (Worcestershire) *CSPD*, 6/6/50, consider whether fit to demolish; 11/6/50, survey and consider loss to owner; 19/4/51, is it untenable?; 5/5/51, militia commissioners to make sure it is untenable.

Maxstoke (Warwickshire) *CSPD*, 20/11/51, owner to give surety of £2,000 that castle will not be used or possessed by enemy.

Mersea, Isle of (Essex) *CJ*, 26/2/47, demolish and disgarrison blockhouse in; *CSPD*, 20/10/55, Protector orders Governor to demolish fort.

Middleham (Yorkshire) *CJ*, 30/4/46, 'being inland castle' make untenable; 26/2/47, disgarrison and make untenable; 13/7/47, adhere to decision. (? Some demolition)

Monmouth (Gwent) *CJ*, 1/3/47, disgarrison and slight works; 19/7/47, agree with Lords to disgarrison and slight and dismantle works made since the troubles.

Montgomery (Powys) *CJ*, 11/6/49, totally demolish and compensate Lord Herbert by adjusting delinquency fine; *CSPD*, 11/6/49, confirm demolition; 15/6/49, warrant to demolish; 16/6/49, commission for demolition; 29/9/49, materials to be sold for paying costs; 19/1/50, allow Lord Herbert £1,611/10/– still unpaid of delinquency fine for compensation. (Largely demolished, see Appendix 4)

Mulgrave (Yorkshire) *CJ*, 30/4/46, make untenable; 19/7/47, disgarrison and slight new works; *Rushworth* (v, 513), Oct. 1648, County Committee order slighting; *CSPD*, 31/12/50, view to see if untenable; 6/3/51, militia commission to render untenable and certify; 7/3/51, appointees; 8/3/51, County to assist; 7/6/51, additional appointee. (Extensively demolished)

Nantwich Town (Cheshire) *CJ*, 23/2/47, disgarrison, dismantle and slight; 13/7/47, disgarrison and slight new works.

Newark Castle and Town (Nottinghamshire) *CJ*, 28/4/46, when captured fortifications will be slighted and castle made untenable; 1/3/47, disgarrison fort at river, slight and dismantle. (Some demolition – C. J. Morris (ed.), *The Journeys of Celia Fiennes* (London 1947), 71. In 1697 'then demolished so that only the ruinated walls remaine')

Newcastle Emlyn (Dyfed) *CJ*, 3/3/47. Speaker to discuss with owner what assurance he can give that it will not be used against Parliament. (? Demolition)

Newcastle upon Tyne *CSPD*, 13/9/55. Petition for materials if Council think fit to demolish.

Newport Pagnell (Buckinghamshire) *CJ*, 11/7/46, slight garrison; 28/1/47, E. Association Committee to take care to slight effectually.

Northampton Town *CJ*, 1/3/47, disgarrison and slight new works.

Nottingham Castle and Town *CJ*, 1/3/47, disgarrison town and slight works, keep garrison in castle; *CSPD*, 9/5/51, castle to be demolished and troop of dragoons sent

to do it; 9/6/51, report approved and orders issued, Governor, Mayor etc. to start within 14 days and castle, all outworks and fortifications to be demolished before 10/11/51; 10/6/51, remove ordnance, arms etc. (Demolished. *Memoirs of Life of Colonel Hutchinson* (ed. J. Sutherland, p. 203 'speedily executed'; *Evelyn's Diary*, ed. de Beer, 14/8/54, '. . . reliques of an ancient castle . . . ')

Oxford *CJ*, 2/3/47, disgarrison, slight and dismantle new works; *CSPD*, 8/9/51, 'citadel' and works to be wholly slighted. (Some demolition)

Pembridge (Herefordshire and Worcestershire) *CSPD*, 15/4/46, proposal to slight and abandon.

Plymouth (Devon) *CJ*, 18/2/48, continue garrison, but demolish works about Plymouth; *CSPD*, 6/4/49, demolish fortifications.

Pontefract (Yorkshire) *CJ*, 30/4/46, maintain garrison of 100 men; 26/2/47, after two votes House decides it shall be made untenable; 14/4/47, prayer for £500 to be spent on repairs; 27/3/49, forthwith totally demolish; *CSPD*, 7/8/49, deliver timber from Pontefract Castle for repairs at Hull. (Demolished. *Evelyn's Diary* (ed. de Beer, iii, 127), 16/8/54, 'was now demolishing by the rebels . . .'; R. Holmes, *The Sieges of Pontefract Castle* (Pontefract, 1887) 328–32)

Powis Castle (Powys) *See* Red Castle.

Raby (Durham) *CJ*, 26/2/47, slight new works and disgarrison.

Raglan (Gwent) *CJ*, 25/8/46 ' . . . the Castle of Ragland, the works about it, and the House and Buildings thereof, be forthwith pulled down and demolished . . . Committee of the County of Monmouth to take care that the same be totally demolished and all materials thereof sold and disposed of for the best advantage of the State deducting the charges for pulling it down.' (Extensive demolition of keep, walls etc.)

Red Castle (Powis Castle, Powys) *CSPD*, 22/3/53, Irish and Scottish Committee to consider how garrison may be slighted. (Outworks demolished, walls breached by order 28/4/60, *10th Report Historical Manuscripts Commission* (1885), App. iv, 395)

Reigate (Surrey) *CSPD*, 10/7/48, render indefensible. (? Partial demolition)

Rhuddlan (Clwyd) *CJ*, 22/12/46, disgarrison and slight; 3/3/47, disgarrison and demolish; 19/7/47, disgarrison and demolish. (? Outer curtain and gates demolished: J. C. Halliwell (ed.), *A Short Relation of a Journey . . . 1652* (London, 1859), 12)

Rockingham (Northamptonshire) *CSPD*, 4/5/46, slight and render untenable but do not demolish or spoil house; *CJ*, 11/11/46, slight works and make untenable forthwith. (? Some demolition)

Rose (Cumberland) *CJ*, 23/2/47, disgarrison and slight new works. (? Some demolition)

Ruthin (Clwyd) *CJ*, 22/12/46, disgarrison and slight; 3/3/47, disgarrison and demolish; 19/7/47, disgarrison and slight new works. (? Some demolition)

Salcombe Fort (Devon) *CJ*, 25/2/47, disgarrison and slight.

Sandal (Yorkshire) *CJ*, 30/4/46, make untenable.

Scarborough (Yorkshire) *CSPD*, 13/7/49, to be demolished but new platform to defend harbour; 9/5/51, to be demolished; 9/5/51, company of foot from Hull to be sent to demolish; 12/6/51, referred back, all former orders suspended; *CJ*, 5/12/51, modest garrison agreed. (Partial demolition of keep and ? curtain)

Sheffield (Yorkshire) *CJ*, 30/4/46, make untenable; 26/2/47, new works to be demolished and house made untenable; 13/7/47, confirmed; *Rushworth* (vi, 513), 16/10/48, York Committee order slighting. (? Demolished partially)

Sherborne (Dorset) *CJ*, 27/9/42, Earl of Bedford to raze to the ground; 24/10/42, Dep. Lieutenant forthwith to demolish; 1/11/42, authority to sell lead, iron, boards; *Rushworth* (v, 536–7), 15/8/45, stormed after mining, and slighting ordered. (Extensively damaged)

Sherborne House (Dorset) *CJ*, 2/3/47, disgarrison, slight works and make indefensible.

Shrewsbury Town (Shropshire) *CJ*, retain castle garrison but slight north works.

Shropshire C. H. Firth and R. S. Rait, *Acts and Ordinances of the Interregnum, 1642–60* (HMSO, 1911), 13/8/46, disband all garrisons except Shrewsbury and Ludlow.

Skipton (Yorkshire) *CJ*, 27/2/47, disgarrison and make untenable. (Some demolition)

Southampton Town (Hampshire) *CJ*, 2/3/47, disgarrison and slight new works.

Stafford Castle *CSPD*, 22/3/53, Irish and Scottish Committee to consider how garrison may be slighted; 11/4/53, stop disgarrisoning.

Sterborough (Surrey) *CJ*, 4/7/48, make indefensible; *CSPD*, 30/6/48, garrison; 4/7/48, render untenable; 10/7/48, make indefensible; 17/7/48, now demolish. (Largely demolished)

Stockton on Tees (Cleveland) *CJ*, 26/2/47, make untenable, slight works and disgarrison; 13/7/47, agree with Lords that works made since the troubles be slighted and dismantled.

Sudeley (Gloucestershire) *CSPD*, 6/1/46, great damage done by breaking down wainscotting, to be stopped; *CJ*, 28/7/46, garrison to be presently slighted; *CSPD*, 19/5/48, withdraw after making untenable; 15/11/48, so far to slight to render it incapable of being held by an enemy; 6/4/49, still not untenable; 16/4/49, 14 days allowed to start unfortifying; 24/4/49, certificate of demolition required; 29/9/49, work approved; 21/3/50, consider compensation; 6/6/50, further inquiry. (Extensive demolition)

Swansea (Glamorgan) *CJ*, 3/3/47, disgarrison and slight works.

Tamworth (Staffordshire) *CSPD*, 13/7/49, forthwith demolish. (Extensive demolition)

Tattershall (Lincolnshire) *CSPD*, 4/4/49, brick keep to be demolished by Earl of Lincoln who can keep materials; 27/4/49, Earl wants to remove just floors and roof but Council of State from 'many experiences in the late war' want tower demolished; *CJ*, 20/6/49, Council report that Earl deserves some compensation by analogy with Belvoir, and told to consider with Goodrich; *CSPD*, 21/8/49, approve Governor of Boston securing castle, and demolition of tower to start within 10 days; 29/9/49, demolition within a month; 12/10/49, nothing done; 17/11/49, JPs in area to assist Governor; 1/1/50, Governor to render untenable, up to £60 allowed; 4/3/50 inquiry into state of work; 25/3/50, pay £60 to Governor; 29/3/50, pay money to John Wincap; 25/1/53, is Earl of Lincoln entitled to compensation? (Tower still stands but were walls, gatehouse etc. demolished?)

Taunton (Somerset) *CJ*, 14/8/46, slight and

dismantle; 2/3/47, keep garrison in town and castle; *CSPD*, 13/10/51, make untenable with all speed; 27/10/51, refer to Committee; 30/10/51, proceed, charge to County, materials to owner; 14/11/51, demolish forthwith; 25/11/51, refer to Irish and Scottish Committee. (Demolition of keep and other parts)

Tewkesbury Town (Gloucestershire) *CJ*, 28/7/46, slight garrison.

Thurland (Lancashire) *CJ*, 18/11/43, approve Col. Rigby's action in demolition and will save him from indemnity. (Demolished)

Tickhill (Yorkshire) *CJ*, 30/4/46, 'being inland castle' make untenable; *CSPD*, 13/11/46, disgarrison. (? Demolition of keep and other parts)

Tutbury (Staffordshire) *CJ*, 2/3/47, make untenable; 19/7/47, adhere to vote. (? Some demolition. For demolition see *Guide* by Sir R. Somerville (1960) p. 12)

Wallingford (Berkshire) *CJ*, 23/2/47, slight and dismantle; 13/7/47, slight all works since the troubles; *CSPD*, 17/11/52, to be demolished and works effectually slighted; *VCH, Berks.*, iii, 530, 30/3/58, cost of demolition £450/5/8, and sale of materials yielded £516/17/11. (Demolished)

Wareham (Dorset) *CJ*, 5/3/46, slight garrison forthwith.

Winchester (Hampshire) *CSPD*, 11/6/49, consider how to make untenable without loss to owner; 11/9/49, engineer to be sent; 26/9/49, order to proceed according to engineer's advice; 29/5/49, £5 to engineer for report; 16/12/50, Governor of Southampton to summon County to demolish castle and wall about it; 30/12/50, proceed without delay; 13/1/51, proceed to demolition at charge of county; 21/2/51, not yet done but to be done within 14 days of assizes and certified; 28/3/51, work of making untenable started, if orders obeyed would have been done long ago. (Only the hall of the castle survives)

Windsor (Berkshire) *CJ*, 23/2/47, all new works about it to be slighted.

S. Wingfield Manor (Derbyshire) *CJ*, 25/2/47, demolish new works and disgarrison house. (Tower and some parts partially demolished)

Worcester Town *CJ*, 3/3/47, disgarrison, slight new works, pull down forts, fill up ditch, pull down drawbridges; 19/7/47, agree with Lords to leave out page about making untenable; 19/3/51, in response to advice from Council of State forthwith make untenable. (? Extensive demolition)

Wressel (Humberside) *CJ*, 11/12/45, slight outworks and new fortifications; 26/2/47, disgarrison and make untenable; *CSPD*, 14/8/49, demolish and use materials to defray costs; 20/8/49, is total demolition necessary?; 21/8/49, only make untenable and retain living quarters; 24/8/49, Earl of Northumberland says he has ordered it to be done; 6/12/49, certificate to be sent to Earl; 25/2/50, to be demolished by 7/4/50 and Earl to do it. (Substantial demolition)

York *CJ*, 26/2/47, Clifford's Tower to be kept as garrison, but town disgarrisoned and new works slighted and demolished; 14/7/47, agreed with Lords.

Appendix 4

Demolition of Montgomery Castle, Powys, June to October 1649

The document selectively transcribed below is a daily account of expenditure on demolition at Montgomery Castle from June to October 1649, from the records at Powis Castle, used here by kind permission of the Trustees of the Powis Castle Estate. Mr J. K. Knight of the Welsh Office who drew my attention to it kindly sent me a photocopy of the original.

On the death of his father in 1648, Richard Lord Herbert of Chirbury (*c.* 1600–55), who was the second holder of the title, compounded for his estate (*DNB*, 954). Total demolition of Montgomery Castle was insisted upon by the Council of State in an order of 11 June 1649 but compensation for loss was to be allowed (*10th Report of the Historical MSS Commission*, App. iv, 395). In January 1650, £1,611/10/– was regarded as allowable of his unpaid delinquency fine against £4,000 estimated loss on the demolition (*CPCC* (HMSO, 1891), iv, 1682). Work was on a large scale during the four months, miners being employed and up to 150 labourers. The employment of craftsmen, as well as the entry 'watching materials' at the end leaves no doubt that material was being carefully taken down and stacked for re-sale or re-use. The profit, not recorded here, was probably substantial. The castle, which had been a royal foundation of 1223, consisted of three wards extending along a spur, the latest structure being a large brick building, the 'Black Hall', erected by the first Lord Herbert in 1622–5 (J. Knight, 'A Castle of the Welsh March, 1223–49', *Château Gaillard Report*, xi (1983), 169–74).

The account, measuring 18 by 29 cm, consists of a title page and sixteen pages of daily wage payments and weekly payments to Lord Herbert's staff acting as overseers. There is a total on each page (fig. 100) and ancillary expenses recorded at the end. This transcript covers the totals on each page with a number of full daily entries selected to show the mounting and then falling scale of work. Omission of one or more daily entries is indicated thus . . . The sharp reduction of wage rates from 17 September is evidently to be attributed to shorter daylight reducing the hours of work.

The full title (fig. 114) reads:

> A Booke of what
> Chargs the Right Honorable
> Richard Lord Herbert hath
> bene at, about and in the demo-
> lishinge of Montgomery Castle
> by order from the Commissioners
> Authorised from the Councill of
> State beginninge the 26 of
> June 1649.
>
> By Richard Thompson & Edward Allenn,
> Overseers of the same.

114 The titles on the cover of the booklet recording expenditure by the overseers of Lord Herbert on demolition at Montgomery Castle in June to October 1649.

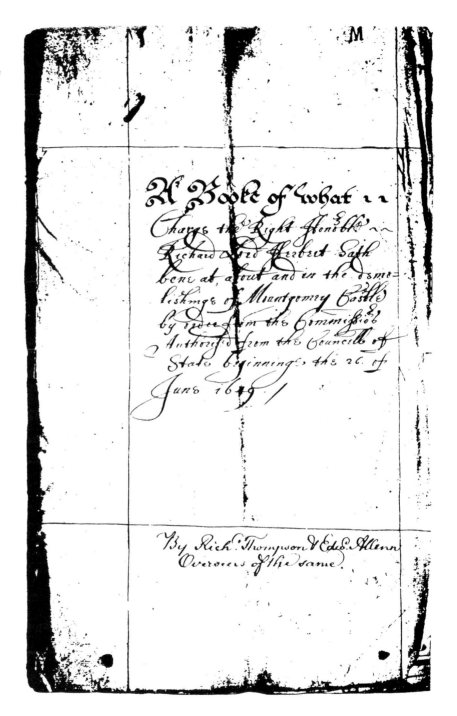

(p. 1)		£	s	d
June				
26	10 Carpenters at 2 s. 6d. per diem	01	05	00
1649	20 labourers at 12 d. per diem	01	00	00
	8 Masons at 1s. 6d. per diem	00	12	00
27	10 Carpenters	01	5	00
	8 Masons	00	12	00
	30 labourers—	01	10	00
29	10 Carpenters at 2 s. 6.d. per diem	01	05	00
	8 Masons at 1 s. 6 d. per diem	01	05	00
	30 labourers at 12 d. per diem	01	10	00
July				
10th, 1649	In 6 Carpenters at 2s 6d. per diem	00	15	00
	6 Masons at 1 s. 6 d. per diem	00	09	00
	14 Labourers at 12 d. per diem	00	14	00
July 11	12 Carpenters at 2 s. 6 d. per diem	1	10	00
	12 Masons at 1s. 6 d. per diem	00	18	00
	80 Labourers at 12 d. per diem	04	00	00
12th	12 Carpenters at 2 s. 6d. per diem	01	10	00
	12 Masons at 1 s. 6 d. per diem	00	18	00
	120 Labourers at 12 d. per diem	06	00	00
13th	12 Carpenters at 2 s. 6 d per diem	01	10	00
	12 Masons at 1 s. 6 d. per diem	00	18	00
	150 Labourers—	07	10	00
14th	12 Carpenters at 2 s 6d. per diem	01	10	00
	12 Masons at 1 s. 6 d. per diem	00	18	00
	130 Labourers at 12 d. per diem	06	10	00
		45	14	00
(p. 2)				
July				
14th	For the attendance of Thomas Herbert and 5 more of the sayd Lord Herbert's servants overseers extraordnary for this worke this weeke	05	00	00
July 16	12 Carpenters at 2 s. 6 d. per diem	01	10	00
	12 Masons at 1 s. 6 d. per diem	00	18	00
	10 Myners at 2 s. per diem	01	00	00
	110 Labourers at 1 s. per diem	05	10	00
	. . .			
July 19	14 Carpenters at 2 s. 6 d. per diem	01	15	00
	12 Masons at 1 s. 6 d. per diem	00	18	00
	10 Myners at 2 s. per diem	01	00	00
	113 labourers at 1 s. per diem	05	13	00
July 20	14 Carpenters at 2 s. 6 d. per diem	01	15	00
	12 Masons at 1 s. 6 d.	00	18	00
	10 Myners at 2 s. per diem	01	00	00
	113 labourers—	05	13	00
		49	09	00

		£	s	d
(p. 3)				
July 21st	14 Carpenters at 2 s. 6 d. per diem	01	15	00
1649	12 Masons at 1 s. 6 d. per diem	00	18	00
	10 Myners at 2 s. per diem	01	00	00
	113 Labourers at 1 s. per diem	05	13	00
	. . .			
July 25	12 Carpenters at 2 s. 6 d.	01	10	00
	12 Masons at 1 s. 6 d. per diem	00	18	00
	10 Myners at 2 s. per diem	01	00	00
	130 labourers at 1 s. per diem	06	10	00
July 26	12 Carpenters at 2 s. 6 d. per diem	01	10	00
	12 Masons at 1 s. 6 d. per diem	00	18	00
	10 Myners at 2 s. per diem	01	00	00
	130 labourers —	06	10	00
		53	18	00
(p. 4)				
July 27	12 Carpenters at 2 s. 6 d. per diem	01	10	00
1649	12 Masons at 1 s. 6 d. per diem	00	18	00
	10 Myners at 2 s. per diem	01	00	00
	130 labourers—	06	10	00
	. . .			
31th July	12 Carpenters at 2 s. 6 d. per diem	01	10	00
	10 Myners at 2 s. per diem	01	00	00
	12 Masons at 1 s. 6 d. per diem	00	18	00
	140 labourers	07	00	00
August 1	12 Carpenters at 2 s. 6 d. per diem	01	10	00
1649	12 Masons at 1 s. 6 d. per diem	00	18	00
	10 Myners at 2 s. per diem	01	00	00
	140 Labourers at 1 s. per diem	07	00	00
		56	00	00
(p. 5)				
August	12 Carpenters at 2 s. 6 d. per diem	01	10	00
2.1649	12 Masons 1 s. 6 d. per diem	00	18	00
	10 Myners at 2 s. per diem	01	00	00
	140 labourers at 1 s. per diem	07	00	00
August 3	12 Carpenters at 2 s. 6 d. per diem	01	10	00
1649	12 Masons at 1 s. 6 d. per diem	00	18	00
	10 Myners at 2 s. per diem	01	00	00
	140 labourers at 1 s. per diem	07	00	00
	. . .			
August 7	12 Carpenters at 2 s. 6 d. per diem	01	10	00
	12 Masons at 1. s. 6 d. per diem	00	18	00
	10 Myners at 2 s. per diem	01	00	00
	70 labourers—	03	10	00
		50	00	00

		£	s	d
(p. 6)				
August 8	12 Carpenters at 2 s. 6 d. per diem	01	10	00
1649	12 Masons at 1 s. 6 d. per diem	00	18	00
	10 Myners at 2 s. per diem	01	00	00
	90 labourers at 1 s. per diem	04	10	00
	. . .			
August 11	12 Carpenters at 2 s. 6 d. per diem	01	10	00
	12 Masons at 1. 6 d. per diem	00	18	00
	10 Myners at 2 s. per diem	01	00	00
	90 labourers—	04	10	00
	For the attendance of Mr Thomas Warren and the rest of his Lordship's servants this weeke	05	00	00
	. . .			
August 15	10 Carpenters at 2 s. 6 d. per diem	01	05	00
	10 Masons at 1 s. 6 d. per diem	00	15	00
	10 Myners at 2 s. per diem	01	00	00
	80 labourers at 1 s. per diem	04	00	00
		57	12	00
(p. 7)				
August 16	10 Carpenters at 2 s. 6 d. per diem	01	05	00
1649	10 Masons at 1 s. 6 d. per diem	00	15	00
	10 Myners at 2 s. per diem	01	00	00
	80 labourers—	04	00	00
	. . .			
August 23	10 Carpenters at 2 s. 6 d. per diem	01	05	00
	10 Masons at 1 s. 6 d. per diem	00	15	00
	10 Myners at 2 s. per diem	01	00	00
	80 labourers at 1 s. per diem	04	00	00
August 24	10 Carpenters at 2 s. 6 d. per diem	01	05	00
	10 Masons at 1 s. 6 d. per diem	00	15	00
	10 Myners at 2 s. per diem	01	00	00
	80 labourers—	04	00	00
		61	00	00
(p. 8)				
August 25	8 Carpenters at 2 s. 6 d. per diem	01	00	00
1649	8 Masons at 1 s. 6 d. per diem	00	12	00
	10 Myners at 2 s. per diem	01	00	00
	70 labourers at 1 s. per diem	03	10	00
	For the attendance of Mr Thomas Warren and the rest of his Lordship's servants this weeke	05	00	00
	. . .			
September	8 Carpenters at 2 s. 6 d. per diem	01	00	00
1 1649	8 Masons at 1 s. 6 d. per diem	00	12	00
	10 Myners at 2 s. per diem	01	00	00
	70 labourers at 1 s. per diem	03	10	00
	For the attendance of Mr Thomas Warren and the rest of his Lordship's servants this weeke	03	10	00
		50	14	00

			£	s	d
(p. 9)					
September	6 Carpenters at 2 s. 6 d. per diem		00	15	00
3 1649	6 Masons at 1 s. 6 d. per diem		00	09	00
	6 Myners at 2 s. per diem		00	12	00
	24 labourers at 1 s. per diem		01	04	00
	. . .				
September	6 Carpenters at 2 s. 6 d. per diem		00	15	00
10	6 Masons at 1 s. 6 d. per diem		00	09	00
	6 Myners at 2 s. per diem		00	12	00
	24 labourers at 1 s. per diem		01	04	00
			24	00	00
(p. 10)					
September	6 Carpenters at 2 s. 6 d. per diem		00	15	00
11 1649	6 Masons at 1 s. 6 d. per diem		00	09	00
	6 Myners at 2 s. per diem		00	12	00
	24 labourers at 1 s. per diem		01	04	00
	. . .				
September	8 Carpenters at 2 s. per diem		00	16	00
18	6 Masons at 1 s. 4 d. per diem		00	08	00
	6 Miners at 1 s. 8 d. per diem		00	10	00
	30 labourers at 10 d. per diem		01	05	00
			23	18	00
(p. 11)					
September	8 Carpenters at 2 s. per diem		00	16	00
19	6 Masons at 1 s. 4 d. per diem		00	08	00
1649	6 Myners at 1 s. 8 d. per diem		00	10	00
	30 labourers at 10 d. per diem		01	05	00
	. . .				
	For the attendance of Mr Thomas Warren and the rest of the overseers extraordinary of this worke this weeke		03	00	00
	. . .				
September	8 Carpenters at 1 s. 8 d. per diem		00	13	04
26	6 Masons at 1 s. 3 d. per diem		00	07	06
	6 Myners at 1 s. 6 d. per diem		00	09	00
	40 labourers at 10 d. per diem		01	13	04
			24	14	06

		£	s	d
(p. 12) September 27	8 Carpenters at 1 s. 8 d. per diem	00	13	04
	6 Masons at 1 s. 3 d. per diem	00	07	06
	6 Myners at 1s 6d per diem	00	09	00
	40 labourers at 10 d. per diem	01	13	04
	. . .			
	For the attendance of Mr Thomas Warren and the rest of the Overseers extraordinary this weeke	03	00	00
October 1st 1649	8 Carpenters at 1 s. 6 d. per diem	00	12	00
	6 Masons at 1 s. per diem	00	06	00
	6 Myners at 1 s. 6 d. per diem	00	09	00
	40 labourers at 10 d. per diem	01	13	07
	. . .			
4	8 Carpenters at 1 s. 6 d. per diem	00	12	00
	6 Masons at 1 s. per diem	00	06	
	6 Myners at 1 s. 6 d. per diem	00	09	00
	40 labourers at 10 d. per diem	01	13	09
		24	10	00
(p. 13) October 5. 1649	8 Carpenters at 1 s. 6 d. per diem	00	12	00
	6 Masons at 1 s. per diem	00	06	00
	6 Myners at 1 s. 6 d. per diem	00	09	00
	40 labourers at 10 d. per diem	01	13	04
	. . .			
13th	8 Carpenters at 1 s. 6 d. per diem	00	12	00
	6 Masons at 1 s. per diem	00	06	00
	6 Myners at 1 s. 6 d. per diem	00	09	00
	40 labourers at 10 d. per diem	01	13	04
		27	02	08
(p. 14)	For the attendance of Mr Thomas Warren and the rest of the overseers extraordinary this weeke	03	00	00
October 15 1649	8 Carpenters at 1 s. 4 d. per diem	00	10	08
	6 Masons at 1 s. per diem	00	06	00
	6 Myners at 1 s. 4 d. per diem	00	08	00
	40 labourers at 10 d per diem	01	13	04
	. . .			
	To Mr Thomas Warren and the rest of the overseers extraordinary this weeke	03	00	00
		23	08	00

		£	s	d
(p. 15)				
22	8 Carpenters at 1 s. 3 d. per diem	00	10	00
	6 Masons at 1 s. per diem	00	06	00
	6 Myners at 1 s. 4 d. per diem	00	08	00
	40 labourers at 10 d. per diem	01	13	04
	...			
27	8 Carpenters at 1 s. 3 d. per diem	00	10	00
	6 Masons at 1 s. per diem	00	06	00
	6 Myners at 1 s. 4 d. per diem	00	08	00
	40 labourers at 10 d. per diem	01	13	04
	For Mr Thomas Warrens attendance with the rest of the overseers extraordinary for this worke this weeke	03	00	00
		20	07	00

	£	s	d
(p. 16)			
For Roapes that were used to take downe the Tymber in bothe the Castles[a]	06	13	04
To the Tylers for untyleinge both the Castles	10	00	00
To the Glaziers for unglazinge the sayd Castles	05	00	00
for Ladders	05	00	00
for Iron Crowes[b] Mattocks and pickaxes with other Iron tooles and the mendinge of them	30	00	00
disburst at severall meetings about the demolishing the sayd Castle	12	00	00
for watching the materialls	05	00	00
	73	13	04

(p. 17, the back of the book)

The charge – The Demolishing – of Montgomery Castle begun 26th June 1649 and ended 27th Oct: 1649

£675:18:2

[a] 'bothe the Castles' – presumably means both the wards of the castle, the courtyards into which it was divided.

[b] 'Crowes' – crowbars.

Notes

Key to the abbreviated titles may be found on page vi.

1 Introduction

1 Y. Christ (ed.), *Dictionnaire des châteaux de France*, V (1981), 19.

2 D. J. King, *Castellarium Anglicanum* (New York, 1983).

3 C. Tillman, *Lexikon der Deutschen Burgen und Schlösser*, 4 vols. (Stuttgart, 1958), I, viii.

4 R. A. Brown, 'A List of Castles, 1154–1216', *EHR*, lxxiv (1959), 249–80.

5 M. W. Thompson, 'Monasteries Associated with Castles: a Tentative List', *AJ*, cxliii (1986), 305–21.

6 P. E. Curnow and M. W. Thompson, 'Excavations at Richard's Castle, Herefordshire, 1962–6', *JBAA*, xxxii (1969), 105–27.

7 *Pipe Roll Society*, xix, 117 and xxi, 50; *VCH, Hants*, ii, 130.

8 M. W. Thompson, *Farnham Castle Keep, Surrey* (HMSO, 1961).

9 Brown, as in note 4.

10 *VCH, Beds.*, ii, 28–9.

11 *VCH, Yorks., N. Riding*, i, 530.

12 J. M. Lewis, *Carreg Cennen Castle, Carmarthenshire* (HMSO, 1960).

13 M. W. Thompson, *Kenilworth Castle, Warwickshire* (HMSO, 1976).

14 M. W. Thompson, *Pickering Castle, Yorkshire* (HMSO, 1959).

15 *CIM*, vii, 169.

16 M. W. Thompson, 'Recent Excavations in the Keep of Farnham Castle, Surrey', *MA*, iv (1960), 81–94.

17 *VCH, Wilts.*, xi, 29; *VCH, Hants.*, iii, 418.

18 M. W. Thompson, 'The Date of Fox's Tower, Farnham Castle, Surrey', *Surrey Archaeological Collections*, lvii (1960), 85–92.

2 Fifteenth-century contrasts

1 A. Emery, *Dartington Hall* (Oxford, 1970), 103ff.

2 J. M. W. Bean, *The Estates of the Percy Family* (Oxford, 1958), 105.

3 J. Parker, *Some Account of Domestic Architecture in England from Richard II to Henry VIII*, 2 vols. (London, 1859), vol. II, 403–22; C. L. H. Coulson, 'Structural Symbolism in Medieval Castle Architecture', *JBAA*, cxxii (1979), 73–90; 'Hierarchism in Conventual Crenellation', *MA*, xxvi (1982) 135–9.

4 *WW*, 20–1, 140, 242–3, 262–3, 397–400. According to Richard Carew (1602) the creation of a single royal Duchy deprived the main Cornish castles of their original function and so 'could not guard them against the battery of time and neglect' and '. . . from foul reparations are now sunk into utter ruin'; F. E. Halliday (ed.), *Richard Carew of Anthony: the Survey of Cornwall* etc. (London, 1953), 153.

5 T. Rymer, *Foedera*, iv, pt II, 54–5.

6 *Rotuli Parliamentorum*, vi, 8.

7 *Calendar of State Papers (Venetian)* (HMSO, 1864), 261. Camden Soc. (1898), i, 25.

8 C. A. Sneyd (ed.), *A Relation of the Island of England about the Year 1500* (Camden Society, 1847), 39.

9 W. Camden, *Britannia* (1695 edition), 847.

10 C. J. Bates, *The Border Holds of Northumberland* (Newcastle, 1891), 13ff., 28ff.; D. L. W. Tough, *The Last Years of a Frontier, a History of the Borders during the Reign of Elizabeth* (Oxford, 1928).

11 D. MacGibbon and T. Ross, *The Castel-*

lated and Domestic Architecture of
Scotland, 5 vols. (Edinburgh, 1887–92).

12 W. Camden, as in note 9, 1020; H. G.
Leask, Irish Castles (Dundalk, 1941).

13 J. Longnon, Les très riches heures du duc
de Berry (London, 1969).

14 E. T. Hamy, Le livre de la description des
pays de Gilles de Bouvier, dit Berry,
1388–1456, Recueil de Voyages et de
Documents . . . xxii (Paris, 1908). H. Pyne
(trans.), England and France in the
Fifteenth Century: the contemporary
French tract entitled 'The Debate between
the Heralds of France and England'
presumed to have been written by
Charles, Duke of Orléans (London,
1870).

15 P. Gringore, The Castell of Labour
(Roxburghe Club, Edinburgh, 1905),
lines 2, 520–3.

16 J. Stevenson (ed.), Letters and Papers
Illustrative of the Wars of the English in
France during the Reign of Henry VI
(Rolls Series 22, 1860), i, 404ff.; ii, 44ff.

17 C. Enlart, Manuel d'archéologie français
(Paris, 1932), vol. ii, pt. ii, 713–870.

18 R. Ritter, Châteaux, donjons et places
fortes (Paris, 1953), 122.

19 G. Henoteaux et le Duc de la Forge,
Histoire du Cardinal de Richelieu (Paris,
1893), vi, 350.

20 P. des Forts, 'Le Château de Rambures',
Bulletin Monumental (1903), 240–66.

21 M. Jones, 'The Defence of Medieval
Brittany', AJ, cxxxviii (1981), 149–205.

22 H. Couasnon, 'Château de la
Hunaudaye', Congrès archéologique de
France (1949), 280–94.

3 Warfare in England and France

1 C. Plummer (ed.), Sir John Fortescue, The
Governance of England . . . (London,
1885), 115.

2 Ibid., 125.

3 W. Hardy (ed.), J. de Waurin, Recueil de
chroniques et anciennes histoires . . .
(Rolls Series, 39 (French), 40 (English),
HMSO, 1879).

4 Ibid., ii, 184–7.

5 Ibid., iii, 157.

6 J. Stevenson (ed.), Letters and Papers, ii,
579.

7 J. Stevenson (ed.), Narratives of the

Expulsion of the English from Normandy
(Rolls Series, 32, 1863), ii, 536.

8 F. P. Barnard (ed.), The Essential Portions
of Nicholas Upton, De Studio Militari,
translated by John Blunt (Oxford, 1931),
46.

9 M. Jones (ed.), P. de Commynes, Memoirs
of the Reign of Louis XI (Hardmonds-
worth, 1972), 353.

10 For example: A. Goodman, The Wars of
the Roses: Military Activity and English
Society, 1452–97 (London, 1981);
J. Gillingham, The Wars of the Roses
(London, 1981).

11 J. Gairdner (ed.), The Paston Letters
1422–1509, 5 vols. (Cambridge, 1898), i,
250–3; v, 36–73; cf. also WW, 190–1.

12 F. J. Giles, The Chronicles of the White
Rose of York (London, 1843), lxxxxvii–
ix, 12; J. Halliwell (ed.), John Warworth's
A Chronicle of the First Thirteen Years of
the Reign of Edward IV (Camden Society,
1839), 2–3.

13 Goodman, as in note 10, 181.

14 Ibid., 30.

15 J. Bruce (ed.), Historie of the Arrivall of
Edward IV (Camden Society, 1838), 19,
29.

16 KW, i, 448–9.

17 O. F. G. Hogg, English Artillery, 1326–
1716 (London, 1963), chaps 1, 5;
P. Contamine, War in the Middle Ages
(Oxford, 1984), 137–50, 193–208. The
two authors do not agree on the question
of fifteenth-century improvements in
cannon.

18 J. Kenyon, 'Early Artillery Fortifications
in England and Wales . . . ', AJ, cxxxviii
(1981), 205–40.

19 G. Brereton (ed.), The Chronicles of
Froissart (Harmondsworth, 1968),
303–8.

20 Hogg, as in note 17, 12.

21 E. Viollet-le-Duc, Dictionnaire raisonné
de l'architecture française du xie au xvie
siècle (Paris, 1875), iii, 167–9; Congrès
archéologique de France (1901), 20–8.

22 A. Masier, 'Le Château de Ham (Somme)',
Bulletin Monumental (1914), 232–315.

4 A rival – the courtyard house

1 M. W. Thompson, 'The Construction of
the Manor at South Wingfield, Derbyshire', Problems in Economic and Social

Archaeology, ed. by G. de G. Sieveking *et al.* (London, 1976), 417–38.

2 P. A. Faulkner, 'Domestic Planning from the Twelfth to the Fourteenth Centuries', *AJ*, cxv (1958), 150–84.

3 L. G. Wickham-Legg, 'Windsor Castle, New College, Oxford, and Winchester College: A Study in the Development of Planning by William Wykeham', *JBAA*, 3rd series iii (1938), 83–95.

4 H. E. Poole (ed.), *Thoughts before Building taken from the Writings of Andrew Boorde* (Canterbury, 1961), 12.

5 *RCHM, City of Cambridge*, ii, 147ff.

6 *KW*, ii, 872–82.

7 *RCHM, Oxford*, plan opp. p. 88. The replacement of the church in the monastic plan by the hall, a place of eating and self-indulgence, raised problems for a quasi-religions body like a college. At Oxford the ranges of the earliest court at Merton were set cloister-wise to the south of the eastern arm of the chapel; Wykeham found an ingenious solution by putting hall and chapel in tandem, both here at New College and at Winchester. This device has dogged the Oxford college plan ever since, although hall and chapel by their very different functions can hardly be described as happy bedfellows.

8 A. Emery, *Dartington Hall* (Oxford, 1970).

9 P. A. Faulkner, 'Some Medieval Archi-episcopal Palaces', *AJ*, cxxvii (1970), 130–46.

10 M. Biddle, L. Barfield and A. Millard, 'The Excavation of the Manor of the More near Rickmansworth, Hertfordshire', *AJ*, cxvi (1959), 136–99.

11 J. H. Parker, *Domestic Architecture*, 264–6; J. Britten, *The Architectural Antiquities of Great Britain* (London, 1814), iv.

12 R. W. Chambers (ed.), *A Fifteenth-century Courtesy Book*, Early English Text Society, cxlviii (1914), 15.

13 Thompson, as in note 1. See also A. Emery in *AJ*, cxlii (1985).

14 B. Bettisfield (ed.), *The Expences of Sir John Howard, Kt. 1462–1469 and Accounts and Memoranda of Sir John Howard, 1463–1471* (Roxburghe Club, 1841), 252, 286–7, 582–6.

15 A. R. Myers, *The Household of Edward IV: the Black Book and Ordi-nance of 1478* (Manchester, 1959).

16 M. K. Dale and V. B. Redstone (ed.), *The Household Book of Dame Alice de Bryene Sept. 1412–Sept. 1413* (Ipswich, 1931); C. Ross, 'The Household Accounts of Elizabeth Berkeley, Countess of Warwick, 1420–21', *Trans. Bristol Glos. Arch. Soc.*, lxx (1951), 81–105.

17 W. H. Dunham, 'Lord Hastings' Indentured Retainers, 1461–87: the Lawfulness of Livery and Retaining under the Yorkists and Tudors', *Transactions of the Connecticut Academy of Arts and Sciences* (New Haven), xxix (1955).

5 A martial face

1 C. Platt, *The Castle in Medieval England and Wales* (London, 1982), chaps. 7, 8.

2 M. Keen, *Chivalry* (New Haven and London, 1984); J. Vale, *Edward III and Chivalry: Chivalric Society and its Context, 1270–1350* (Woodbridge, 1982). The term 'Chivalry' in contemporary usage meant the secular nobility (dukes, earls, barons, knights, esquires); see D. M. Brodie (ed.), *The Tree of Commonwealth, A Treatise Written by Edward Dudley* (Cambridge, 1948), p. 44.

3 *Ibid.*, 93.

4 *KW*, i, 337–95; A. J. Taylor, *Caernarfon Castle* (HMSO, 1957).

5 *KW*, ii, 870–2; G. Brereton (ed.), *Froissart Chronicles*, 66–7.

6 D. Simpson, *The Building Accounts of Tattershall Castle, 1434–72* (Lincoln Record Society, 1960).

7 *VCH, Warwicks.*, viii, 452ff.

8 *Leland*, ii, 40.

9 A. J. Taylor, *Raglan Castle* (HMSO, 1950); A. Emery, 'The Development of Raglan Castle and Keeps in late Medieval England', *AJ*, cxxxii (1975), 151–87; E. Viollet-le-Duc, *Dictionnaire*, i, 425–36; ii, 174–8; viii, 429–38.

10 *Norfolk Archaeology*, xxx (1952), 178–88; *Ant J*, xxx (1952), 35–51.

11 *Ibid.*, 44–8.

12 *Ant J* (1942), 110–22; *Cal Charter Rolls*, vi, 13.

13 *CP*, xi, 479–81.

14 *VCH, Beds.*, iii, 270.

15 *Leland*, iv, 133.

16 *RCHM, Herefordshire (East)*, ii, xxvi, 74.

17 *Leland*, ii, 55–6.

18 *VCH*, *Herts.*, iii, 370; T. P. Smith, 'Rye House, Hertfordshire, and Aspects of Early Brickwork in England', *AJ*, cxxxii (1975), 110–50. Dr Peter Richards has kindly drawn my attention to the illustration of Rye House (plan and view) published in 1685 in the second edition of T. Sprat, *A True Account and Declaration of the Horrid Conspiracy against the Late King* (London, 1685, front of volume), but the small group of buildings immediately adjoining the gatehouse, including a multi-gabled hall, appears to be a sixteenth- and seventeenth-century contraction within the large rectangular moat area, perhaps intended for two courtyards with a hall in the cross-range.

19 M. W. Thompson, *Tattershall Castle* (National Trust Guidebook, 1974); Simpson, as in note 6.

20 *DNB*, Supplement, ii, 90; A. Emery, Ralph, Lord Cromwell's Manor at South Wingfield (1439–50), *AJ*, cxlii (1985).

21 *RCHM*, *Essex*, ii, 69–72.

22 B. Elliott, *William, First Lord Hastings* (Leicester, 1984), 14–15; T. L. Jones, *Ashby de la Zouch Castle* (HMSO, 1953).

23 *CCR*, ii, 242.

24 C. Peers, *Kirby Muxloe Castle* (HMSO, 1917).

25 *CA*, 248.

26 *Ibid.*, 245.

27 *Ibid.*, 115, 123; E. B. Powley, *The House of de la Pomerai* (Liverpool, 1944), 108.

28 *KW*, ii, 680–1.

29 *RCHM*, *Huntingdonshire*, 34–8.

30 Thompson, 'Fox's Tower', Farnham Castle, Surrey, *Surrey Arch. Coll.*, lvii (1960), 81–94.

31 A. L. Bedingfeld, *Oxburgh Hall, Norfolk* (Nat. Trust Guidebook, 1972).

6 Accelerating decay

1 M. W. Thompson, *Ruins, their Preservations and Display* (London, 1981), 9.

2 *KW*, i, 299.

3 C. J. Bates, *The Border Holds of Northumberland* (Newcastle upon Tyne, 1891), 12.

4 B. L. James (ed.), *Rice Merrick, Morganiae Archaeogaphia, A book of the Antiquities of Glamorganshire*, S. Wales Rec. Soc., i (1983), 75–6, 89–122.

5 *KW*, iii, 169–86, 225–336; H. M. Colvin, 'Castles and Government in Tudor England', *Eng. Hist. Rev.*, lxxxiii (1969), 125–39.

6 *England, Wales, Scotland and Ireland Described and Abridged . . .* (London, 1627).

7 H. Owen (ed.), *The Description of Pembrokeshire by G. Owen*, Cymmrodorion Society, Record Series, I (London, 1892–7), pt 2, 401–2.

8 *Ibid.*, I, 76.

9 Sir W. Brereton, *Notes of a Journey through Durham and Northumberland in the Year 1635* (Newcastle, 1844); L. G. W. Legg (ed.), *A Relation of a Short Survey of 26 Counties Observed . . . in 1634* (London, 1904); *id.*, *A Relation of a Short Survey of the Western Counties . . . in 1635* (Camden Miscellany, xvi, 1936).

10 M. W. Thompson, 'The Abandonment of the Castle in Wales and the Marches', in *Castles in Wales and the Welsh Marches: Essays presented to David King*, ed. by J. R. Kenyon (Cardiff, 1987), 205–16.

11 G. Edelen (ed.), *The Description of England by W. Harrison* (New York, 1968), 20. The absence of fortifications in England was also commented upon by a visiting German party in 1602, *Trans. Royal Historical Society*, NS VI (1892), p. 39.

12 F. J. Fisher (ed.), *The State of England (1600) by Sir Thomas Wilson* (Camden Miscellany, xvi, 1936).

13 *Ibid.*, 12. Quotations in notes 13, 14 and 15 with permission of Royal Historical Society.

14 *Ibid.*, 14.

15 *Ibid.*, 43.

16 *KW*, iii, 173–7.

17 J. Caillert, *De l'Administration en France sous le Ministère de Cardinal de Richelieu* (Paris, 1857), 124–6; the law in question is Jourdan, Decrusy, Sambert, *Recueil général des anciennes lois de France . . .* vol. xvi, 192. Frontier fortifications were excluded. The Code Michaud (274–5, 282) forbad keeping unnecessary arms, powder or lead and instructed that cannon were handed over to the royal arsenal. See also M. de Caumont, *Cours d'antiquités monumentals professés a*

Caen en 1830 (Paris, 1835), pt v, 236, 330, 350. Richelieu may have been responsible for demolition at Pierrefonds: D. L. M. Avenel (ed.), *Lettres, instructions diplomatiques et papiers d'état du Cardinal de Richelieu* (Paris, 1874), vol. vii, 365.

18 *KW*, iv, 1–39, 367ff., map on 372.

19 C. Duffy, *Siege Warfare, the Fortress in the Early Modern World, 1499–1660* (London, 1979), chaps. 1–5; J. R. Hale, 'The Early Development of the Bastion: an Italian Chronology *c.* 1450–1534', in *Europe in the Late Middle Ages* (London, 1965), 466–94.

20 I. MacIvor, *The Fortifications of Berwick upon Tweed* (HMSO, 1972).

21 Brereton, as in note 9, 34. The normal word for bastion at this time was 'bulwark', see *Faerie Queene*, 11, ci, 14:
    Against that Castle restless siege did lay
    And evermore their hideous Ordnance
    Upon the Bulwarks cruelly did play
    That now it gan to threaten new decay.

7   A continuing theme

1 J. A. Du Cerceau, *Les plus excellents bastiments de France*, ed. H. A. Detailleur, 2 vols. (Paris, 1868).

2 H. E. Poole (ed.), *Thoughts before Building*, 13.

3 For some references on moated ponds see: M. W. Thompson, 'The Excavation of two Moated Sites at Cherry Holt, Grantham and at Epperstone near Nottingham', *Lincolnshire Architectural and Archaeological Society Reports and Papers* vi (2) (1956), 72–82.

4 J. Moret, *Le Magnifique Château de Richelieu* (Paris, 1678).

5 D. Simpson, *Craigievar Castle* (National Trust of Scotland, 1978).

6 *RCHM, Essex*, ii, 158–61.

7 *Vetusta Monumenta*, ii (1789), xxiv shows Nonsuch (not Richmond); note the two gatehouses.

8 M. Girouard, *Robert Smythson and the Architecture of the Elizabethan Era* (London, 1966), pl. 63, 64.

9 *RACHM, Anglesey*, 124.

10 *RACHM, Glamorgan*, iv, 263.

11 *Ibid*, 262–8.

12 *RCHM, Dorset*, ii, 146–9.

13 *RCHM, Dorset*, i, 67.

14 M. W. Thompson, *Kenilworth Castle,*

Warwickshire (HMSO, 1976).

15 R. W. Goulding, *Bolsover Castle*, 6th ed. (1936); P. Faulkner, *Bolsover Castle, Derbyshire* (HMSO, 1972); Girouard, as in note 8, chaps. 6, 7.

8   Destruction

1 A. L. Leach, *The History of the Civil War (1643–49) in Pembrokeshire* (London, 1937), 60.

2 A good example: M. W. Thompson, *Conisbrough Castle, Yorkshire* (HMSO, 1959).

3 *CSPD*, 29/10/1644.

4 J. Sutherland (ed), *Memoirs of the Life of Colonel Hutchinson, by Lucy Hutchinson* (London, 1973), 83.

5 F. J. Varley, *Cambridge during the Civil War, 1642–46* (Cambridge, 1935), 164.

6 *CSPD*, 5/1/1645.

7 *Ibid.*, 8/12/1644.

8 *Rushworth*, v, 330; *CSPD*, 15/5/1644, 21/7/1644, 30/9/1644.

9 S. R. Gardiner, *A History of the Great Civil War, 1642–49*, 3 vols. (London, 1886), ii, 381.

10 C. H. Firth (ed.), *The Memoirs of Edmund Ludlow* . . . (Oxford, 1894), i, 59.

11 *CSPD*, 2/11/1644.

12 Gardiner, as in note 9, i, 510.

13 *CJ*, 12/10/1645.

14 *CJ*, 20/10/1645.

15 *CJ*, 19/6/1646.

16 *CJ*, 23/2–3/3/1647.

17 *CJ*, 14/5/1647.

18 *CJ*, 25/11/1648.

19 *CJ*, 19/3/1651.

20 *CJ*, 27/8/1659; *CSPD*, 3/9/1659. For Booth's rising see D. Underdown, *Royalist Conspiracy in England, 1649–60* (New Haven, 1960), 254–85; for Chirk Castle see W. M. Myddleton, *Chirk Castle Accounts, AD 1605–1666* (St Albans, 1908), pp. viii–ix, 98. Hussey wished to make the cross-range Elizabethan (*Country Life*, xi (1951), 899, 980, 982, 1064–6), but in the provinces mullioned and transomed windows of this kind occur until *c.* 1690 (cf. *RCHM, Northants.*, VI, 40–1; *Herefordshire*, I, 80, 155, II, 35 (pl. 20); *City of Salisbury*, I, pl. 68–70; *Glamorgan*, IV, map 20, figs. 83, 84, pl. 21; E. Mercer, *English Vernacular Houses* (RCHM, 1975), pl. 108–9. Cf. also the

houses erected in *c.* 1660 in Hay on Wye and Rockingham Castles.)

21 M. W. Thompson, *Tattershall Castle* (National Trust Guide, 1974).

22 *Id.*, *Kenilworth Castle, Warwickshire* (HMSO, 1976).

23 For this and subsequent statements without references see Appendix 3 under the name of the castle.

24 *VCH, Berks.*, iii, 530–1.

25 R. Holmes, *The Sieges of Pontefract Castle* (Pontefract, 1887), 326–32.

26 Mr J. K. Knight has very kindly sent me a photostat of these accounts. If there was substantial profit from the lead etc. and he had been credited with £1,600 from his delinquency fine, Lord Herbert lost less from this demolition than might have been thought.

27 M. W. Thompson, *Ruins, their Preservation and Display* (London, 1981), pl. 17, 19, 20.

28 *CSPD*, 25/1/1645.

29 *Ibid.*, 6/4/1646.

30 *Ibid.*, 6/1/1646.

31 *CJ*, 29/4/1646.

32 *CJ*, 3/8/1648.

33 H. F. Abell, *Kent and the Great Civil War* (Ashford, 1901); A. Everitt, *The Community of Kent and the Great Rebellion* (Leicester, 1973).

34 For demolition at Denbigh see Myddleton, as in note 20, 88–9. The walls of Gloucester were 'razed' on orders of Commissioners appointed for regulation of Corporations: T. Rudge, *The History and Antiquities of Gloucester . . .* (Gloucester, 1811), 156, 158. For Coventry see *VCH, Warwicks.*, viii, 23.

35 *Sixth Report of Royal Commission on Historical MSS.* (1877), 473.

36 Dr A. J. Taylor has very kindly drawn my attention to his publication of the letters between Lord Conway and his agent: *TAMS* NS, xxix (1985), 81–9.

37 M. W. Thompson, *Farnham Castle Keep, Surrey* (HMSO, 1961).

38 C.-L. Salch, *Dictionnaire des châteaux et des fortifications du Moyen Age en France* (Strasbourg, 1979).

9 Nostalgia

1 G. Webb (ed.), *The Complete Works of Sir John Vanbrugh* (London, 1928), iv, *The Letters*, 14. Quoted by permission.

2 W. S. Lewis (ed.), *Selected Letters of Horace Walpole* (London, 1973), 19.

3 P. Toynbee, *Strawberry Hill Accounts* (Oxford, 1927), 174–95.

4 H. Walpole, *A Description of the Villa of Mr Walpole . . .* (Strawberry Hill, 1784).

5 *Ibid.*, iii.

6 H. Walpole, *The Castle of Otranto, A Gothic Story*, ed. by W. S. Lewis (Oxford, 1969).

7 K. K. Mehrotra, *Horace Walpole and the English Novel: A Study of the Influence of 'The Castle of Otranto'* (Oxford, 1934); I. Railo, *The Haunted Castle, A Study of the Elements of English Romanticism* (London, 1927).

8 I. MacIvor, *Fort George* (HMSO, 1970).

9 A. J. Rowan, 'The Castle Style in British Domestic Architecture in the 18th and 19th Centuries' (Unpublished Ph.D. thesis, Cambridge University (5162), 1965).

10 D. Watkin, *The English Vision: the Picturesque in Architecture, Landscape, and Garden Design* (London, 1982).

11 M. W. Thompson (ed.), *The Journeys of Sir Richard Colt Hoare through Wales and England, 1773–1810* (Gloucester, 1983), 109.

12 *Ibid.*, 179, 181.

13 *RCHM, City of York, The Defences* (HMSO, 1972), 28–9.

14 Thompson, as in note 11, 200.

15 A. D. Saunders, *Tilbury Fort, Essex* (HMSO, 1960).

16 M. Girouard, *The Victorian Country House* (London, 1979).

17 G. G. Scott, *Remarks on Secular and Domestic Architecture, Present and Future* (London, 1858).

18 E. Viollet-le-Duc, *Dictionnaire raisonné*, viii, 14–34.

19 P. Floud, *Castell Coch, Glamorgan* (HMSO, 1954).

20 The volume which belongs to the Welsh Office has been deposited on loan in the Department of Art of the National Museum of Wales.

21 Girouard, as in note 16, 418.

22 M. Trinick, *Castle Drogo, Devon* (National Trust Guide, 1978).

23 Girouard, as in note 16, 418.

24 P. J. Perry, *British Farming in the Great Depression, 1870–1914, an Historical Geography* (Newton Abbot, 1974).

Select bibliography

Anglo, S. *Spectacle, Pageantry and Early Tudor Policy* (Oxford, 1969)

Bates, C. J. *The Border Holds of Northumberland* (Newcastle upon Tyne, 1891)

de Beer, E. S. (ed.) *The Diary of John Evelyn*, 6 vols. (London, 1955)

Botfield, B. (ed.) *Accounts and memoranda of Sir John Howard Kt, AD 1463–AD 1471* (Roxburghe Club, 1841)

Brereton, G. (ed.) *The Chronicles of Froissart* (Harmondsworth, 1968)

Brown, R. A. 'A List of Castles, 1154–1216', *English Historical Review*, lxxiv (1959), 249–80

Broxar, E. *The Great Civil War in Lancashire (1642–51)* (Manchester, 1910)

Bruce, J. (ed.) *Historie of the Arrivall of Edward IV and the Finall Recouvery of his Kingdoms from Henry VI, AD MDCCCCXXI* (Camden Society, 1838)

Calendars of State Papers, Domestic, 1642–1660 (HMSO)

Du Cerceau, J. A. *Les plus excellents bastiments de France*, ed. H. A. Detailleur (Paris, 1868–70)

Colvin, H. M. (ed.) *A History of the King's Works*, i–iv (HMSO, 1963–82)

'Castles and Government in Tudor England', *English Historical Review*, lxxxiii (1969), 125–39

Contamine, P. *War in the Middle Ages* (London, 1984)

Coulson, C. L. H. 'Structural Symbolism in Medieval Castle Architecture', *Journal of the British Archaeological Association*, cxxxii (1979), 73–90

'Hierarchism in Conventual Crenellation', *Medieval Archaeology*, xxvi (1982), 69–100

A Handlist of English Royal Licences to Crenellate, 1200–1578 (in manuscript)

Dale, M. J. and Redstone, V. B. (ed.) *The Household Book of Dame Alice de Bryene of Acton Hall, Suffolk, Sept. 1412–Sept. 1413* (Ipswich, 1931)

Dictionnaire des châteaux de France (general editor Y. Christ), 18 vols. (Paris, 1978–), vols. ii, iii, iv, v, x

Duffy, C. *Siege Warfare: the Fortress in the Early Modern World, 1499–1660* (London, 1979)

Dunham, W. H. 'Lord Hastings' Indentured Retainers, 1461–87: the Lawfulness of Livery and Retaining under the Yorkists and Tudors', *Transactions of the Connecticut Academy of Arts and Sciences* (New Haven, USA), xxxix (1955)

Eastlake, C. L. *A History of the Gothic Revival*, 2nd ed. by J. M. Crook (Leicester, 1970)

Emery, A. *Dartington Hall* (Oxford, 1970)

Enlart, C. *Manuel d'archéologie française depuis les temps mérovingiennes jusqu'à la Renaissance*, vol. ii, pt ii, 2nd ed. (Paris, 1932)

Faulkner, P. A. 'Domestic Planning from the Twelfth to the Fourteenth Centuries', *Archaeological Journal*, cxv (1958), 150–84

'Some Medieval Archiepiscopal Palaces', *Archaeological Journal*, cxxvii (1970), 130–47

Ferguson, A. B. *The Indian Summer of English Chivalry* (Durham, N.C. 1960)

Firth, C. H. (ed.) *The Memoirs of Edmund Ludlow, Lieutenant General of the Horse in the Army of the Commonwealth of England, 1625–72* (Oxford, 1894)

Firth, C. H. and Rait, R. S. *Acts and Ordinances of the Interregnum*, 3 vols. (HMSO, 1911)

Fisher, F. J. (ed.) 'The State of England' (1600) by Sir Thomas Wilson, *Camden Miscellany*, xvi (1936)

Gairdner, J. *The Paston Letters, 1422–1509,*

5 vols. (Camabridge, 1898)

Girouard, M. *Robert Smythson and the Architecture of the Elizabethan Era* (London, 1966)

The Victorian Country House (London, 1979)

Goodman, A. *The Wars of the Roses: Military Activity and English Society, 1452–97* (London, 1981)

Hamy, E. T. (ed.) *Le livre de la description des pays de Gilles de Bouvier dit Berry* (Paris, 1908)

Hardy, W. (ed.) *Recueil des croniques et anciennes histories de la Grant Bretagne, 1388–1456, à present nommé Engleterre par Jehan de Waurin, Seigneur du Forestal*, 8 vols. (Rolls Series 39 (French), 40 (English), HMSO, 1864–92)

Harris, J. Orgel, S. and Strong, R. *The King's Arcadia: Inigo Jones and the Stuart Court* (London, 1973)

Harvey, J. H. (ed.) *William Worcester, Itinerarii* (Oxford, 1969)

Hogg, A. H. and King, D. L. C. 'Early Castles in Wales and the Marches', *Archaeologia Cambrensis* (1963), 77–124

'Masonry Castles in Wales and the Marches', *Archaeologia Cambrensis* (1967), 71–132

Hogg, O. F. C. *English Artillery, 1326–1716* (London, 1963)

Holmes, R. *The Sieges of Pontefract Castle* (Pontefract, 1887)

Huizinga, J. *The Waning of the Middle Ages* (Harmondsworth, 1955)

Jones, M. (ed.) *P. de Commynes, Memoirs of the Reign of Louis xi* (Harmondsworth, 1962)

Journal of the House of Commons, 1642–60

Journal of the House of Lords, 1642–8

Keen, M. *Chivalry* (New Haven and London, 1984)

Kendall, P. M. *The Yorkist Age* (London, 1962)

Kenyon, J. R. 'Early Artillery Fortifications in England and Wales: a Preliminary Survey and Re-Appraisal', *Archaeological Journal*, cxxxviii (1981), 205–41

King, D. J. C. *Castellarium Anglicanum, an Index and Bibliography of the Castles in England, Wales and the Islands* (New York, 1983)

Legg, L. G. W. 'Windsor Castle, New College, Oxford, and Winchester College: a Study in the Development of Planning by

William Wykeham', *Journal of the British Archaeological Association*, 3rd ser. iii (1938)

Longman, J. (ed.) *Les très riches heures du Duc de Berry* (London, 1969)

McFarlane, K. B. *The Nobility of Later Medieval England* (Oxford, 1973)

England in the Fifteenth Century, Collected Essays (London, 1981)

MacGibbon, D. and Ross, T. *The Castellated and Domestic Architecture of Scotland*, vols. i–iii (Edinburgh, 1887–92)

Masier, A. 'Le Château de Ham (Somme)', *Bulletin Monumental* (1914), 232–315

Mehrotra, K. K. *Horace Walpole and the English Novel: a Study of the Influence of 'The Castle of Otranto', 1764–1820* (Oxford, 1934)

Myers, A. R. *The Household of Edward IV, the Black Book and the Ordinance of 1478* (Manchester, 1959)

Owen, H. (ed.) *The Description of Pembroke-shire by G. Owen* (Cymmrodorion Society Record Series I), pts 1 and 2 (London, 1892, 1897)

Parker, J. H. *Some Account of Domestic Architecture in England from Richard II to Henry VIII*, 2 vols. (Oxford, 1859)

Platt, C. *The Castle in Medieval England and Wales* (London, 1982)

Plummer, C. (ed.) *Sir John Fortescue, The Governance of England: otherwise called the Difference between an Absolute and Limited Monarchy* (London, 1885)

Poole, H. E. *Thoughts before Building taken from the Writings of Andrew Boorde* (Canterbury, 1961)

Pursell, S. (ed.) *The Poems of Charles of Orleans* (Cheadle, 1973)

Raile, E. *The Haunted Castle: a Study of the Elements of English Romanticism* (London, 1927)

Ritter, R. *Châteaux, donjons et places fortes: l'architecture militaire française* (Paris, 1953)

Rushworth, J. (ed.) *Historical Collections, Abridged and Improved*, 6 vols. (London, 1703–8)

Smith, L. T. (ed) *The Itinerary of John Leland in or about the Years 1535–45*, 5 vols. (London, 1910)

Smith, P. *Houses of the Welsh Countryside* (HMSO, Cardiff, 1975)

Speed, J. Theatre of the Empire of Great Britain (London, 1611)

Sprigge, L. Anglia Rediviva, England's Recovery (London, 1647)

Stevenson, J. (ed.) Letters and Papers Illustrative of the Wars of the English in France during the Reign of Henry VI, 2 vols. (Rolls Series 27, 1861)

(ed.) Narratives of the Expulsion of the English from Normandy (Rolls Series 32, 1863)

Sutherland, J. (ed.) Memoirs of the life of Colonel Hutchinson by Lucy Hutchinson (London, 1973)

Thompson, M. W. 'The Date of "Fox's Tower" ', Farnham Castle, Surrey, Surrey Archaeological Collections, lvii (1960), 85–92

'The Construction of the Manor at South Wingfield, Derbyshire' in Problems in Economic and Social Archaeology, edited by G. de G. Sieveking et al. (London, 1976), 417–38

'The Architectural Significance of the Buildings of Ralph, Lord Cromwell' (1399–1456) in Collectanea Historica, ed. A. Detsicas (London, 1981), 156–62

'The Abandonment of the Castle in Wales and the Marches', in Castles in Wales and the Marches: Essays presented to D. J. King, ed. by J. Kenyon (Cardiff, 1987)

'Monasteries Associated with Castles, a Tentative List', Archaeological Journal, cxliii (1986), 305–21

Tillman, C. Lexikon der Deutschen Burgen und Schlösser, 4 vols. (Stuttgart, 1958)

Tough, D. L. W. The Last Years of a Frontier, a History of the Borders during the Reign of Elizabeth (Oxford, 1928)

Underdown, D. Royalist Conspiracy in England, 1649–60 (New Haven, 1960)

Somerset in the Civil War and Interregnum (Newton Abbot, 1973)

Viollet-le-Duc, E. Dictionnaire raisonné de l'architecture française du xie au xvie siècle, 10 vols. (Paris, 1875)

Wood, M. The English Medieval House (London, 1965)

The source of the illustrations is given in brackets with grateful acknowledgement to those who have given permission for their use.

Frontispiece. Caister Castle, Norfolk, round keep of brick castle built in 1430s (*RCHM*)

1 Gatehouse of Wingfield Castle, Suffolk (A. E. Thompson) *page* 3
2 A map of Norman mottes in Great Britain and Ireland (D. K. Renn) *page* 5
3 The abandoned motte at Ely in 1611 with a windmill on top (Speed) *page* 6
4 The abandoned castle at Worcester in 1611 (Speed) *page* 7
5 Eighteenth-century view of castle/college at Mettingham, Suffolk (S. and N. Buck) *page* 10
6 The great castle mound at Thetford, Norfolk, abandoned after demolition in the twelfth century (A. E. Thompson) *page* 12
7 The castle at Huntingdon abandoned after demolition by Henry II (A. E. Thompson) *page* 12
8 Ruins of Bedford Castle in 1611 (Speed) *page* 13
9 Tower at Enniskillen in Ireland in 1611 (Speed) *page* 22
10 Map of tower-houses in British Isles (P. Smith/*RCAHM* Wales) *page* 23
11 Dacre Castle, Cumberland (J. Parker) *page* 24
12 Dacre Castle, Cumberland (J. Parker) *page* 24
13 Comlongon Castle, Dumfriesshire (MacGibbon and Ross) *page* 25
14 Comlongon Castle, Dumfriesshire (MacGibbon and Ross) *page* 25
15 Clara Castle, Kilkenny (H. G. Leask) *page* 26
16 Clara Castle, Kilkenny (H. G. Leask) *page* 26

17 Rambures Castle, Somme (E. Sadoux) *page* 29
18 Rambures Castle, Somme (Société Française d'Archéologie, Bulletin Monumental, 1903) *page* 29
19 Rambures Castle, Somme (Société Française d'Archéologie, Bulletin Monumental, 1903) *page* 29
20 Hunaudaye Castle, Brittany (Société Française d'Archéologie, Congrès archéologique, 1949) *page* 30
21 Lodgings at Josselin Castle, Brittany (E. Sadoux) *page* 31
22 External face of wall behind the lodgings in fig. 21 (Boulard) *page* 31
23 Gunports at Cooling Castle, Kent (A. E. Thompson) *page* 36
24 Gunports on gatehouse of Bodiam Castle, Sussex (A. E. Thompson) *page* 37
25 A gunport on the West Gate, Canterbury (A. E. Thompson) *page* 37
26 Viollet-le-Duc's reconstructed view of Bonaguil Castle, Lot-et-Garonne *page* 39
27 Ham Castle, Somme, reconstructed view (Société Française d'Archéologie, Bulletin Monumental, 1914) *page* 40
28 Ham Castle, Somme, section of keep (Société Française d'Archéologie, Bulletin Monumental, 1914) *page* 41
29 Ham Castle, Somme, plan (Société Française d'Archéologie, Bulletin Monumental, 1914) *page* 41
30 Harlech Castle, Gwynedd, plan (Cadw-Welsh Historic Monuments, Crown Copyright) *page* 45
31 Stokesay Castle, Shropshire, plan (Shropshire Archaeological Society) *page* 46

32 Treago Castle, Worcester and Hereford (Royal Commission on Historical Monuments) *page* 46

33 Pembroke College, Cambridge, in the late seventeenth century (Loggan) *pages* 48, 49

34 Windsor Castle, plan of upper ward (Sir W. H. St John Hope) *pages* 50, 51

35 Dartington Hall, Devon, plan (A. Emery, *Dartington Hall*, Clarendon Press, 1970) *pages* 52, 53

36 Dartington Hall, Devon, in the eighteenth century (S. and N. Buck) *page* 54

37 Eltham Palace, Kent, plan (Copyright Historic Buildings and Monuments Commission for England) *page* 56

38 Knole, Kent (Kip) *pages* 58, 59

39 Gainsborough Old Hall, Lincolnshire, plan (P. A. Faulkner/Royal Archaeological Institute) *page* 60

40 Haddon Hall, Derbyshire, plan (P. A. Faulkner/Royal Archaeological Institute) *page* 61

41 Thornbury Castle, Gloucestershire (Pugin) *page* 62

42 Thornbury Castle, Gloucestershire (S. & N. Buck) *page* 63

43 South Wingfield Manor, Derbyshire, plan (Ferrey with additions) *page* 65

44 South Wingfield Manor, Derbyshire, south porch of hall and adjoining window of great chamber (A. E. Thompson) *page* 66

45 Tretower Castle and Court, Gwent, from the air (Cambridge Air Photographic Library) *page* 69

46 Warwick Castle, Guy's Tower, late fourteenth century (A. E. Thompson) *page* 75

47 Warwick Castle, Caesar's Tower (A. E. Thompson) *page* 76

48 Warwick Castle, gatehouse (A. E. Thompson) *page* 76

49 Warwick Castle, Richard III's artillery tower (S. and N. Buck) *page* 77

50 Raglan Castle, a gunport on the keep (A. E. Thompson) *page* 78

51 Raglan Castle, the 'slighted keep (A. E. Thompson) *page* 79

52 Raglan Castle, Gwent, the gatehouse (A. E. Thompson) *page* 79

53 Viollet-le-Duc's reconstructed view of bastilles at Lübeck *page* 80

54 Caister Castle, Norfolk, plan (Society of Antiquaries of London) *page* 81

55 Caister Castle, Norfolk, aerial view (Crown copyright) *page* 82

56 Herstmonceux Castle, Sussex, gatehouse (A. E. Thompson) *page* 84

57 Herstmonceux Castle, Sussex, an eighteenth-century view (S. and N. Buck) *page* 85

58 Sudeley Castle, Gloucestershire, plan by W. H. Godfrey (Sudeley Castle Estate) *page* 86

59 Rye House, Hertfordshire, gatehouse (A. E. Thompson) *page* 88

60 Tattershall Castle, Lincolnshire, an eighteenth-century view (S. and N. Buck) *page* 89

61 Tattershall Castle, Lincolnshire, the keep (A. E. Thompson) *page* 90

62 Tattershall Castle, Lincolnshire, the keep (A. E. Thompson) *page* 90

63 Faulkbourne Hall, Essex, plan (*RCHM*) *page* 92

64 Faulkbourne Hall, Essex, north front (B. T. Batsford) *page* 92

65 Ashby de la Zouch Castle, Leicestershire, north side of keep (A. E. Thompson) *page* 93

66 Ashby de la Zouch Castle, Leicestershire, south side of keep (A. E. Thompson) *page* 93

67 Kirby Muxloe Castle, Leicestershire, gatehouse (A. E. Thompson) *page* 95

68 Kirby Muxloe Castle, Leicestershire, north-west tower (A. E. Thompson) *page* 95

69 Kirby Muxloe Castle, Leicestershire, gunports on the gatehouse (A. E. Thompson) *page* 96

70 Buckden Palace, Cambridgeshire (Huntingdonshire), an eighteenth-century view (S. and N. Buck) *page* 97

71 Farnham Castle, Surrey, entry tower (M. W. Thompson) *page* 98

72 Buckden Palace, Cambridgeshire (Huntingdonshire), exterior face of tower (A. E. Thompson) *page* 98

73 Hatfield Bishop's Palace, Hertfordshire, plan (Britton and Bayley) *page* 100

74 Hatfield Bishop's Palace, Hertfordshire, tower over porch (A. E. Thompson) *page* 101

75 Oxburgh Hall, Norfolk, gatehouse (A. E. Thompson) *page* 101

76 Calshot Castle, Hampshire, an eighteenth-century view (S. and N. Buck) *page* 113

77 Kingston upon Hull, Humberside, a

seventeenth-century view (Hollar)
pages 114, 115

78 Berwick upon Tweed, a plan of 1611
(Speed) *page* 116

79 Viollet-le-Duc's reconstruction of
Renaissance windows being inserted
into a medieval castle tower *page* 117

80 Ancy-le-Franc, Yonne, sixteenth-century
plan at basement level (Du Cerceau)
page 118

81 Ancy-le-Franc, Yonne, sixteenth-century
view of château and gardens
(Du Cerceau) *pages* 118, 119

82 Chambord, Loir et Cher, sixteenth-
century plan (Du Cerceau) *page* 120

83 Versailles, Seine et Oise, château as built
by Louis XII (Gombou and Nolhac)
page 121

84 Chambord, Loir et Cher, sixteenth-
century view (Du Cerceau) *page* 122

85–6 Craigievar Castle, Grampian, two
nineteenth-century views (MacGibbon
and Ross) *page* 124

87 Leez Priory, Essex, an eighteenth-
century view (S. and N. Buck) *page* 126

88 Nonsuch Palace, Surrey, in 1611 (Speed)
page 127

89 Layer Marney Tower, Essex, gatehouse
(Q. Lloyd) *page* 128

90 Wollaton Hall, Nottinghamshire, an
eighteenth-century view (Wyatt)
page 129

91 Lulworth Castle, Dorset, an eighteenth-
century view (S. and N. Buck) *page* 130

92 Sherborne Castle, Dorset, plan (*RCHM*)
page 131

93 Longford Castle, Wiltshire, plan
(Britton) *page* 131

94 Bolsover Castle, Derbyshire, an
eighteenth-century view (Kip) *page* 134

95 Bolsover Castle, Derbyshire, the terrace
range (A. E. Thompson) *page* 136

96 Donnington Castle, Berkshire, an
eighteenth-century plan of civil war
defences (Grose) *page* 140

97 Nottingham Castle, an aerial view of site
(Cambridge University Aerial Photographic Library) *page* 144

98 Chirk Castle, Powys, an aerial view
(C. Musson/Clwyd-Powys Archaeological Trust) *page* 145

99 Montgomery Castle, an aerial view of
ruins (C. Musson/Clwyd-Powys

Archaeological Trust) *page* 148

100 Daily labour costs for demolition at
Montgomery Castle in July 1649 (Powis
Castle Estate Trustees) *page* 149

101 Kenilworth Castle, Warwickshire, an
aerial view from north (Cambridge
University Aerial Photographic Library)
page 150

102 Wressel Castle, Humberside, aerial view
of ruin (Cambridge University Aerial
Photographic Library) *page* 151

103 Bolingbroke Castle, Lincolnshire, an
aerial view of the site (Cambridge
University Aerial Photographic Library)
page 152

104 Scarborough Castle, North Yorkshire,
the 'slighted' keep (A. E. Thompson)
page 153

105 South Wingfield, Derbyshire, the
'slighted' tower (A. E. Thompson)
page 153

106 Helmsley, North Yorkshire, an aerial
view of ruin (Cambridge University
Aerial Photographic Library) *page* 154

107 Wimpole Hall, Cambridgeshire,
eighteenth-century folly castle
(A. E. Thompson) *page* 159

108 Esher, Surrey, Bishop Waynflete's gatehouse as altered by Kent in an eighteenth-
century view (S. and N. Buck) *page* 160

109 Hertford Castle, brick gatehouse of the
1460s, with inserted eighteenth-century
windows (A. E. Thompson) *page* 160

110 Twickenham, Greater London, the
library at Strawberry Hill (H. Walpole)
page 161

111 Castell Coch, Glamorgan, view towards
entry of Burges' castle of the 1880s
(Cadw-Welsh Historical Monuments –
Crown copyright) *page* 166

112 Castell Coch, section of existing ruin and
proposed reconstruction by Burges
(Cadw-Welsh Historic Monuments –
Crown copyright) *page* 167

113 Castle Drogo, Devonshire, Lutyens'
granite 'castle' near Dartmoor (National
Trust) *page* 168

114 Cover and title of booklet recording
expenditure on demolition at
Montgomery Castle in June–October
1649 (Powis Castle Estate Trustees)
page 187

Index

The appendices, which are largely alphabetical lists, are not covered by this index. The abbreviation C. stands for Castle or Château, P. for Palace, and H. for Hall or House. Page numbers in italics refer to illustrations.

Abbey Cwmhir H., 139
Abergavenny C., 20
Aberlleiniog C., 129
Aberystwyth C., 144, 151, 155
Adam, Robert, 162
Agincourt, battle of, 32
Alnwick C., 18, 109
Alnwick, Bishop of Lincoln, 97
Ampthill C., 85
Ancy de Franc C., 117, *118*, *119*
Angers C., 38
angled bastion, 113, *116*, 121
Antwerp, 116
Arthurian legend, 72
Arundel C., 108, 155
Ashby de la Zouch C., 73, 91, *93*, 94, 97, 147, 151

Bacon, Sir Francis, 103
Bagworth H., 93
Balmoral C., 157
Bamburgh C., 34
Banbury C., 147
Banqueting H., Whitehall, 136
Barlborough H., 127
Barnet, battle of, 35
Barnstaple C., 105
bartisans, 22, *92*, *93*, 124
Basing H., 139, 142
Bastille, the, 157
bastilles, *80*, 82, 112
Bayeux Tapestry, 5
Beauchamp, Richard, 85
Beauchamp, Thomas, Earl of Warwick, 75
Beaumaris C., 155
Bedford C., 7, *13*, 19
Bedingfield, E., 101
Belvoir C., 142, 146, 150, 156
Beowulf, 43

Bergen, 116
Berkeley C., 11, 109, 156
Berkhamsted C., 105
Berry Pomeroy C., 96
Berwick upon Tweed, 113, *116*, 154
Bindon, Viscount, 129
Bishop's Waltham P., 15, 16
Blenheim P., 158
Bodiam C., 17, 36, *37*, 111, 155
Bolingbroke C., x, 105, 144, *152*
Bolsover C., x, 130–3, *134*, *135*, *136*, 152, 153, 156, 166
Bolton C., 17, 46, 107, 143
bombards, 36
Bonaguil C., 39
Boorde, A., 46, 47, 57
Booth, Sir George, 145
Border Region, 21, 34, 107, 111, 155
Boston, Governor of, 146
Boston, 155
Boteler, Ralph, Lord Sudeley, 73, 86
Bouvier, Gilles de, 27
Brancepeth C., 105
Brereton, Sir William, 116
brick, 74, 81, 84, 87, 91, 94–102
Bristol C., 19, 109, 155
Bronsill C., 85, 86
Buckden P., 73, 97, 98
Buckingham, Duke of, 9
Builth Wells C., 106
bulwarks (*boulevardes*), 39
Burges, W., 137, 165
Burghley H., 2
Bute, Marquess of, x, 133, 137, 165

Caerleon C., 20
Caernarfon: C., 71, 72, 137, 155, 156; town wall, 163
Caerphilly C., 20, 105

Caister C., *Frontispiece*, 34, 73, *81, 82*

Calais, 21, 35

Cambridge: C., 19, 139; Corpus Christi College, 54; King's College Chapel, 18; Pembroke College, 48, *49*

Camden, William, 22, 24

Canterbury: C., 109; West Gate, 36, 37

Carcassone, 164

Cardiff: C., 165; town wall, 163

Carew C., 105

Carisbrooke C., 109, 111

Carlisle C., 109, 154

Carmarthen C., 9, 12, 96, 155

Carreg Cennen C., 14, 165

Castell Coch, x, 133, *166, 167*

Castell of Labour, 27

Castle Drogo, 166, 168, 169

Castle Hedingham, 20, 105

Castle Howard, 158

Castle of Otranto, 160

castles: abandonment of, 4, 6, 16, 19, 103, 104ff., 156; artillery and, 3, 16, 34–42, 111–16; buildings in, 2, 44, 46, 84, 105; coastal defence by, 109–12, 154–6, 163; decay, 10, 19, 104ff., Appendix 1 and 2; definition of, 1; demolition of, 3, 12, 13, 16, 112, 138–57, Appendix 3 and 4; in Glamorgan, 107; fantasy in, 133–7; in France, 27–31, 32ff., 111, 112, 117–21, 156; gunports in, *36, 37, 73, 77, 78, 79*, 85, 94, *95*; in Ireland, 21, 22, 23, 26, 156; Italian writers on, 20, 21; limited slighting of, 151–2; maintenance of, 14, 15; methods of demolition of, 150, 151; numbers of, 4; in Pembrokeshire, 108; and the Picturesque, 157; as prisons, 12; and the Romantic movement, 157; royal, 11, 18, 108, 112, 113; sale of materials from, 147–8; in Scotland, 21, 22, 23, 24, 108, 123–5, 157; 'slighting' of, *see* demolition; as status symbol, 1, 2, 42, 107; Style, 161–2; £10, in Ireland, 26; in Wales, 9, 107, 155; in Yorkshire, 107

Cavendish: Sir Charles, 132, 133; Sir William, Duke of Newcastle, 132

Cawood C., 17

Chambord C., *121, 122, 123*

Charles I, 132

Charles II, 155

Chatsworth H., 151

Cheddar P., 43

chemin de ronde, 76, 84

Chenonceau C., 117

Chepstow: C., 8, 155; town wall, 165

Chester: C., 109; in Civil War, 140

Chirk C., 105, *145*, 146, 156

chivalry, 71, 72, 101, 133, 160

Christchurch C., 155

Clain C., 26

Clara C., 25, 26

Claremont H., 158

Clarendon P., 49

Clyro C., 20

Colchester, St Botolph's Priory, 74

colleges: associated with castles, 9, 10; at Oxford and Cambridge, 9, 51, 67, 126

Comlongon C., 24, *25*

Committee of Both Kingdoms, 141, 142, 143

Committee for Oxfordshire, Buckinghamshire and Berkshire, 142

Compton Wynyates H., 57, 73

Conisborough C., 44, 155

Constantinople, walls, 137

Conway, Lord, 156

Conwy: C., 71, 155, 156, 162–3; town wall, 163

Cooling C., 17, 36, 111

Corfe C., 36

Cork Cathedral, 165

Cornwall, Sir Richard, 85

Council of the Marches in Wales, 20, 111

Council of State, 142, 145, 146

County Committees, 142

Coventry, 156

Craigievar C., 123, *124*, 125

Crayke C., 107

Criccieth C., 107

Crickhowell C., 20

Cromwell, Oliver, 144

Cromwell, Ralph Lord, x, 64–6, 72, 73, 87–91, 98, 133, 136–7

Croydon P., 56

Curzon, Lord, 87, 145

Dacre C., 24

Dartington H., *52, 53*, 54, 79

Dartmouth C., 112

Denbigh C., 155

Derbyshire Committee, 151, 152

Derby House, 142, 145

Devizes C., 15, 106

Dinas Bran C., 105

Doddington C., 18

Donnington C., *139*, 140

Dover: artillery works at, 163; C., 109, 111, 151, 155

Downton C. (Shropshire), 162

Downton C. (Wiltshire), 16

Drewe, A., 169

Drewe, J., 166, 168

Du Cerceau, 117
Dunster C., 156
Durham C., 105
Dursley C., 106

Eccleshall C., 109
Edward I, 9, 45, 71, 111, 112, 137, 145
Edward III, 9, 36, 47, 72
Edward IV, 10, 20, 34, 67, 91
Edward VI, 116
Elmley C., 106
Eltham P., 18, 55, 56, 63
Ely C., 7
Emery, A., x
Enlart, C., 28
Enniskillen C., 22
Esher Tower, 159, 160
Etampes C., 27
Evelyn, John, diarist, 148
Exeter C., 140

Farnham C., x, 13, 16, 81, 91, 98, 99, 100
Fastolf, Sir John, 19, 34, 73
Fauconberg, Bastard of, 34
Faulkbourne H., 73, 91, 92
Ferte-Milon C., 27
feudalism, contract, 68–9
Fiennes, James, 83
Fiennes, Sir Roger, 83
Fitzherbert, J., 103
Flint, C., 11, 151, 155
flushwork, 3, 75
Forbes, W., 21, 32
Fortescue, Sir John, 21, 32
Fort George, 161
forts, Henry VIII's coastal, 1, 17, 18, 111, 113, 115
Fotheringhay C., 109
Francis I, 120
Froissart, 36
Fulbrook C., 106

Gainsborough: in Civil War, 141; Old Hall, 57, 60
garrisons after Civil War, 142ff.
Garter, Order of, 72
gatehouses, 47, 73, 74, 83, 87, 94, 95, 99, 101, 125, 126
George, Sir Ernest, 166
Girouard, M., 164
Gloucester town wall, 156, 164
Glyndŵr, Owain, 20, 95, 107, 165
Goodrich C., 146
Gorges, Sir Thomas, 129
'Gothic Revival', 164ff.

Gravelin, 116
Gravour, a master mason, 81
Greenhalgh H., 96
Greystoke C., 109
Grimsthorpe C., 158

Haddon H., 57, 61
Hadleigh, Deanery at, 102
Ham C., 40, 41
Hardwick New H., 127, 151
Harewood C., 17
halls, 43, 44, 67
Hampton Court, 117, 125
Hanley C., 106
Harfleur, siege of, 33
Harlech C., 34, 45, 71, 84, 155
Harrison, W., 105, 156
Hastings, William Lord, 68, 73, 91, 93, 94, 95
Hatfield P., 99, 100, 101
Hawkesworth, Major, 147
Helmsley C., 143, 151, 154
Hemyock C., 17
Henry II, 6, 12, 16, 18
Henry V, 33
Henry VI, 29, 69
Henry VIII, 111, 112, 125
Henry IV of France, 3, 112
Henry of Blois, Bishop of Winchester, 15
Herbert, Lord, 145
Hereford: C., 105, 106, 109; town wall, 163
Herstmonceux C., 73, 75, 83, 84, 85, 155
Hertford C., 98, 160
High Ercall H., 151–2
Hinderskelf C., 107
Hoare, Sir Richard Colt, 162–3
Holbein Gate, Whitehall, 125
Hornby C., 107
houses: country, 17, 161–2; courtyard, 9, 43–70, 81, 85, 126–7; hall in, 43ff., 62; 'prodigy', 127; tower-, 2, 21–6, 73–4, 123–5, 126
Howard, Sir John, 66, 67
Huizinga, J., 71
Hull: fortifications at, 112, 114, 115, 155; Holy Trinity Church, 74
Hussey, Christopher, 162
Hutchinson, Col. and Mrs, 138, 153

James of St George, 137
Jehan de Waurin, 32
Josselin C., 30, 31
Jonson, Ben, 132
Journal of the House of Commons, 142ff.

Kafka, F., 157

Kenilworth C., 14, 17, 44, 132, 147, 148, *150*, 155, 156
Kent, Countess of, 146
Kent, William, 158
Kimbolton C., 158
King's Lynn, 154
Kip, T., *56*, 157
Kirby Muxloe C., 91, 93, 94, *95*, *96*
Knaresborough C., 107
Knight, J. K., x
Knight, Richard Payne, 162
Knole P., *56*, *57*, *58*, *59*

Lambert, Major General, 145
Lancaster C., 12, 96, 147
Lancaster, Duchy of, 11, 108
Langley, Batty, 158–9
Lathom H., 96
Laugharne C., 20
Layer Marney H., 125, 128
Leez Priory, 125, *126*
Leicester, Robert, Earl of, 132
Leland, John: 2, 10, 14, 15, 19, 20, 73, 77, 86, 104–7, 155, 156; problems of his *Itinerary*, 104; his description of castles, 104
Lewes C., 109
licences to crenellate, 18, 60, 83, 87, 93, 96
Lichfield Close, 142
Limbourg brothers, 11
Lincoln: C., 11; P., 44, 97; Earl of, 146
Little Wenham H., 74
Liverpool C., 155
livery and maintenance, 21, 68
Llandovery C., 20
Llawhaden C., 20
lodgings, cellular, 46–57, 63–70, 77, 94, 125
London, fortifications of, 154
Longford C., 130, *131*
Longleat, 2
Louis XIII, 121
Louis d'Orléans, 27
Louvre C., 27
Lübeck, *80*
Ludford Bridge, 34
Ludlow, Colonel, 140
Ludlow C., 20, 111
Ludwig of Bavaria, 137
Lulworth C., 129, *130*
Lumley C., 17, 109
Lutyens, Sir E., 166, 168
Lyme Regis, 139

Macclesfield, 18
MacGibbon, D., 2, 24, 123
Maidstone P., 105

Malton C., 13–14, 19, *105*
Manchester, Earl of, 158
mangonels, 33
Manorbier C., 20
Marlborough C., 10, *65*
Marney, Lord, 125
Martello towers, 163
masques, 132, 136
Maxstoke C., 156
Mehun-sur-Yevres C., 27
Meldrum, Sor John, 141
Merdon C., 15, 16
Merrick, Rice, 107
Mettingham C. and college, *10*
Middleham C., 107
monasteries, 4, 8, 9, 43, *55*
Monk, General, 156
Monmouth C., 9
Montgomery, Sir John, 91
Montgomery C., 105, 144, 145, 147, 148, *149*, Appendix 4
Morley, Bishop, 156
Morpeth C., 109
Mortimer, Roger, 146
Morton, Cardinal John, 99
mottes, *5*, *6*, *7*, 12
Mulgrave C., 107, 143
Myddleton, Sir T., 145

Napoleon I, 163
Napoleon III, 163, 164
Nappa C., 107
Naseby, Battle of, 142
Nefyn, 73
Newcastle Emlyn C., 105
Newcastle upon Tyne, 155
Newport (Gwent) town wall, 163
Nonsuch P., 125, *127*
Norfolk, Duke of, 34, 81
'Norman Style', 162
Northampton, 38, 109
Northern Earls, Rising of, 107
Norwich: C., 12, 19; Cow Tower, 74
Nottingham C., 105, 109, 138, 143, *144*, 153
Nunney C., 17, 75

Old Wardour C., 17, 139, 140
Orford C., 109
Orléans, siege of, 33
Osborne H., 157
Overton, Prior, 97
Owen, George, 108
Oxburgh H., *101*, 102, 125
Oxford: in Civil War, 140; New College, 40, 47

Paston, John, 34, 80
Peckforton C., 165
Penrhyn C., 162
Penrith C., 18
Philippe de Commynes, 33
Picturesque, cult of the, 162–3
Pickering C., 15, 105, 107
Pierrefonds C., 27, 164
Pilgrimage of Grace, 107
Plas-teg H., 129
Platt, Colin, 71
Plymouth C., 111
Plympton C., 105
Pontefract C., 107, 109, 142, 143, 147
Porchester C., 36
Poussin, N., 162
Powis C., 156
Progresses of Q. Elizabeth, 126, 130
Pugin, A., 164

Queenborough C., 17, 18, 36, 111, 155

Raby C., 17
Radcliffe, Mrs, 160
Raglan C., 73, 74, 78, 79, 80, 89, 96, 151, 155
Raleigh, Sir Walter, 130
Rambures C., 29
rampiring, 38
Ravensworth C., 107
Renaissance, 99
Renn, D. F., x
Restoration, the, 144, 156, 163
Rich, Lord, 125
Richard III, 79, 94
Richard, Duke of Gloucester, 86
Richard's C., 10, 11
Richelieu, Cardinal, 3, 112, 121, 157
Richmond P., 18, 96
Rochester C., 109
Rockingham C., 105
Roger, Bishop of Salisbury, 15
Rosa, Salvator, 162
Ross, T., 2, 24, 123
Rotherham, Bishop of Lincoln, 98
Rousdon H., 168
Royalist conspiracies, 144ff., 154
Ruperra C., 129
Russell, Bishop of Lincoln, 97
Ruthin C., 138
Rutland, Earl of, 146
Rye H., 87, 88

St Albans: 33; Abbey, 74
St Michael's Mount, 34
Sandal C., 107

Saumur C., 27
Scarborough C., 107, 111, 141, 147, 153, 154
Schloss Kempen, 81
Scott, Sir Gilbert, 164
Second Civil War, 143, 155
Serlio, 117
Shakespeare's Henry V, 32, 33
Sheen P., 18, 96
Sherborne: New C., 130, 131; Old C., 139, 141, 148
Sherburn in Elmet P., 56
Sheriff Hutton C., 17, 107
Shrewsbury C., 105, 106
Shropshire Committee, 151
Simpson, Douglas, 81, 87
Slingsby C., 130
Smith, Peter, x
Smythson, family of masons, 132, 137
Snape C., 107
Snodhill C., 20
Southampton: C., 109, 155; town wall, 36, 111
Southwell P., 56
South Wingfield Manor, ix, 1, 2, 43, 64, 65, 66, 72, 82, 89, 95, 151, 153
Speed, John, 6, 13, 22, 116
Spenser's Faerie Queene, 103
Stafford C., 110
Stamford, 7, 33
Stanley, Thomas, Earl of Derby, 96
Stapleton C., 20
Stokesay C., 46
Strawberry Hill, 159, 160, 161
Sudeley C., 86, 87, 151, 152
Swansea town wall, 163

Tamworth C., 105
Tattershall C., x, 72, 74, 87, 88, 89, 90, 91, 98, 133, 137, 141
Taunton C., 15, 109
Tewkesbury, Battle of, 35
Thetford C., 12
Thomas, Earl of Lancaster, 14
Thornbury C., 9, 60, 62, 63
Thorne C., 107
Thornton C. (Leics.), 93
Thornton Abbey (Lincs.), 74
Tilbury Fort, 163
Totnes C., 105
towers, great, 73–5, 86, 88–90, 93, 94, 97–9
Tower of London, 12
town walls, 163
Treago C., 46
trebuchets, 33
Tresham, Sir Thomas, 130

Très riches heures of Duke of Berry, 27
Tretower C., 20, *69*, 70
Triangular Lodge (Northants.), 130
Tynemouth C., 154

Union, Act of, 1707
Usk C., 20

Vanbrugh, Sir John, 158
Vergil, Polydore, 21
Versailles C. and P., *121*
Victoria, Queen, 157
Vincennes C., 7
Viollet-le-Duc, E., 39, 117, 120, 156, 164, 165

Wallingford C., 147
Walpole, Horace, 72, 159–61
warfare: archery in, 32, 39; artillery in, 33,
    35–42, 112–15; in the Civil War, 138–9; in
    France, 32ff., 79, 109; in the Low
    Countries, 109, 115; sieges in, 33–5, 81; in
    French Wars of Religion, 121, 122; in Wars
    of the Roses, 34
Warkworth C., 18, 110
Warwick C., 17, *75*, *76*, *77*, 94, 106, 109, 155

Wasserburg, 81
Wayneflete, William, Bishop of Winchester,
    98, 159
Welbeck Abbey, 132
Westminster P., 12, 44
West Tanfield C., 107
William II, 11
Wilson, Sir Thomas, 109, 110
Winchelsea, 111
Winchester: C., 109, 147, 150, 155; College,
    50; Pipe Rolls, 15; town gate, 36; Wolvesey
    P., 15, 156
Windsor C.: 9, 12, 17; lodgings in, 46, 47, *50*,
    51, 72, 159; St George's Chapel in, 9
Wingfield C. (Suffolk), 1, *3*, 17, *55*
Wollaton H., 127, *128*
Worcester, William, 19
Worcester: C., 7, 19; in the Civil War, 140,
    145
Wressell C., 107, 149, *151*

Yarmouth, Great, 155
Yeavering P., 43
yett, 22, 93
York: C., 11, 19, 107, 110; town wall, 163